DEFENDING ANCIENT SPRINGS

KATHLEEN RAINE

Defending Ancient Springs

London
OXFORD UNIVERSITY PRESS
NEW YORK   TORONTO
1967

Oxford University Press, Ely House, London W.1.

GLASGOW NEW YORK TORONTO MELBOURNE WELLINGTON
CAPE TOWN SALISBURY IBADAN NAIROBI LUSAKA ADDIS ABABA
BOMBAY CALCUTTA MADRAS KARACHI LAHORE DACCA
KUALA LUMPUR HONG KONG TOKYO

*Printed in Great Britain
by the Bowering Press, Plymouth*

CONTENTS

ACKNOWLEDGEMENTS

I wish to make acknowledgements to the editors of the following periodicals in which these essays first appeared, though many of them have since been much rewritten: *Adam, The Anglo-Welsh Review, Antaios, The Dublin Magazine, Encounter, The Sewanee Review, The Southern Review, The Texas Quarterly*, and *Tomorrow* (now *Traditional Studies*). Most of the essays were first prepared as lectures for some particular occasion, as 'Yeats's Debt to Blake' for the Yeats Centenary Summer-School at Sligo. To Mr. Alan Clodd my thanks for keeping track of these ephemerae, and also for typing several of them; and to Mrs. Willa Muir for reading proofs, besides more important and less tangible help.

LONDON, JULY 1966

I

EDWIN MUIR

When Edwin Muir died, in January 1959, at the age of seventy-one, he was still at the height of his poetic powers, and many of his finest poems are among his last. Time, that so remorselessly fades some poems which in their day seemed impressive, makes others, at first little noticed, seem to glow with some inner light. Edwin Muir's poems belong to the second kind: time does not fade them, and it becomes clear that their excellence owes nothing to the accidental circumstances of the moment at which the poet wrote, or we read, his poems; they survive, as it were, a change of background, and we begin to see that whereas the 'new' movements of this or that decade lose their significance when the scene changes and retain only a historical interest, Edwin Muir, a poet who never followed fashion, has in fact given more permanent expression to his world than other poets who deliberately set out to be the mouthpieces of their generation.

He was not a political poet; and yet his record of the state of Europe before and after the Second World War is not only more imaginatively perceptive, but more first-hand than that of the political poets of the thirties. He belonged to no church and subscribed to no formulated doctrine; yet he has written poems that sound depths of certain Christian themes never touched by poets of the Anglican revival. He was not a Scottish nationalist, and after some early exercises never wrote in any Scots dialect; and yet he stands out as the greatest, and perhaps also the most typical, Scots poet of his time. All this because of an unswerving inner certainty, an integrity, an indifference to fashion, that made him never seek to impress or please, but only to bear witness to the truth that was in him.

It is easier to explain why we admire some poem than why it moves us; for what is finally moving is just that in it which cannot be explained. The final Yes that we give to a living poem is more than an intellectual response – though it includes intellectual assent as well. It involves both the conscious and the unconscious mind. Muir, at all events, would have accepted some such statement. He once described to me a dream that at the time seemed to convey to him the deepest truth about writing. The dream was a very simple one: it consisted of a semicolon. The meaning of this semicolon, as it revealed itself to the dreamer, was that the poet never knows all that he writes; he writes only, as it were, as far as the semicolon; beyond the statement is something more, that completes his meaning. We can never define it, yet it is part of the poem, and part of what the poet communicates to the reader.

In one of his first published works, *Latitudes*, there is an essay entitled 'Against Being Convinced'. In this essay Muir criticizes the philosopher, as one who can 'give an answer with certainty – certainly at least by definition – to the question "what is thought?" but he can give no certain answer to the question "what is life?" ' Though he does not say so, he implies that to answer this question belongs to the poet; the poem communicates life, essence, which is indefinable; for the opposite of the philosopher, he says, would be 'a thinker of an incredible simplicity, a spontaneity which would appear to be a piece of nature's carelessness'. 'A philosopher is a man who thinks in and out of season,' he wrote in the same essay; and he knew with a sureness given to few poets how to entrust himself to the wisdom that has nothing to do with dialectic but everything to do with life. In one of his last poems, 'The Poet', he wrote of the poet's task.

> What I shall never know
> I must make known.
> Where travellers never went
> Is my domain.
> Dear disembodiment
> Through which is shown
> The shapes that come and go
> And turn again.

In many poems, as in 'Day and Night', he writes of the two wisdoms, that of the conscious day, and that of the night, ancestral, impersonal, yet deeply familiar, and wise with the wisdom of countless generations. Of this wisdom the poet is not the author but the transcriber; 'the authors', as Blake says, 'are in eternity'.

The last poem that Muir wrote opens with the line 'I have been taught by dreams and fantasies,' and ends with a declaration of faith

> That Plato's is the truest poetry
> And that these shadows
> Are cast by the true.

But the dreams and fantasies came long before Muir had studied the Platonic philosophy. The world of ideas for him was not a doctrine but an experience. In his *Collected Poems*, published in April 1960 but chosen, all but some fragments left unpublished when he died, by Muir himself, he has reprinted two early poems, 'The Ballad of the Soul' and 'The Ballad of the Flood'. Technically they are not very successful exercises in the tradition of the supernatural ballad, and the influence of 'The Ancient Mariner' is strong – a poem that might also have been called 'The Ballad of the Soul', and no doubt Muir recognized that Coleridge had seen into the same world as himself; for these poems are an attempt to describe in verse a vision, whose circumstances are described in the poet's *Autobiography*. This vision seems to have been his poetic initiation, an opening of the imaginative eye that he never afterwards forgot. He seemed – not in sleep, but in a state of waking trance – to be the spectator and participator of a great cosmic drama. Years later, he was able to write that he remained certain that 'it was not I who dreamed it but something else which the psychologists call the racial unconscious, and which has other names': Jung's Collective Unconscious, Yeats's *Anima Mundi*, Blake's world of Imagination, or Plato's of Ideas. It is the test of the authentic poet at all times that his work should draw its inspiration from this source.

Muir was, in this traditional sense of the word, a true poet. At the present time much that is called poetry is little more than the autobiography of the artist; it is the critical fashion to discount the imagination and to make 'sincere' feeling or 'realistic' description the test of merit. Writers of such verse may have a merit of their own, but, as Blake said, such writing is of a 'distinct and inferior' kind, and the categories must be recognized as different and incommensurable, 'for the sake', as he said, 'of eternal life' – which, of course, is lost sight of altogether when the two kinds of poetry are held to be upon the same level.

What Muir saw in his vision that was to shed its peculiar light upon all his subsequent poems he called the Fable, and entitled his first autobiography *The Story and the Fable*. In that title we again find the distinction between the wisdom of the day and of the night, the sleeping and the waking mind, that which comes before and after the semicolon. For the Story is the life of the individual – of any individual; but the Fable is that which every life seeks, more or less imperfectly, to realize, to reflect, to embody – something we know by inheritance, a pattern built up, it may be, by the endlessly repeated experience of the race. He wrote:

It is clear that no autobiography can begin with a man's birth, that we extend far beyond any boundary line which we can set for ourselves in the past or the future, and that the life of every man is an endlessly repeated performance of the life of man. It is clear for the same reason that no autobiography can confine itself to conscious life, and that sleep, in which we pass a third of our existence, is a mode of experience, and our dreams a part of reality. In themselves our conscious lives may not be particularly interesting; but what we are not and can never be, our fable, seems to me inconceivably interesting. I should like to write that fable, but I cannot even live it. And all I could do if I related the outward course of my life would be to show how much I have deviated from it; tho' even that is impossible, since I do not know the fable, or anybody who knows it.

But the Fable is enacted and reflected, again and again, in the differing situations of time and in history. If this were not so, individual life would be meaningless and poetry unnecessary – a few old myths would have said all. But the Fable is both old and ever new, and must be rediscovered, retold, reclothed in every age, indeed in every life. Edwin and Willa Muir were the translators of Kafka, the most contemporary, in the dress in which he clothes the Fable, of all symbolist writers; Kafka's supernatural labyrinth is superimposed upon a bureaucratic modern European society with such imaginative power that the symbolism gives meaning to the actual while at the same time the actual gives to the Castle and the Courts of Judgment the aspect of the contemporary. The two early ballads I have mentioned are, as Muir himself must have realized (for he did not reprint them for many years) interesting failures. They are so because the archetypes are not sufficiently incarnated; but,

while the visionary insight remains as strong as ever at every
return to his cosmic revelation, Muir added some new human
or historic concreteness, wedding the archetypal to the real as
only those poets can do for whom the real is the *signature* of the
Mystery.

A very great proportion of his poems are about history and
about politics (as were Yeats's also), but always he sees the
events of history as episodes in the Fable: and this enabled him
often to see the immediate with a steadier gaze than, say, the
political poets of the thirties, whose sense of proportion was less
true for want of that imaginative orientation. Certainly Spender
and Day Lewis felt strongly about world events; and Auden
equals, indeed surpasses, Muir in descriptive vividness; but in
Muir alone do we find 'those hard symbolic bones' that Yeats
found in Dante and Blake – political poets also – that give events
their enduring aspect.

Edwin and Willa Muir passed like pilgrims through some of
the worst horrors of Europe; in Czechoslovakia before the
Anschluss and after – they returned there as the tide of German
occupation had barely receded, and in time to witness the Communist *coup d'état* – but in such poems as 'The Cloud' we may
see how the perception of the Fable enabled the poet to see man
in a given political situation, if not unmoved, then at all events
unshaken. The anonymous man of the modern collective farm
is none the less a child of Adam and his great spiritual destiny
for not knowing himself to be so; the belief that man is only
'dust of the earth' does not make this true, though millions share
the error:

> At a sudden turn we saw
> A young man harrowing, hidden in dust; he seemed
> A prisoner walking in a moving cloud
> Made by himself for his own purposes.

It was in German literature, from his early readings of Heine
and Nietzsche, to his later studies of Kleist, Hölderlin, Kafka,
and Hofmannsthal, that he probably found his deepest affinities.
He expresses, in his own work, much rather the European than
the English experience of the war years. The invasion of human
feeling and natural kindness by those successive tides of ideology and power which reached England only as hearsay, Muir
saw, and felt, at first hand.

If Edwin and Willa Muir passed through the world like pilgrims, that argues a certain kind of detachment, but not, certainly, the detachment of the privileged unparticipating
observer. They were always poor, and Edwin Muir came from
the poorest of the poor. He was the son of a small farmer on the
small island of Wyre, in the Orkneys. There he lived only long
enough to learn what was to be, for him, the landscape of Eden,
that recurs in so many of his poems, always with that peculiar
radiance in which the imagination clothes the childhood of
poets,

> That dread country crystalline
> Where the blank field and the still-standing tree
> Were bright and fearful presences to me.

It was no sheltered life he lived there; his father was driven from
the first farm by the exactions of a bad landlord, and after a
succession of poorer farms, off the land altogether. As boyhood
ended, Orkney was exchanged for Glasgow; he was to learn
that there is poverty and poverty.

Glasgow gave him a precise imagery of Hell. There is a
passage in the *Autobiography* that captures the terror of that
landscape:

The same attraction to squalor drew me to the football matches
on Saturday afternoon. Crosshill was a respectable suburb, but
there were vacant lots scattered about it, chance scraps of waste
ground where the last blade of grass had died, so that in dry weather
they were as hard as lava and in wet weather a welter of mud. On
these lots teams from the south side played every Saturday afternoon
with great skill and savage ferocity. . . . Some of the teams had boxers
as their supporters; these men stood bristling on the touchline and
shouted intimidations at the opposing players. I first saw one of these
games shortly after I came to Glasgow, a brown fog covered the
ground, and a small tomato-red sun, like a jelly fish floating in the
sky, appeared and disappeared as the air grew thicker or finer. . . .
There was a grimy fascination in watching the damned kicking a
football in a tenth-rate hell.

Years later some such memory became infused into the poem
whose title is 'Milton'; but the poet is in truth Muir himself.
He does not, as Auden would have done, describe Glasgow;
though from the prose description quoted, we cannot doubt his
descriptive powers. For him, that 'tenth-rate hell' is but a sym-

bol, and in two lines he evokes only as much of its essence as he
needs:

> . . . a mass of blackened stone
> Crowned with vermilion fiends like streamers blown
> From a great funnel filled with roaring flame.
> Shut in his darkness these he could not see,
> But heard the steely clamour known too well
> On Saturday nights in every street in Hell.

He uses only as much imagery as is needed to give a Here and
Now to the symbolic statement and to remind us that the Fable
goes on, in the world we inhabit, never more realized than in
those regions that have most forgotten it.

Both the Orkneys and Glasgow, the places that give Muir the
landscape of his poetry are, of course, Scotland, not England.
He wrote in English, but when he wrote of England, or of
English writers, he wrote as a Scot, seeing all south of the border
as a country whose ways of thought were alien to him – perhaps
more alien than those of other European countries. The Scottish Nationalist movement held it against Muir that he did not
write in what is nowadays called 'lallans' – lowland Scots. But
the question of language was one of which he was deeply
aware; and he even wrote that 'No writer can write great English who is not born an English writer and in England – and
born moreover in some class in which the tradition of English is
pure, and it seems to me, therefore, in some other age than this.'
(This last quiet phrase is characteristic of his almost imper-
ceptible manner of making quite devastating critical pronouncements.) 'It is improbable', he added, 'that Scotland will
produce any writer in English of the first rank – or at least that
she will do so until her tradition of English is as common, as
unforced and unschooled as if it were her native tongue.' He
criticized the alien facility of Stevenson; yet he had to write in
English, for he regarded 'lallans' as an artificial language. He
himself came, besides, from the Orkneys, where the speech is as
remote from lowland Scots as English is; a speech and a language whose affinities are Norse. History made the use of English for him inevitable; in the same way as he felt that for the
political problems of Scotland – the problem of Glasgow, for
example – Socialism, not Scottish Nationalism, could now provide the only answer. We have to go forward in time.

In *A Note on the Scottish Ballads* he defined some of the attributes most characteristic of Scottish poetry as he saw it, 'this terrific sad, and simple vision of life'. English poetry, he believed, most excels when most subtle, delicate, and complex, Scottish when most intensely simple; the best English poetry is the work of an aristocratic culture, whereas the great poetry of Scotland – and not only her ballads – has been produced by men in the ordinary sense uncultivated, the sons of the land and of the sea. Muir himself was thus in the tradition of his race, the son of a farmer, and deeply wedded to the rocks and isles of Scotland. He writes, besides, from, and for, a tribe, a race. The Fable belongs to the race, to the ancestors; but so does Muir's speech, so do his images, and his loyalties.

There is an archaic splendour, as of the ballads, in his heraldic images of animals, flowers, roads, mountains, images strengthened and clarified by the imaginative simplification of those experiences most intensely and universally shared. The genius of the race is not for the subtle deviation but for the simple essence. 'The unquenchability of desire, the inexorability of separation, the lapse of time, and all these seen against something eternal and as if, expressed in a few lines, they were what human beings have felt from the beginning of time and must feel till time ends: these things, uttered with entire simplicity, are what at its best Scottish poetry can give us.' At his best, Muir achieved a poetic language at once powerfully mythological, yet concrete; symbolic, yet poignant with a particular joy or anguish.

In Muir's poetry the personal gives immediacy to the universal, which in turn gives meaning and stature to the personal. There are poems equal to 'The Brothers' – one of the last he wrote – but none which better realizes that synthesis of the story and the fable, an individual talent and an imagination at one with that of a race. The poet describes a vivid dream of his two brothers, long dead, as they had been as boys; yet the image is at the same time simple in its universality, and written within the tradition of a people that still attaches to blood-kinship a kind of formal dignity almost unknown in modern society. The vividness of the supernatural that exceeds in its intensity anything in nature is perhaps common to all primitive races; but the image of the two radiant children picks up purely Scottish echoes, from such ballads as 'The Cruel Mother' – a story of the unwedded girl who bears twin children, and kills and buries them to cover her shame. As she returns home,

> She lookit out owre her castle wa'
>> Fine flowers in the valley
> And saw twa naked boys at the ba'.
>> And the green leaves they grow rarely.

> 'O bonny boys, gin ye were mine,
> I wad clad you in silk and sabelline.

> O I would dress you in the silk
> And wash you ay in morning milk.'

And they reply that it was not so when they lived,

> 'O mother dear, when we were thine,
> You didna prove to us sae kind.

> O cruel mother, we were thine
> And thou made us to wear the twine.

> But now we're in the heavens hie,
>> Fine flowers in the valley
> And ye have the pains o' hell to drie
>> And the green leaves they grow rarely,
>> Ten thousand times good night and be wi' thee!'

Muir's poem is different in tone, but it plays upon an imagination whose contours have been formed by such burning images:

> Last night I watched my Brothers play,
> The gentle and the reckless one,
> In a field two yards away.
> For half a century they were gone
> Beyond the other side of care,
> To be among the peaceful dead.
> Even in a dream how could I dare
> Interrogate that happiness
> So wildly spent yet never less?
> For still they raced about the green
> And were like two revolving suns;
> A brightness poured from head to head,
> So strong I could not see their eyes
> Or look into their paradise.
> What were they doing, the happy ones?
> Yet where I was they once had been.

The poet then takes us beyond that age-old magic of the supernatural, into the metaphysical, in a statement moving in its simplicity, of the incorruptibility of the soul:

> I thought how could I be so dull
> Twenty thousand days ago
> Not to see they were beautiful?
> I asked them were you really so
> As you are now, that other day?
> And the dream was soon away,

Still keeping close to the pattern of the old ballad and its intensity of guilt as the individual confronts the eternal, he brings the archetypal image to bear upon the actual world:

> For then we played for victory
> And not to make each other glad.
> A darkness covered every hand,
>
> Frowns twisted the original face,
> And through the mask we could not see
> The beauty and the buried grace.

Muir possessed a birthright rare in the modern world, and perhaps irrecoverable, in being able to write for his tribe, to speak with the voice of the ancestors. Modern man lives as though without a past; but Muir wrote, 'I think that if any of us examines his life, he will find that most good has come to him from a few loyalties, and a few discoveries made many generations before he was born.' Fast vanishing in Ireland and Scotland, all but gone in England and America, this vital sense of the life of a race that bears, as if a single life, a destiny to unfold and fulfil, is still to be found among those Jews who are loyal to their inheritance; and many of Muir's finest poems take the Hebrew patriarchs for themes – Moses on Pisgah Hill watching his people below entering the Promised Land; the nomadic wanderings of Abraham, Isaac, and the still-journeying, still-suffering race.

Time, and the continuity of man through time, the poignancy of the individual life that for a while bears the burden, the calm patient continuance of the race from Adam – and before Adam – to the return to Eden at the end of the journey, these things were the essence of his vision. Often the poet writes in the first person plural – 'we'; but his 'we' is not, as with Auden (another poet much given to this plural) a group of friends or like-thinkers, or a political team, but the greater 'I' of the tribal life of Man. Conversely his 'I' embraces 'we', as the journeying spirit that travels from the beginning of the cosmos to its end.

In writing his Fable of Man, Muir turned naturally to those great symbolic figures who are not men, but Man – Adam, and Prometheus; the Israelites, with their strange god-bearing destiny; and, inevitably, the figure of Christ, though that figure emerges late in Muir's verse. History itself becomes a symbolic story as a pattern emerges, or is imposed, by the human experience repeated time and again. The eternal battlefield of Troy, the flight of Hector, the sack of the city, the constancy of the wife who waits. It is Penelope, wife to the wanderer, not the static Platonic image of Helen, who is Muir's figure of woman. In 'Telemachus Remembers', he writes of the weaving and unweaving of the unfinished figures of the loom, as an emblem of that daily life which is always an imperfect realization of the Fable. The loom cannot, indeed must not, be finished, yet life must never be relinquished. Penelope's greatness lies in her acceptance of the imperfection, and her loyalty to the task of producing the partial, the imperfect, the never completed.

> A horse's head, a trunkless man,
> Mere odds and ends about to be,
> And the thin line of augury
> Where through the web the shuttle ran.

Woman as the weaver of lives is an old theme; but again, it is a Scottish theme; Gray's 'Fatal Sisters' is based upon the story of 'a man from Caithness' who saw women in a hollow hill weaving men's entrails into the web of fate; but Muir could take such symbols, and in his hands they seem neither old nor new. The homeliness of 'odds and ends about to be' makes us accept the 'thin line of augury' as something no less simple and inevitable – as indeed it is; though Yeats, one reflects, would have said it differently. Muir never mounted 'that high horse'; it is often only on a second or a third reading that we realize just how much he has said.

But the story of the Journey goes back long before man; and perhaps Muir's greatest poem is the sequence he called *The*

B

Journey Back that opens with the line, 'I take the journey back to seek my kindred,' and traces the long travelling through the animals, the earth itself, to the stars and the first stuff of the material world.

It may be that modern man's sense of chaos comes in part from his loss of that pattern of which his necessarily fragmentary individual life is a part. Blake writes of the 'chaos' of the individual experience, which he contrasts with the beautiful order of 'eternity'. Have we lost our sense of that order because we have let go the myths that best embody it, or have we relinquished the myths because we have lost sight of the order that they exist to make known? Yeats, it may be, rediscovered the order through the study of myth and symbol; but Muir's poetry springs in the first place from intuitive perception. At first his poetic images arose within his dreams, and owed little to religious or aesthetic tradition. 'I do not know the fable, or anybody who knows it', he wrote, but then he added, 'One or two stages in it I can recognize: the age of innocence and the Fall and all the dramatic consequences of the Fall. But these lie behind experience, not on its surface; they are not historical events; they are stages in the fable.' Here the poet is acknowledging that the Fable has in part been known, in part stated in those mythological forms we inherit: Eden and Adam, and 'those dramatic consequences', the Incarnation and the Redemption.

Rather late in life a friend pointed out to Muir that he was a Christian. It had not occurred to him, yet, when put to him, he acknowledged that this was so. Some writers on his work have made too much of this; for if he was a Christian poet he was so by convergence of symbol, not (as for example T. S. Eliot) by subscription to doctrine. His wine could never be measured in any pint-pot of orthodoxy; for in revealing in part the mystery, he leaves it still a mystery. The most certain thing he knew of it was that it is unknowable. He did in fact increasingly use a traditional symbolism as he discovered that his vision itself placed him within age-old traditions; that what he had glimpsed in dreams had been man's theme for countless centuries.

His poem of the Annunciation is as profoundly spiritual, in its way, as Fra Angelico (whose painting he had in mind), yet it is not because he was a Christian but because he rediscovered the symbols from within that this is so. For him, the meeting of the Angel and the woman is essentially a poem about the eternal nature of love, not a poem describing an unique historical event. The theme is none the less holy for that; for Muir, like Plato, understood that lovers are winged – that is to say uplifted into a spiritual order, whose mystery is reflected in the earthly event:

> See, they have come together, see,
> While the destroying minutes flow,
> Each reflects the other's face
> Till heaven in hers and earth in his
> Shine steady there. He's come to her
> From far beyond the farthest star,
> Feathered through time. Immediacy
> Of strangest strangeness is the bliss
> That from their limbs all movement takes.

Muir never employed so great a wealth of traditional symbols as did Yeats; yet inevitably he discovered that in exploring the Fable he was travelling in a frequented land; for the symbolism of all religions and mythologies, not least Christianity, exists only to make that country known. He discovered late what was known early to Dante and Milton, and discovered in the course of their poetic thought by Coleridge, Shelley, Blake, and Yeats, the great symbolic language of tradition. The world-tree and its fruits, the birds of the soul, sun, moon, river, loom, dragon, gate, and dark tower, may be likened to words of that language, whose meanings, though not otherwise definable, are exact. Knowledge of these symbols is essentially a kind of learning, but it is the learning of the imagination, not of the merely conceptual mind. It is the learning of the poets. Muir came to the great source of vision without this learning, with little knowledge of the traditional forms. He was a symbolist poet by natural gift, not one who, like Yeats, had 'Set his soul to study in a learned school'. But the learning of tradition, for him, was less important than for Eliot, less than for Yeats, just because that which tradition preserves and transmits was so much nearer to him. 'We receive it from the past, on which we draw with every breath, but also – this is a point of faith – from the source of the mystery itself.'

But even when his symbols are drawn direct from *Anima Mundi* they are never vague, never obscure. Muir in his own way insisted as strongly as Yeats did on the necessity of form.

In *A Vision,* Yeats speaks of the symbol as 'uniting the sleeping with the waking mind', and Muir would have agreed with him; the symbol masters the unknown and the chaotic. He criticized D. H. Lawrence, whom in many respects he admired, because he saw in him an expression of the tendency of the time towards chaos, towards allowing the 'human form divine' to be lost in some vague life-force. What Lawrence expresses (and Muir links him in this respect with Shaw) 'is faith in all life that is not the life of personality, of synthesis, of order, of fulfilment . . . they are nihilists and the more dangerous for not knowing it. Their popularity is disquieting; it points to a disintegration of personality which must be general.'

But no symbolist artist can ever be on the side of vagueness, of disintegration. Muir's 'wisdom of the night' is not a capitulation to chaos. It is, he believed, man's characteristic vital achievements, *as man,* to give form, to impose pattern and order upon what he experiences and perceives. Plato held that form belongs specifically to intellectual order; that matter, until the mind projects upon it those forms, is mere chaos, *non-ens.* Mathematical relations – the triangle, the square, and the rest – belong to the order of the mind. And Muir, with his love of clarity of form likewise cites mathematics as a pure instance of the peculiarly human gift of imposing harmonious order upon the chaos of the world.

I think he loved the heraldic imagery he so often uses for some such reason, for every heraldic form both defines and celebrates some mastery over the natural and animal flux and chaos that is around and within man.

> Who curbed the lion long ago
> And penned him in this towering field
> And reared him wingless in the sky?
> And quenched the dragon's burning eye,
> Chaining him here to make a show
> The faithful guardian of the shield?

But these still, heraldic forms are not merely invented in order to master the flux: they are pre-existent, they belong to the order of the Fable that was and is 'in the beginning' – whatever the beginning may be:

> The frieze of fabulous creatures winged and crowned,
> And in the midst the woman and the man –

Lost long ago in fields beyond the Fall –
Keep faith in sleep-walled night and there are found
On our long journey back where we began.

In the imagination the creatures are 'winged', as Plato's lovers
or angels are, with spiritual life, and 'crowned' with all that
kingship conveys of glory, uniqueness, inherent power and entire
reality, overwhelming presence and entity. It is the poet who
can reveal their, as Blake would say, 'eternal lineaments'.

I am one of those who hold the unfashionable belief that talent
cannot make a poet, and that the *what* of art is more important
than the *how*; and also that 'technique' does not exist in itself
but only as a means to an end, an idea that is to be realized.
Nor are all poetic ideas of equal value. Donne or Dryden cannot
be as great as Milton or Dante because these poets do not
attempt themes that bring into play so great a range of imaginative experience. The themes of major poetry are epic, and cosmic; Muir wrote no epic nor could he have attempted a coherent
whole on the scale of the *Sagas* or the *Iliad*, yet an epic sense
haunts his work; and nearly all he wrote has the luminosity of
an inspired vision.

His themes – here again he is in the tradition of the Scottish
and border ballads – are epic themes, the tribe, its wanderings
in exile, its cities and their fall, its heroes and those anonymous
bearers of its destiny who watch and remember. Beyond the epic
lies the cosmic, the world of the gods in whose presence the
human scenes take their due proportion. 'Religious' poetry is
not necessarily of this kind. The devotional poets of the seventeenth century, or Hopkins, are beautiful minor poets whose
experiences of the divine are (in no moral or pejorative sense)
self-centred; whereas Blake, Milton, Dante, and the author of
'Byzantium' speak from beyond the human personality, from
that life of which the individual man is no more than a form or
organ. Visionary as he was, Muir is perhaps at his surest when
he writes of middle earth; yet he never writes of the human
scene without some haunting of the larger presences of the gods;
and sometimes he writes of the gods themselves, catching an
echo from Hölderlin:

About the well of life where we are made
Spirits of earth and heavens together lie.
They do not turn their bright heads at our coming.

So deep their dream of pure commingled being.
So still the art and the level beam that flows
Along the ground, shed by the flowers and waters
All above and beneath them a deep darkness.
Their bodies lie in shadow or buried in earth,
Their heads shine in the light of the underworld
Loaded with fear and crowned with every hope
The born stream past them to the longed-for place.

1961

2

VERNON WATKINS AND THE BARDIC TRADITION

I first heard the poetry of Vernon Watkins praised in the nineteen thirties, by Dylan Thomas, who then said that he was probably the finest poet then writing in Britain (unless Thomas himself). This was not an obvious judgment at the time of writing, and might have been put down partly to sympathy and affinity; but it is clearly true at the time of writing, not only because since then so many fine poets have died, or like David Gascoyne stopped writing, but because Vernon Watkins has during the intervening years perfected himself in the poetic art as none of his contemporaries has done. Nor is this development a matter of style alone (style can in any case develop only in relation to the matter of the poetry) but also in poetic content.

Vernon Watkins is a Welsh poet, product of the same influences that formed Dylan Thomas, only perhaps more so, since he has lived from early childhood in Wales and in the Gower Peninsula. Of himself he writes:

> I have been luckier than
> All others in one thing,
> Devoted secret time
> To one love, one alone

– and to that theme he often returns:

> Let each whose soul is in one place
> Still to that place be true.

This was in 1941 a most unfashionable prayer; and my own perhaps belated respect for the poet who, having roots, knew that he must not tear them up is the greater for having myself been for years dazzled and bedevilled by an alternative he unhesitatingly rejected. Vernon Watkins made a brief sortie into Cambridge as an undergraduate at William Empson's very college, at the time

I was myself a student at Girton; but his clear-sightedness in making a choice by which, from a worldly point of view, he lost so much and gained so little demonstrates not only his integrity but his intelligence: he returned to Swansea after a term or two.

Perhaps he understood even then that tradition has more to give a poet than education has; and perhaps, in the light of that tradition, divined the other great lack in the Cambridge 'scientific' school of literary criticism of Richards, Empson and (already) Leavis, the denial of the imagination. I. A. Richards has since proved to be a Platonist, but the Cambridge trend, then and since, has been anti-imaginative, for the very good reason that Cambridge humanism is a by-product of the Cambridge scientific schools and the positivist philosophy of Russell and Wittgenstein. Years later Vernon Watkins wrote a ballad on Abram and Sodom; but at the time he acted like Lot and quickly left a town past praying for. He was not deceived by the prestige of ignorance in high places.

He chose tradition (vital memory) as against education, and inspiration as against the new positivist spirit of the age; he remained true, as Yeats said poets must, to 'certain heroic and religious truths, passed on from age to age, modified by individual genius, but never abandoned'. One may say that he was lucky to be able to make the choice at all; Yeats, coming to the same realization, had to re-graft himself within the tradition of Ireland; Edwin Muir brought from his 'distant isle' (Orkney) only memories; and other poets know themselves exiled beyond all possibility of return to ancestral roots. What those values were which Vernon Watkins chose early he defines in the poem which gives its title to his last volume, *Affinities*.

> I find them in the wings of every age
> While fools and rhetoricians hold the stage.
>
> They know instinctively that speculation
> Will never reach a single true equation.
>
> There is no theory, however strict,
> A work of genius cannot contradict.
>
> Who pulls tradition down, and sets up fashion?
> Pretence is one thing, and another, passion.
>
> In every smith whose work I come across
> Tradition is the ore, fashion the dross.

They who skim ice cannot afford to stumble;
If pausing they went through, they might grow humble.

Pretenders mock the dead to make their mark,
As little children shout who fear the dark.

'His work is new. Why, then, his name encumber
With ancient poets?' He is of their number.

Complain against the dead, but do not sue.
They never read you, much less injured you.

Must it be anarchy to love that nation
Which counts among its assets inspiration?

The view of poetry he is here defending is, after all, that of the greatest poets of all ages, discovered and rediscovered again and again. It is Milton's and Blake's and Coleridge's view of the imagination and 'inspiration' as against such theories as have lately been current. To the positivist who denies the source of inspiration (whether within or beyond the human soul) its springs must necessarily remain inaccessible and poetry seem the product of conscious art, the association of ideas which William Empson has described with so much subtlety; or of the 'sincere' feelings of the shabby mortal individuality which refers everything in heaven and earth to its own responses, as touchy as an earthworm forever being prodded by a straw. It is inevitable that we should judge in the light of such knowledge as we have, unaware of its limitations; and never has there been a time when in the arts greater knowledge has been so much at the mercy of less or the verdicts of ignorance so decisive. Poetry, both present and past, is misread in the light of theories which deny imagination. But whereas there is nothing in positivist thought and theories not perfectly comprehensible to a Blake or a Coleridge or a Yeats (or to our poet), the reverse is not the case. Yet by their reiteration of faith in the imagination the English poets, from Spenser to Milton, from Blake and Coleridge to Keats and Shelley, from Yeats to Edwin Muir and Vernon Watkins, have preserved in English culture a knowledge obscured by her philosophers (Locke, Blake's enemy, was the type of all later positivists who believe man to possess no knowledge except through the senses) and indeed by her religion, which has taken the bias of a temperamental pragmatism. Without knowledge of this mind and access to its fountains no true poetry can be written, but only an imitation which, while it may appear indistinguishable to those deaf to the 'other' voice, cannot for a moment deceive those attuned to it. Thus it is that in discussions of verse with such people one so often has the sense of talking of two different things. To those who rule out life an acorn is a poor kind of pebble: the difference is not of degree but of kind.

Vernon Watkins is familiar with Coleridge's thought and with Blake's, with Plotinus and the Platonic philosophers who were their teachers as they were Yeats's. He is also well acquainted with the parallel history of German poetry; he himself has published a volume of fine translations of Heine, and a sequence of poems to Holderlin. But one may guess that it was not by way of learning of this kind that the initiatory knowledge of the poet came to him first; but rather, as he implies, by way of the vital memory of the Welsh bardic tradition. This tradition transmits, as surely as Plato or Coleridge or Blake, the doctrine of poetic inspiration.

This 'other' mind of inspiration is beautifully expressed in the Welsh mythological story of the poet-child Taliesin, a theme to which Vernon Watkins often returns. Taliesin dies and reincarnates, unageing and indestructible: his knowledge is as old as the world. Robert Graves and Charles Williams have given versions of the famous 'Lay of Taliesin', and Vernon Watkins descants on the theme in 'Taliesin and The Mockers' (*Affinities*, 1962):

> Before men walked
> I was in these places.
>
> I was here
> When the mountains were laid.
>
> I am as light
> To eyes long blind,
> I, the stone,
> Upon every grave.
>
> I saw black night
> Flung wide like a curtain.
>
> I looked up
> At the making of stars.

> I stood erect
> At the birth of rivers.
> I observed
> The designing of flowers.

This spirit of the divine wisdom is also in the Taliesin legend identified with the prophetic tradition both Christian and pre-Christian. The same wisdom that was present when the mountains were laid was present at the Crucifixion, and inspires all prophetic (that is to say poetic) utterance:

> I was a lamp
> In Solomon's temple;
> I, the reed
> Of an auguring wind.
>
> What do you seek
> In the salmon river,
> Caught in the net
> What living gold?

(an allusion to the Celtic Salmon of Wisdom). The poetry of Taliesin is the only true poetry:

> Mock me they will
> Those hired musicians,
> They at Court
> Who command the schools.
>
> Mock though they do,
> My music stands
> Before and after
> Accusing silence.

The argument is identical with that of Milton's Jesus defending the Jewish tradition of prophetic inspiration against Satan's last temptation, human learning.

Through his participation in a still living tradition, Vernon Watkins commands great advantages over poets whose sources are solely literary. Inseparable from the poetic doctrine of Taliesin is the mythical story itself and the symbols associated with it; and in using these the poet is assured of being understood by those to whom his poems are most immediately addressed. A second advantage is that the dress of his mythology is identical with the natural world of present Wales. All Taliesin's stars and birds and rivers, and also the Hebrew and Christian themes of the 'Lay', remain contemporary. The Welsh poet has even the advantage over the Irish poets who, led by Yeats, attempted to revive ancient Irish mythology, for Taliesin's symbols are cosmic and timeless in themselves. There is doubtless an esoteric meaning within the Bardic tradition which is perhaps not to be understood apart from the Druid learning perpetuated presumably in the Taliesin poems; yet it is certainly true that, while loaded with the riches of the past, these symbols are no less appropriate to the present.

How very much within this tradition Vernon Watkins was and was to remain may not have been apparent to readers who saw in his early 'Ballad of the Mari Lwyd' a *tour-de-force* (which it is) evoked by a picturesque custom which the poet remembers from childhood. On the last night of the old year a mare's skull decked with ribbons was carried from house to house by 'a party of singers, wits and impromptu poets who, on the pretext of blessing, boasting of the sanctity of what they carried, tried to gain entrance to a house, for the sake of obtaining food and drink. The method they used was to challenge those within to a rhyming contest.' Thus our poet's first experience of the art of verse was in a context at once popular and sacred. The horse (which in other Celtic countries also is associated with the dead) is the symbolic vehicle of all those powers outside the world of the living who in every tradition seek to gain admittance. Perhaps (as Y. Evans-Wentz argues in his *Fairy Faith in Celtic Countries*) reincarnation was part of the teaching of the Druids and therefore part of the Bardic tradition which has lingered into the modern world as folklore. Be this as it may, for Vernon Watkins the dead and the unborn are near akin. Yeats in his later years said that the only two themes to hold the interest of an intelligent man are, finally, the mysteries of sex and the dead; and the mystery of life and death is, seen now from the side of birth, now of death, the central theme of Vernon Watkins's poetry, expressed on many levels and in many moods.

The wits and impromptu poets who carried the *Mari* from house to house boasted of 'the sanctity of what they carried'. The *Mari* is a sacred cult object associated with the dead who themselves are the memory of the world immortal in the 'other' mind. Must we not perhaps define the sacred as whatever comes from that world, speaks from it, is born from it or returns to it? Since the bard is the oracle of that mind, that world, his office was traditionally held to be sacred, and is so still in so far as his inspiration comes from that fountain. It is no doubt precisely this different (though traditional) conception of the role of the poet which sets Vernon Watkins apart in the profane modern world. He is a true initiate; his theme is bardic sacred lore.

The evocation of the 'other' mind by incantatory rhythms is as old as mankind; and whatever the reason may be, the gift of lyrical and incantatory speech seems at all times to accompany 'inspired' utterance and to be the natural gift of those who know how to tap the springs. Plato in the *Ion* describes this characteristic of inspired speech of the poets, who in their sober minds are incapable of rhapsodic utterance. Vernon Watkins has this gift to a marked degree. His 'Ballad of the Mari Lwyd' is a poem which seems rather given than made, the utterance rather of the race than of an individual poet. It is by the compulsion of their incantation that the dead strive to break down the defences of the living:

> There were jumping sausages, roasting pies,
> And long loaves in the bin,
> And a stump of Caerphilly to rest our eyes,
> And a barrel rolling in.

> But dry as the grave from Gruffydd Bryn
> We are come without one rest;

> And now you must let Mari in:
> She must inspire your feast.'

> Midnight. Midnight. Midnight. Midnight.
> Hark at the hands of the clock.

> 'For she knows all from the birth of the Flood
> To this moment where we stand
> In a terrible frost that binds the blood
> In a cramp that claws the hand.

> Give us rhyme for rhyme through the wood of the door
> Then open the door if you fail.
> Our wit is come from the sea-wave's roar,
> The stars, and the stinging hail.'

The knowledge of the *Mari* and her head is Taliesin's knowledge. With a subtle change of rhythm the sacred pleads for admission

in images at once holy and homely, familiar and fraught with
the riddling wisdoms of the mystery:

We bring from Cader Idris
And those ancient valleys,
Mari of your sorrows,
Queen of the star fillies.'

You'll not play skittles with us,
White Spirit. Spray of malice;
Froth from an old barrel:
Tell us if that be holy.

'Hers the white art that rouses
Light in the darkest palace,
Though black as a mole's burrow;
Truly we come to bless.'

You come from drunkard's houses
And bent, picklock alleys.
You come to thieve or borrow:
Your starved loins poke and press.

'Great light you shall gather,
For Mari here is holy;
She saw dark thorns harrow
Your God crowned with holly.'

Have you watched snowflakes wither?
They fasten, then fade slowly,
Hither and thither blowing:
Your words are falling still.

'Deeper sadness knowing
Than death's great melancholy,
We journeyed from Calgarw,
From that skull-shaped hill.'   [Calvary]

A white horse frozen blind,
Hurled from a sea-wave's hollow,
Fostered by spray and wind,
Profane and priestlike thing!

'She has those precious secrets
Known to the minstrel solely,
Experienced in the marrow,
Quick to tame beasts unruly.'

She should have been a whistle
For that tames our collie;
He darts on like an arrow,
Then he creeps up slowly.

'O, if she were a whistle
She would not call your collie,
But through this keyhole narrow
Try, your wits to rally.'

Go back to Cader Idris,
To your Dry Bones Valley.
Death shall pounce tomorrow
And break upon your folly.

So it is at all times with the 'other' mind and its wisdom; the
world of common consciousness is reluctant to admit it, holy and
obscene, blessed and accursed, too great a burden of knowledge
for the living to bear.

The Mari's shadow is too bright,
Her brilliance is too black.
None can bear that terror
When the pendulum swings back.

This poem seems an initiation which the poet has received from
the ancestors, which has continued to fertilize all his future work.

David Jones in an essay, 'The Myth of Arthur', has described
the characteristic evanescence, melting and mingling of contours
and planes of reality which characterize the Celtic genius. 'A
half aquatic world . . . it introduces a feeling of transparency and
interpenetration of one element with another, of transposition
and metamorphosis.' Both Dylan Thomas and Vernon Watkins
share this delicate, intricate and dazzling web of intermingled
elements as they weave the texture of a world less concrete than
that of the English, more like the glittering veil of *maya* as conceived by the Indian metaphysics, a system made up not of solid
substances but of appearances. Yeats and the Irish poets turned
to India for a metaphysics to match their own Celtic inheritance
of subtle myth and a cosmic sense of the whole implied in every
separate part – the past and future in the present, the dead in the
living and rebirth in decay – rarely found in England. Vernon
Watkins lets fall the names of Plotinus, Blake and Yeats; he
always gives the impression that he writes from a great reserve

of knowledge. Initiate he is: and in this he perhaps differs from Dylan Thomas, for whom nevertheless the word 'holy', which he so often used, had a personal meaning whose emotion colours all he wrote. But if Dylan Thomas surpassed his friend in dazzling richness and the fullness of the flow of life in his work, Vernon Watkins has the greater metaphysical sense.

It would be wrong to suppose that, a friend and contemporary, Vernon Watkins is the same kind of poet as Dylan Thomas, only not quite so good; neither judgment would be true, although there are, of course, resemblances.

. . . O lead me that I may drown
In those earlier cobbles, reflected; a street that is strewn with palms,
Rustling with blouses and velvet. Yet I alone
By the light of the sunflower deepening, here stand, my eyes cast down
To the footprints of accusations, and hear the faint, leavening
Music of first Welsh words; that gust of plumes
'They shall mount up like eagles,' dark-throated assumes
Cold-sunned, low thunder and gentleness of the authentic Throne.

– this might be Dylan Thomas – or from 'The Spoils of War' (the theme is almost the same as Thomas's 'Ceremony After a Fire-Raid'):

She sprang, luminous on a wish, to the trivial
Tread of her gallows-drop, reaching for a cushion for her child in the shelter to sleep on,
Crossed her own tombstone, then all the stars ran in
And the world shot back like a ball;
Dropping from nowhere from a whirlwind of skies and eyes,
Casting the vesture and tidings of those calamities,
To a shrouded, most mute place, to her inmost call.

These examples are from *The Lady with the Unicorn* (1948), the collection in which the resemblances to Dylan Thomas seem most frequent. They have in common that prodigality of dazzling images declaimed in what Blake called 'the voice of a true orator', a voice perhaps made possible for both by the emotional climate of Wales, in which such voices do not go unheard, as in England they are likely to do.

But all along Vernon Watkins has adhered to his symbols with a more conscious dedication to their sacred and traditional content. All life is foaled by the sacred *Mari*:

And whoever watches a foal sees two images,
Delicate, circling, born, the spirit with blind eyes leaping
And the left spirit, vanished, yet here, the vessel of ages
Clay-cold, blue, laid low by her great wide belly the hill.

– or (in Horatian Alcaics), writing of human birth,

O returning child, not knowing why you were born,
Not understanding world's beauty the dead sustain,
The sharpness of colour, the clearness of water are yours;
The love there shadowed you know not.
What first I feared as a rite I love as a sacrament.
The spring returns. I look. There is no dissembling.
The brook falters, runs on. I divine those meanings,
Listening to tongues that are silent.

In the fine poem 'Niobe' the bereaved mother turned to stone
is herself a landscape, a threshold between life and death; she is
the dark face of the cosmic mystery, arrested, in mourning, under
its aspect of tragedy:

The winged grief taloned in the place of death
Is she.
The frozen wintry stream's enchanted breath
Is she.
She is the stinging herb, the barb that rends.
She is the anchor of the winds and clouds.
She is the crag that bends
The stormcloud to its point that forms the floods.

Who knows the threshold of her secrecies,
And who can enter
The place that grief has forced with its own tears?
Where grief is true it is the earth that dies;
The image of one loved outweighs the Earth.

Why should she read the sundial's old degrees
Who knows a timeless birth,
Whose heart is fixed in rock beneath time's centre?
She cannot, like old trees,
Stretch forth a pattern from unwounded years.

Like the *mari*

'Bright is her midnight, but her day is sable'

At a time when it is so widely assumed that no more is needed
in poetry than the description of something perceived by the
c

senses or some emotion felt by the poet, or a complexity of images
and feelings (at which point Dylan Thomas frequently was content to remain), it is necessary to point out that a characteristic
of Watkins's poetry is the presence of some organizing idea which
can only be apprehended poetically, some true cosmic or metaphysical apprehension of what Coleridge calls 'the eternal in and
through the temporal'. Inevitably, either everything in nature
has this dimension or nothing has; no poet can be sometimes
merely descriptive of physical or emotional sensations, and sometimes writing 'symbolically'. The symbol one may call the measure of wisdom, since its reach is in depth, in virtue of the analogy
by which every plane of reality expresses and reflects every other;
and Vernon Watkins's soundings are deep. In *The Lace-maker* he
employs, as does Blake, whose women are all weavers of the
texture of the world, or Edwin Muir, whose Penelope wove
human lives upon the loom of history, the images of weaving
for the purposes of a symbolic statement; this is but normal traditional practice and only at an abnormal time has it become
necessary to point to so obvious a usage. The lace-maker's hand
is weaving, like light, the 'minute particulars' of the veil of the
visible, quietly accomplishing the triumph of light over darkness:

> And your shadowing, birdlike hand,
> Migrated from a young land,
> Brings, like a midnight lark,
> Whiter than whitest sand,
> Light running out of dark.

The bird suggests, perhaps, the musical harmony which runs
through the universe, and the 'young land' some Tir-nan-og
remembered beyond merely individual youth. The implicit
equation of 'particles' of light to sand in an hourglass leads on to
that old image of material mutability, the sea, and the white
of lace –

> Sea, for one hour, one place,
> One moment caught in a knot.

This is not mere complexity of wit; it is sacred lore. The thread
foam of lace is *maya* itself,

> No sooner come than gone;
> So light it is not weighed down
> By any thought that will stay.
> You have seen time's flood that would drown
> Surpassed in butterflies' play.

The next poem in order of publication, 'The Butterflies', takes up this thought of subtle weaving; the delicate verse-form is as perfect in its way as Herrick's:

> High, lost in air, they pair,
> Butterflies blue, so fair,
> Blind in stopped flight,
> Twined on a thread,
> Then drop where light, effaced,
> Shuts, in the dread
> Secret of sepalled air.
> Their petals chaste.

Light is the woven thread; butterflies, delicately and minutely articulated as lace, are an apt image alike of the perfection and the transience of the souls they symbolize. Space and time are woven by the reception of the light of the sun in their consciousness, eye and antennae:

> Hid, meadow-masked from sight,
> Hushed near the pulse of light,
> They magnify
> With round big eye
> Antennae'd, that gold place
> From which the sky
> Seizes their still delight,
> Inventing space.

I should like to quote the whole of the poem for its beauty, the only quality to which the realists might object in it, for so subtle is its descriptive mask that those who wish to look no farther need not do so; it can be enjoyed, like Shelley's 'Cloud' or 'Skylark', for its imagery, even though the images are themselves words in the language of imaginative discourse, the means not the ends of poetic statement. Beauty and nobility are at all times the distinguishing mark of traditional poetry: necessarily so, since such poetry is concerned with the 'sacred' themes of the cosmos and not with mortality. Irony and vulgarity, so often associated with modern realism (and mistakenly regarded as more 'truthful' than beauty and nobility), are never to be found in any poem of Vernon Watkins's, nor for that matter in the work of Dylan Thomas.

Another characteristic gift of the 'other' mind, lyrical form, is perhaps Vernon Watkins's most outstanding mark as a poet. But if the gift is innate it has certainly been perfected through practice. To a naturally gifted poet knowledge is attracted like iron filings to a pre-existing magnetic field. Thus we find Vernon Watkins using with ease Sapphics and Alcaics, besides many free or strict English lyric and ballad forms. His favourite borrowed form seems to be the Sapphic metre, which in his hands never sounds like an exercise. He does not use, so far as I know, Welsh metrical forms or those assonances borrowed from the Welsh by Hopkins; but in the subtle cadences of the 'Ballad of the Mari Lwyd' one catches the voice of Wales. In all his verse one finds something David Jones points to as characteristic of 'the Celtic thing', 'an elusive hardness, a bent towards the intricate and abstract' – characteristic also, though differently, of Dylan Thomas.

Yeats's influence is often present, riding the feminine Welsh *Mari* like the high horse of Ireland, sometimes with effect:

> Fierce is the music, loud the shouting of Tamburlaine
>   tearing the throats of kings.
> Antigone sees her father; a great light Oedipus brings
> Out of the trodden darkness; the mountain speaks through
>   the springs.

At other times Yeats's influence is unfortunate, and makes apparent the difference between the gossamer-light weaving and interweaving which is Watkins's Welsh native bent, and the proud stateliness of Yeats; as in this passage from 'The Conception', which invites comparison with 'Leda and the Swan' to its own disadvantage:

> Are not the stars of heaven like this one seed,
> And does not Earth revolve within the womb?
> What mandrake screamed? What shudder shakes the tomb?
> What infant crying out in mortal need?
> What sacred pattern, leaping from time's loom,
> Breaks, for the opulence of the breast to feed?

The rhetorical questions, the ponderous word 'opulence' seem too static for Dr. Watkins's essentially fluent patterns. It is not in the direction of Yeats that Vernon Watkins's natural development seems to lie. Rather it is to some modern return to a poetry like that of the English metaphysicals, especially Herbert and Vaughan, whose roots also were Welsh. It seems that Dr. Watkins has been for a long time moving from pagan rite to Christian sacrament; his lyricism tends more and more to diverge from the abundant rhapsodic image-laden poetry of his own youth and that of Dylan Thomas; his themes, as they become more austere in feeling and image at the same time become more complex and more reflective. Like Vaughan and Herbert 'one place' suffices to give him themes whose complexity is all in depth. Yeats was in this sense a more worldly poet. So, curiously enough, was Edwin Muir, whose visionary poems embraced the European history of his time in a way not Auden himself, most extraverted of poets, has done. Every poet has his limitations, but this is not necessarily a weakness; it merely defines his field. Certainly Vernon Watkins's field is, in a worldly sense, a narrow one; but I do not find his poetry so any more than that of those earlier metaphysical poets who by choice withdrew from the world to seek for wisdom in depth rather than knowledge in extent.

The Death Bell (1954) is a return to the theme of the *Mari Lwyd*, the two worlds of the dead and the living. This poem could never have the popularity of the earlier incantatory magic. It is more austere, restrained, profound and, though less immediately impressive, a more finely written poem. It is also, so it seems to me, a better poem than Dylan Thomas's 'Do not go Gentle into that Good-night' because subtler and more sober in its searchings, as it is in its expression, of the themes of death and immortality. Dylan Thomas assumes annihilation, and for those who share his view of death his emotional response to the situation of his father's blindness and impending death must seem as sufficient in its content as it is natural in its intensity. Vernon Watkins's theme (also occasioned by the death of his father) is not so much death as the mystery of immortality. The image of the bell, swinging between the two extremes of dust and spirit, hope and despair, is used with that exhaustive searching of every possible implicit symbolic analogy which characterizes the metaphysical poets of the seventeenth century.

The bell itself is more than an instrument. It is involved with all for whom it has tolled, and its resonance has the power to beckon everyone whom its sound has touched. Before it rises, it must sink to its full weight at the end of the rope, and lie there, as a dead body must, under a single thread, expecting resurrection. The harmony within the bell, and within the dead body, is musically controlled, and depends upon the mercy and judgment of the heavenly scales for its peace. These scales are discernible everywhere in nature, but they may be discerned only by intuition, not by the reason.

Let us admit it, Dr. Watkins's theme is not only unfashionable at this time: it is difficult and profound, embodying a knowledge not to be bought at the cheap rate which this age demands. Thought and language alike suggest Herbert or Vaughan (far more than Donne from whom the theme of the death bell – 'It tolls for thee' – is taken):

> All is conjecture here
> And affirmation there.
> Here is the bell man-rung
> And there the angel's tongue.
> Ah, could the skies reveal
> Two spirits in one peal;
> But great design hath hid
> Foreknowledge from the lid.
> Here is the reckoning
> But there the austere scales swing
> Where last is counted first
> And confidence reversed
>
> .   .   .
>
> There is no bell that swings
> Though swift as angels' wings,
> But answers to the mould
> Fiery, primaeval, cold,
> In which it first was cast.
> Though resurrection's blast
> Thrill the resounding nave
> And call from niche and grave,
> Where sunbeams fall aslant,
> Each holy celebrant,
> There is no temporal flight
> Can raise mankind to light
> Save where the font is laid.
> Cooled and prepared by shade
> Each must achieve his own
> Deliverance from stone,
> Pulled by the world to make
> True answer, nor to break,
> But rise to heaven through weight,
> Weaned of an earth made great
> Crowning with man-pulled ropes
> Those efficacious drops.

The complexity of the ideas here interwoven, within the terms of a symbolism of ponderosity, musical resonance, font, rope and

bell, is in form, even in vocabulary, as timeless as its themes, perhaps because the vocabulary of our subtler thought changes
more slowly than the words of common usage. We are reminded
of the perfect manner of Herbert and Vaughan, who in writing
upon the most intimate themes never intrude their own personality or attempt to address ours.

The elusive figure of Taliesin unites pre-Christian with
Christian themes; and in 'Taliesin and the Spring of Vision' the
prophetic Bardic spirit itself seeks baptism; the cosmic spirit is
reluctant to leave the freedom of timeless nature for human history, yet he makes the choice:

And you are my constant, who have endured all vicissitudes
In the cradle of sea, Fate's hands, and the spinning waters.
The measure of past grief is the measure of present joy.
Your tears, which have dried to Chance, now spring from a secret.
Here time's glass breaks, and the world is transfigured in music.

'Taliesin took refuge under the unfledged rock' from time and
history; but realization comes to him that the time-bound human
condition taught Shakespeare and Dante and Blake; the cosmic
voices seek to hold the poet to a world of perfection which for
that very reason falls short of human perfection:

Taliesin answered: 'I have encountered the irreducible diamond
In the rock. Yet now it is over. Omniscience is not for man.
Christen me, therefore, that my acts in the dark may be just,
And adapt my partial vision to the limitation of time.'

Vernon Watkins's Christianity is thus a seed or acorn into which
the essence of the pagan cosmic sense, which filled with blossom
and bough, with sea foam and rock and wings his earlier poetry,
has been distilled; the tree of life has been diminished to a grain
which in its simplicity holds the potential complexity of the tree
both as memory and as promise. The 'sanctity' of the old mare's
skull is deepened into the exploration of themes which will set
him even farther apart from contemporary profane English
culture. It may be that his deliberate baptism of the bardic spirit
is reflected in his attempt in his last volume, *Affinities*, to write on
human rather than natural themes, odes to poets dead and living,
friends or strangers. 'Revisited Waters' was written for the
Quatercentenary of Repton School – an unpromising subject,
though Gray immortalized the Eton playing fields. Surprisingly,
this occasional poem is a very fine one. I would expect Vernon

Watkins in the nature of things to follow in the future religious themes to their source, 'out of nature'. If he becomes more explicitly a religious poet, he is likely to be less appreciated than ever; but his choice was made long ago, and its price known.

> O dark, interior flame,
> O spring Elijah struck:
> Obscurity is fame:
> Glory and praise are luck.
> Nothing can live so wild
> As those ambitious wings
> Majestic, for love's child
> Defending ancient springs.

What we did not know thirty years ago was how extreme would be the isolation of those who hold to tradition. It then seemed that there were at least some values which were agreed upon between the profane positivist world and the world of the 'ancient springs'. Now we know that this is not so, perhaps was never so. At all events, we can now no longer deceive ourselves. It seems that there no longer exist any common terms or common values; beyond a certain point of divergence communication becomes impossible. Relative ignorance may still recognize and aspire towards knowledge; absolute ignorance is perfectly complacent. Tradition, which recognizes a difference between knowledge and ignorance, cannot come to terms with a world in which there are no longer any standards by which truth and falsehood may be measured.

1964

3

DAVID GASCOYNE AND THE PROPHETIC ROLE

'Genius, Poet: do we know what these words mean? An inspired Soul, once more vouchsafed as, direct from Nature's own great fire-heart, to see the Truth, and speak it, and do it.'
Carlyle, *Past and Present*. Bk. II. Ch. 9.

The publication, in 1965, of the *Collected Poems* of David Gascoyne[1] has brought to the notice of a generation to whom his name is unfamiliar (for his last work, *Night Thoughts*, was published in 1955) the work of an outstanding poet.

David Gascoyne was born in 1916. His father was a bank-clerk (subsequently for a time manager of a bank in the small town of Fordingbridge between Salisbury and Poole) and on his mother's side he is related to the actress, Winifred Emery. Many, even most writers of the present time (and among them poets) have come from lower middle-class suburbs; talent is at home anywhere, and numbers of writers have described suburban life in terms of suburban or working-class values; have made those values articulate, comprehensible, acceptable. Some would see in this articulation the sole task of literature.

But true imagination is an alien presence in any society. Always it seems to manifest itself in a way which cannot be explained, and there is perhaps no section of society, and no kind of society into which some bearer of this supernatural gift has not at some time been born. There is nothing, in David Gascoyne's kind and quality of imagination, which is typical of, expressive of, suburban values or modes of thought; he is no more of the world into which he was born than the angel Tolstoy's cobbler found naked in the snow behind a church, and brought into his house to learn shoe-making.

[1] Edited and introduced by Robin Skelton and published by Oxford University Press.

I first met David Gascoyne when he was, I suppose, about seventeen or eighteen years old; he had already published a novel – *Opening Day*[1] (to which he no longer refers, but which contains nevertheless some remarkably interesting biographical material) and a volume of verse – *Roman Balcony and Other Poems*[2]. Tall, possessed as he still was of the androgynous beauty of adolescence, his blue eyes expressive of great depth of feeling and imagination, his vulnerable mouth not yet brought into an expression of sorrow, he had, even then, a dignity, a presence, as if of a being from another world. His voice was deep and musical, though his speech was rapid and nervous. David Gascoyne, whose unusual gentleness and charity would never utter a reproach against any person (what seems to him evil he regards never as the real person, but as a failure of that person to become real) is himself a reproach: nothing false or ugly is unexposed in his presence. In his writings there is (whenever he has achieved what he has at all times attempted) little or nothing that is personal; his gift has been rather genius than talent.

In his novel *Opening Day* the sixteen-year-old author has drawn, obviously, upon his own memories; and without a trace of vanity notes the loneliness which is the inevitable lot of the young child of genius 'born in exile':

'. . . he had taken his loneliness as a matter of course, but seeing more of other children made him wish for that companionship that because of his unusual nature he was seldom to have.'

Adaptation to environment is deemed a virtue in this world; but the imagination, whose kingdom is 'not of this world', must wage a bitter struggle against 'adaptation', compromise, and ultimate forgetfulness. The poet, who in infancy 'lived in the strange and antique solemnity of semi-consciousness, through the bright dreams of which only those things that were especially pleasing, beautiful or new, unpleasant, horrible or terrifying could penetrate', called such adaptation by another name – spiritual death, 'the gradual sinking of his individuality, his thwarted talents, to the drab level of this mundane suburb that for ever sprawled beneath an ashen sky'; a death many have had to die, compelled by necessity to join that long procession of black-coated city workers of whom Eliot in Dante's words exclaimed:

---

[1] Published by Cobden Sanderson, London, in 1933.
[2] Published by Lincoln Williams, in 1932.

'I had not known death had undone so many.'

In 1935, in *A Short Survey of Surrealism*[1], the poet looks back upon the world from which he has himself so barely and so recently escaped, and re-affirms the refusal of the imagination to adapt itself to that sad man-made Hades:

Confined from early childhood in a world that almost everything he ever hears or reads will tell him is the one and only *real* world and that, as almost no-one, on the contrary, will point out to him, is a prison, man – l'homme moyen sensuel – bound hand and foot – not only by those economic chains of whose existence he is becoming ever more and more aware, but also by chains of second-hand and second-rate *ideas*, the preconceptions and prejudices that help to bind together the system known (ironically, as some think) by the name of 'civilization', is for ever barred except in sleep from that, other plane of existence where stones fall upwards and the sun shines by night, if it chooses, and where even the trees talk freely with the statues that have come down for ever from their pedestals – a world to which entrance has generally been supposed, up till now, to be the sole privilege of poets and other madmen (p. ix).

To say that imagination loves and seeks out whatever is beautiful, shrinks from what is ugly, is a tautology, since the beautiful might be defined as what the imagination finds congruent to itself. The hero of Mr. Gascoyne's novel discovered, as childhood can, whatever beauty his world afforded him. He noticed how the sandy cart-track, not yet a road,

constituted a maze of miniature streams and perilous cataracts down which to float straws or matchboxes. Along the edge of the road grass grew at random under the sharp-edged flints and with it clusters of small, spark-like yellow blossoms that he learnt to know by the name of 'Lady's Slipper'. The name appealed to his imagination and stuck in his memory.

Paradise perhaps always retains the aspect of whatever images first reflected it back to us; and (though he knew natural beauty under other forms – the pine and rhododendron woods near Bournemouth, the haunts of heron by the river at Fordingbridge) it is notable that 'nature' most often appears in his poems as a dispossessed unheeded beauty – the quarry, the urban park, London trees at night – an image of lost paradise, on the outskirts of the human and urban world. In 'The Gravel-Pit Field'

[1] Published by Cobden Sanderson, in 1935.

one such 'nondescript terrain' receives (with Traherne's 'orient
and immortal wheat' and Muir's industrial stone 'clean at the
heart') its apotheosis:

> The shabby coat of coarse grass spread
> Unevenly across the ruts
> And humps of bumpy soil; the bits
> Of stick and threads of straw; loose clumps
> Of weeds with withered stalks and black
> Tatters of leaf and scorched pods: all
> These intertwined minutiae
> Of Nature's humblest growths persist
> In their endurance here like rock.
> As with untold intensity
> On the far edge of Being, where
> Life's last faint forms begin to lose
> Name and identity and fade
> Away into the Void, endures
> The final thin triumphant flame
> Of all that's most despoiled and bare.
> So these least stones, in the extreme
> Of their abasement might appear
>
> Like rare stones such as could have formed
> A necklet worn by a dead queen
> Of a great Pharaoh, in her tomb. . . .

Nature is that inviolate and healing principle which silently
repairs all man-made devastation. In 'Spring MCMXL':

> Still must a punctual goddess wake to ascend
> The rocky stairs, up into earth's chilled air
> And pass upon her mission through those carrion ranks
> Picking her way among a maze of broken brick
> To quicken with her footsteps the short sooty grass between.

The adolescent of the novel, always scanning his drab world
for whatever redeeming images of the beautiful it would yield,
notices, on a railway-journey into London, some nasturtiums
growing in a tin bath outside a block of tenement buildings; and
years later that image he tried to catch, 'to hold it and taste it
slowly, to crystallize it for ever' has perhaps helped to create in
'Fragments Towards a Religio Poetae' the lines:

> Though towards the suburbs the city becomes wan
> And dark with the weariness of women who have to queue
> Outside the horse-butcher's or for the home-bound bus,

On even the busiest days the sun sometimes paints propaganda
For the possibility, of the Kingdom of Heaven on earth
Over the prices scrawled in white on the shops' plate-glass
And the attic window-boxes above the market
Offer a tribute of happy beauty to the omniscient Heavenly Eye.

From an extremely early age the poet 'trained himself consciously to annotate and classify for future contemplation the passing sights, sensations and sounds of each moment of existence' (*Opening Day*). Yet far from becoming therefore a 'realist', a camera-eye, David Gascoyne (scanning all with the eye of the imagination) discerned always the qualitative essence; not for him the too prevalent obscuring of all distinctions between the vile and the sublime, the beautiful and the ugly upon which a pseudo-scientific 'detachment' prides itself: these distinctions, on the contrary, become apparent only to the qualitative discernment of imagination; and if they often lie otherwise than as the world sees, that is nothing new:

> The Sermon on the Mount is just as often misconstrued
> By Marxists as by wealthy congregations, it would seem.
>
> ('A Vagrant')

The greater part of his novel is in fact a meticulous qualitative record of all the poet's eye saw from the windows of bus and train on a journey from Cambridge Park to Waterloo Station. Commenting upon the obscuring of such observation which happens when we are preoccupied with our own concerns, he writes that trees, houses, people, 'appear to us individually to be comparatively not worth our attention because the universal law of appearance decrees it so, because otherwise all life would be tuned up to one high level of supreme importance, the strain of which no human mind could stand'. That intense degree of experience of the real world has nevertheless been David Gascoyne's especial gift.

Naturally enough the poet as a boy kept the ugliness at bay with the aid of whatever beauty he could lay hold of in the artificial paradises of music and poetry and the other arts. As a chorister at Salisbury choir-school he was attuned to the splendour of the great cathedral:

'Out of the grass it rose like a tremendous tree, petrified and sterilized in all its diversity of ornamental foliage by some antique winter of prodigious violence' – so begins a passage of 'fine

writing' in his novel, suggestive in its style of the writings of
Pater, whom he at that time (along with Beardsley, Ruskin,
Emerson and Poe) admired. He also at that time received his first
education in music:

> Evening service was to him a wonder. At Evensong, when a
> subdued and vernal twilight penetrated the very ancient windows,
> bathing the tombs in beauty, they sang long and dramatic operatic
> anthems by Steiner and Sullivan, or passages taken from the *Elijah*
> or the *Messiah*.

At sixteen a prodigious reader (already reading in French
Baudelaire, Rimbaud, Gide, Mallarmé and the Symbolists) he
discovered his world also in the paradises of Debussy and Ravel
and Chopin; already he played the piano-music of Schönberg,
as later of Satie and Poulenc. 'This was his taste. Van Gogh;
Rimbaud; Beardsley. This was his method of escape.' From the
arts of music and poetry he created for himself an interior environment, in which he could take refuge from the world of
'spiritual death'.

There are a hundred motives, good and bad, for the reading of
books; and 'education' is, at worst, a process of acquiring a mass
of information which others have decided constitutes some field
of necessary knowledge. But the poet reads what he himself
hungers for as his food. It might occur to no one to call David
Gascoyne learned; yet there must be few learned men who have
read more books than he, or retained from their reading so much,
or to better purpose. So we see the sixteen-year-old boy taking
down from the shelves of the public library books chosen for
mere love; never in order to 'evaluate'. If he saw faults in some
novel by Huysmans, or in the poems of minor contemporaries of
Rimbaud, he none the less received with gratitude what they
had to give. Imagination finds its food, or does not find, merely
disregarding what is not to its purpose. David Gascoyne was
from his boyhood a supremely imaginative reader; for years he
made a habit of copying into notebooks passages which pleased
or impressed him – another part of that gathering, 'for future
reference', of the material he so early felt the poet would some
day require. Whether in poetry, mysticism or metaphysics he
read always the originals, never works 'on' those authors among
whom he moved, even as a boy, as an equal among equals.

Creation flowed naturally from this great intake of the arts.

'All this dream-spun beauty (external to him once, but that had now been read by him, heard by him, and therefore become as it were, digested by him and a part of him) formed an entirely original synthesis and of this synthesis was born the desire to create' (*Opening Day*). With that desire came the instinct of the cygnet to seek out the other swans, to be with his own kind; and in a surprisingly short time he had found his place in the literary circles of London, and, soon after, Paris, where the surrealist movement was at that time the growing-point of the arts.

The anti-social and subversive aspect of that movement commended itself to the still adolescent poet whose struggle to escape from lower middle-class suburbia had cost him dear. There is a strong vein of merely adolescent subversiveness in Huysmans, Jarry and Lautréamont, difficult to take seriously at a later age; and this subtly, imperceptibly merging into the genius of Rimbaud on the one hand (imagination seeking its freedom) and on the other the pure nihilism of *Dada*. Perhaps in every revolution these two elements are strangely confused – the forces of life which seek expression, and those 'devils' which had possessed Pyotr Stepanovitch and his friends, whose only purpose is to destroy; and whose agents often do not themselves know whom they are serving. Thus we find David Gascoyne (in his *A Short Survey of Surrealism*) praising 'the masterpiece of Jarry, *Ubu Roi*' who is 'a monster, representing under the guise of the most far-fetched cruelty and stupidity, forces of bourgeois law, order and respectability' (p. 15). With the innocence of his inexperience he writes with approval:

Negativism, revolt, the destruction of all values, Dada was a violent protest against art, literature, morals, society. It spat in the eye of the world. Life was a disgusting riddle, but we can ask harder ones, was the dadaist attitude. To many intelligent men at this time, suicide seemed to be the one remaining solution to the problem of living, and Dada was a spectacular form of suicide, a manifestation of almost lunatic despair (p. 23).

'Bourgeois', as David Gascoyne uses the word, means not so much any class in particular but all that in society is contrary to the imagination, the ultimate reality no less of *l'homme moyen sensuel* than of the poet. It was in Germany that the 'sacrilegious, subversive and altogether outrageous' aspects of Dada reached their extreme expression; an exhibition at Cologne, in 1929, was characterized by images of destruction and excrement, at which a young girl dressed as for first communion recited obscene poems: 'Destruction and sacrilege not at all uncommon features of the feverish atmosphere of Germany immediately after the War' (p. 34). David Gascoyne did not know (writing in 1935) that he was in fact describing the state of Germany before a very much worse war. Such evil jokes appear less amusing since Belsen and Buchenwald put nihilism into practice on a mass scale, and the instruments of mechanized warfare made the prophetic nightmares of Ernst seem as old fashioned as Jules Verne. Had such art been after all, cathartic, or had it played its part in the loosing of the devils into a possessed world?

But there were other aspects of surrealism of more positive value to a young poet; above all a return to the springs of imagination, an exploration of the sources of the poetic image, of the poetic language itself.

Surrealism, profiting from the discoveries of Freud and a few other scientific explorers of the unconscious, has conceived poetry as being, on the one hand, a perpetual functioning of the *psyche*, a perpetual flow of irrational thought *in the form of images*, taking place in every human mind and needing only a certain predisposition and discipline in order to be brought to light in the form of written words (or plastic images) and on the other hand a universally valid attitude to experience, a possible mode of living (p. xi).

Like Dostoevsky's 'underground man' the surrealist attitude calls in question the right of discursive reason to dictate to the energies of life; grounds which at least to that extent justify their claim to William Blake among their predecessors as a prophet of the irrational; 'A restatement of the ancient and supposedly discredited notion of inspiration – with a difference' (p. xi). With, indeed, a good many differences.

The crucial difference is the denial of the metaphysical. The psyche was, for the surrealists as for Freud, autonomous and its 'perpetual functioning' and 'irrational flow' envisaged in terms in no way incompatible with materialism. The surrealists were continually professing their solidarity with Communism, unable to see why Moscow withheld its approval; for

the surrealist attitude is totally in accord with the Communist philosophy of dialectical materialism, with its insistence on the synonymity of theory and practice, and . . . only the imminence of proletarian revolution allows surrealism to hope that its aims will ultimately be fulfilled. The surrealist cause is the revolutionary cause (p. xii).

But Russia had her revolution behind her, and wanted no more Pyotr Stepanovitches; were there not already (David Gascoyne with his own revolt against the restrictions of home still fresh in his mind notes with regret) 'such apparent compromises on the part of the Communists as the Franco-Soviet pact and the recent rehabilitation in Russia of the bourgeois conception of the family'? (His novel, however, bears the dedication 'To my Mother').

Those who deny the higher spiritual hierarchies find themselves perforce at the mercy of the lower; as Coomaraswamy at the time said of surrealism. The preponderance, in the surrealist 'irrational' imagery, of 'excrement, blood and putrefaction', of cancerous proliferation of the formless, of machine-like forms of life (insects and arthropods) and mechanisms informed with blind irresistible purpose, is surely the result rather of nihilism than of imagination. Fragmentation characterizes the surrealist world; whereas imagination (as Coleridge, following the Platonic philosophers, understood) is the 'esemplastic power' which gives unity. He would have judged their automatism to be 'fantasy'; lutes and lobsters *ad nauseam.* Yet there seems to be a sort of unconfessed hope that the dreaming mind will organize such material; the Surrealist *Manifesto* declares a belief 'in the omnipotence of the dream and the disinterested play of thought' (First Surrealist *Manifesto*, p. 62,) raising dream into the empty throne of the will, indeed the person. Therefore we cannot also agree that 'surrealism possesses its devotee like the voice of the ancient oracles' (p. 66); for an oracle without a god is not an oracle at all. With the French tendency, besides, towards regarding imaginative material as the mere starting-point for theorizing, whatever was in surrealism oracular, a true expression of the mystery beyond reason, was destroyed before it could manifest itself, through premature rationalization.

Surrealist imagery is not archetypal; often striking, sometimes prophetic, most of what surprised at first by its novelty seems in retrospect the lumber of another age. In the poetry of the most typical (though not, indeed, the best surrealist poets, Eluard and perhaps René Char) every line is a new beginning; and the juxtaposition of image after image, whose shock at first strikes the attention, in the end wearies it for want of an organizing principle;

D

or rather because subjected to the wrong organizing principle, murdered on a Procrustean bed of manifestos and formulations. Mr. Gascoyne wrote a few poems in this style: in 'The Cubical Domes' and 'Rites of Hysteria' images sprawl in monotonous – and derivative – novelty:

> Now the beckoning nudity of diseases putrifies the saloon
> The severed limbs of the galaxy wriggle like chambermaids
> The sewing-machine on the pillar condenses the windmill's halo
> Which poisoned the last infanta by placing a tooth in her ear
> When the creeping groans of the cellar's anemone vanished
> The nightmare spun on the roof a chain-armour of handcuffs
> And the ashtray balanced a ribbon upon a syringe.

Breton noted that this kind of automatism produced 'an illusion of extraordinary verve, much emotion, a considerable assortment of images of a quality we should never have been able to obtain in the normal way of writing' (*A Short Survey of Surrealism*, p. 36). As Paul Eluard said, whoever speaks in another's voice can speak for ever; but such poems were, after all, honest exercises in the *ars poetica* by an adolescent poet.

Paul Eluard was indeed (as David Gascoyne all along realized) a poet of quite another quality, 'one of the most considerable French poets living, a direct descendant of Baudelaire'. Eluard was a revolutionary not of hate but of love. 'The poems of Paul Eluard are pure crystallizations of tenderness and simplicity, of passion and revolt' (p. 76). To his second volume of poems, *Man's Life is This Meat*, David Gascoyne prefaced a translation from Eluard; and one of his own last poems was a magnificent 'Elegiac improvisation' on the death of his early master and friend, which is at the same time a reflection of the style of those Eluard poems, published on the clandestine presses (René Char had one in his country house) which communicated his message:

> Warmly and urgently,
> Simply, convincingly
> Gently and movingly
> Softly, sincerely
> Clearly, caressingly
> Bitterly, painfully,
> Pensively, stumblingly
> Brokenly, heartbreakingly
> Uninterruptedly
> In clandestinity

In anguish, in arms and in anger,
In passion, in Paris, in person
In partisanship, as the poet
Of France's Resistance, the spokesman
Of unconquerable free fraternity.

Eluard had finely written of Baudelaire in a vein more congenial to David Gascoyne's true genius than Péret's destructive and bitter poems some of which (with Humphrey Jennings) he had translated: 'All the powers of unhappiness are on his side. Perhaps there is some chance of winning? Will black and white triumph over grey and dirt? Will the avenging hand finish writing on the walls of the immense prison the accursed sentence that would make them crumble away? But the light is fading, the sentence is interminable.'[1]

The surrealist attack upon the reign of logic remains, in retrospect, as an event of positive value; so, too, must seem another aspect of the movement which strongly appealed to David Gascoyne's already nascent prophetic conception of the poet's role:

'The most vital feature of surrealism is its exclusive interest in that point at which literature and art give place to real life, that point at which imagination seeks to express itself in a more concrete form than words or plastic images' (p. 61). André Breton, the spokesman and moving spirit of the movement, had at one time intended to become a psychiatrist and his understanding of the nature of dreams and the irrational was more than superficial; he it was who took up the cause of the 'insane' against the medical profession, whose 'unbearable and increasing abuse of power' he castigated with the authority of his knowledge. 'Man's imagination should be free, yet everywhere it is in chains' (p. 59) is the theme of the opening pages of the first *Manifesto*; 'even experience has its limits assigned to it. It revolves in a cage from which it becomes more and more difficult to release it' (First Surrealist *Manifesto*, 1924, p. 59). Surrealism as a style, a way of life, was of course confined to members of the movement; but it was not the intention of that few that this should be so. *L'homme moyen sensuel* was to be his own poet and his own painter; no technical skill, 'fine drawing' or craftsmanship is required in the making of a surrealist picture:

[1] *A Short Survey of Surrealism*, p. 6. Quoted from *The Mirror of Baudelaire*, Minotaure, No. 1.

If poetry should be made by all, not one, then everyone should be able to make pictures also. . . . All that is needed to produce a surrealist picture is an unshackled imagination . . . and a few materials: paper or cardboard, pencil, scissors, paste, and an illustrated magazine, a catalogue or a newspaper. The marvellous is within everyone's reach (p. 106).

Herbert Read has since made this idea current; *Education through Art* is a practical, and valuable, outcome of this aspect of surrealist thought; though it remains true that genius is not democratic, and the distinction between (for example) the self-expression of patients under analysis and the art of genius is by no means only a matter of craftsmanship, but much more of the quality and kind of imagination. By October 1934 (the year before the publication of *A Short Survey of Surrealism*, which he had presumably completed when he put surrealism behind him) David Gascoyne had already renounced the theory and practice of automatism; and virtually ceased to be a surrealist. In answer to the question, 'Have you been influenced by Freud?' he wrote in *New Verse*:

'To give oneself up at any time to the writing of poems without the control of reason is, I imagine, to have come under the influence of Freud. I no longer find this navel-gazing activity at all satisfying.' The reason he gives is significant: it is not, as might be thought, because it is inadequate to the requirements of the imagination, but because 'for an English poet with continually growing political convictions it must soon become impossible'.

During the late thirties, the more responsible of the surrealists already felt, in a world so gravely menaced, an evergrowing sense of political responsibility. Louis Aragon had already gone over to orthodox Marxism at the end of 1930; and with the coming of the Second World War, Eluard and Aragon also placed their talents and their lives at the disposal of the French Resistance; and with the advent of those nightmares subliminal fantasies had foreseen, the movement, as such, came to an end.

In June 1925 (in the second number of *The Surrealist Revolution*) Breton had written: 'I believe with all truly free men that the Revolution, even with its abuses, remains the highest and most moving expression that can be given to that love of the Good in which the universal will and individual wills are united' (p. 69).

'The good' was, in England too, identified, during the 1930s, with the cause of the Communist revolution; there too the young poets were politically 'engaged'. Auden, Spender and Day Lewis were not, it is true, concerned with the irrational, nor indeed with the imagination at all; and were, if anything, influenced rather by the official social-realist creed of Marxism. There was, however, for a brief moment, an English counterpart to surrealism (at all events of certain aspects of it) an altogether original variant of the irrationalist movement. Charles Madge, one of the two founders of Mass-Observation, was also much under the influence of Freud; and his friend Humphrey Jennings (painter and film-director) was at the same time one of the most active propagandists for surrealism in England.

Charles Madge originally envisaged 'Mass-Observation' as a technique for recording the subliminal stirrings of the collective mind of the nation; through the images thrown up in such things as advertisements, popular songs, themes in the press, the objects with which people surround themselves (have on their mantel-piece, for example). This idea was akin to (perhaps in part deter-mined by) the surrealist *'objet trouvé'* ('objects functioning sym-bolically') which Dali in particular (anticipating Jung's notion of 'Synchronicity'?) declared could be discovered no less in the objective world than in dreams. Dali defined 'paranoia' (he did not signify by the word a deranged mental state, but rather a peculiarly active one) as 'a mental state enabling the subject, with a superhuman swiftness of mind defying analysis, to draw from the objective world a concrete proof, or illustration of his obsessions, or even of his transitory ideas' (p. 101). So it was that Mass-Observation combined a surrealist conception of the irra-tional with a new kind of sociology. (The other founder of the movement, Tom Harrison, was an anthropologist who had the then novel idea of applying methods of sociology hitherto em-ployed only on savages to the English working-class.) For Charles Madge and Humphrey Jennings the movement had more to do with the nature of the imagination (and the functioning of a collective imagination) than with those Gallup-polls and trade-surveys which have since become commonplace.

This conception made possible a kind of poetic (or pictorial) imagery at once irrational and objective; and it was David Gas-coyne who finally realized and perfected a kind of poetry (written also by Charles Madge and Humphrey Jennings) in which an

imagery of precise and objective realism, gathered from the daily
human (and therefore especially urban) scene, from the habitat
of the common man, is informed with a content not only
supremely imaginative but infused with the imagination of the
collective mind of which it is an eloquent, if unconscious, expression; a listening to the dreaming (for to the dream-state it is,
as Breton said, 'by this time very difficult to set limits' – *Enter the
Mediums*, Littérature No. 6, 1922) – of a nation or a world, itself
unaware of the purport of its own fantasies. Thus the poet re-
assumes the ancient role at once of national prophet, and reader
of the auguries; not from entrails or yarrow-stalks, but from
(literally) the 'writings on walls', the seemingly fortuitous recurring images in the daily records. Anything and everything speaks
to the augur attuned to its meaning. The two apparently irreconcilable opposites are in such poetry brought together: imaginative inspiration, and a realistic objectivity.

'The boundaries of the senses are not often clearly realized.
The Infra and the Ultra are fields easily forgotten. Out of hearing
stays unthought-of; out of sight is out of mind. And yet, how
haunted we all are.'

So in his latest work, *Night Thoughts*,[1] Mr. Gascoyne returns to
a realization which characterized surrealism and, during its
brief moment, Mass-Observation; an enchanted dream-like
consciousness which created for itself, by a confusion and inter-
fusion of inner and outer worlds, in which the waking world was
experienced symbolically, fraught with meanings and messages
of the soul. We create the world continually in the image of our
dreams; and see reflected in the outer, images of inner realities
and preoccupations.

For if from the surrealists Mr. Gascoyne learned to find everywhere mirrored in objective reality, subjective states, it was not
only or principally his own subjectivity he so discovered; the
rebel against the world of the common man returned to articulate
that world's unspoken dreams. If the oracular quality which is
characteristic of his finest poetry passed almost unnoticed at
the time, it was because no one was listening for the prophetic
voice.

The context of Gascoyne's poetic development was swept
away by the war. The communications between the poets of
England and France were broken, never to be resumed; the

---

[1] Published by André Deutsch, London, in 1956.

moment of the Surrealist Exhibition in 1936 (in which both David Gascoyne and Humphrey Jennings were active) marks the climax of the last literary movement to unite the two countries. Philippe Soupault once said to me, 'David Gascoyne is not an English poet, he is a French poet writing in English'. He was in fact bilingual to the point of writing a number of poems in French; and it is a sign of the changed times that his editor did not think it worth including these in his collected edition. (Another omission to which I would like, in passing, to register my regret, is the omission of a number of 'Makeweight poems', light verse which is, some of it, especially 'Le Déjeuner sur l'Herbe', extremely elegant and very funny.)

Humphrey Jennings (who was killed in an accident while climbing in the island of Poros, in 1948) is best known as a director of documentary war-films; but he is remembered by those who knew him as one of the most remarkable imaginative intelligences of his generation. One of I. A. Richard's two most brilliant pupils at Cambridge (the other was William Empson), his wonderful talk fired others to accomplish what he himself (his ideas always running ahead of his achievement) never carried out. Taking as his starting-point 'the surrealist object', he held (and in his war-films brilliantly realized his idea) that 'the image' (he spoke always of 'the image', never of 'the symbol') was valid just in so far as it was not invented, but discovered: never must the poet 'invent' an image; because the kind of truth poetry communicates was, for him, collective, public, and historical. His Churchillian sense of history, and of the present in which he lived as indivisibly one with the glory of England's past, and the 'Pandemonium' (so he himself described it in the title of a never-published compilation) of her Industrial Revolution, led him to 'discover' images of this kind no less in the past (in works of literature and the other arts and also in the works of engineers, scientists and inventors) than in the present. To go on a walk with Humphrey was to see the world come to life, as he discerned and discovered everywhere expressions of the imagination, past and present, of the English race. The meanings with which such images are charged come not from an individual mind; at most a great man (Wren, Brunel or Darwin) can 'tie a knot in the thread of history'. The locomotive is such an image, at once embodying and typifying an aspect of the Industrial Revolution; and in contrast, the horse, its natural antithesis; and the plough, workmanship of the craftsman, and implement of man in a 'normal' relationship with nature which, with the Industrial Revolution, came to an end.

The imagination, according to Jennings, must test itself continually against historical actuality; for such actuality is itself an embodiment of imaginative truth; man creates his world continually in the image of his dreams. In this view (and on its application to the Industrial Revolution) Jennings was indebted to Blake, who so vehemently declared that the 'dark Satanic Mills' of industry are but an embodiment of the mechanistic thought of Bacon and Newton.

It seems worth quoting (since they were only printed privately, by Ruthven Todd, in New York, 1951) one of Jennings's *Reports*; the term, with its implied objectivity, suggests Mass-Observation's 'scientific' records; the title, *I See London,* the first line of a passage from Blake's *Jerusalem* Humphrey Jennings used sometimes to declaim: 'I behold London, a Human Awful Wonder of God'. The juxtaposition of images is surrealist; but the context which lends them dignity is that of Churchill's 'greatest hour':

> I see London at night.
> I look up in the moon and see the visible
> moving vapour-trails of invisible night-fliers
> I see a luminous glow beyond Covent Garden
> I see in mind's eye the statue of Charles the First
> riding in double darkness of night and corrugated iron.
> On the corrugated iron I see wreaths of fresh flowers
> I see the black-helmeted night and the blue-helmeted morning
> I see the rise of the red-helmeted sun
> And at last, at the end of Gerrard Street, I see
> the white-helmeted day, like a rescue-man, searching
> out of the bottomless dust the secrets of another life.
>   (March–April 1941).

> I see a thousand strange sights in the streets of London
> I see the clock on Bow Church burning in day time
> I see a one-legged man crossing the fire on crutches
> I see three negroes and a woman with white face-powder
> reading music at half past three in the morning
> I see an ambulance girl with her arms full of roses
> I see the burnt drums of the Philharmonic
> I see the green leaves of Lincolnshire carried
> through London on the wrecked body of an aircraft.

The burning clock is just such a visual metaphor as Magritte or Ernst might have invented; and doubtless we all select from ever-various reality according to our current taste in painting and the other arts. It is none the less striking that the kind of images which had troubled the uneasy dreams of surrealism were so often prophetic. The 'burnt drums' might have come from Dali and Bunuel's film *Un Chien Andalou*, but were in fact to be seen in London after an air-raid; though the heroic image of the wrecked aircraft crowned with a wreath of leaves from Lincoln-shire seems to belong rather to the world of Inigo Jones's Masks, 'Lycidas', Dryden's *King Arthur* or Handel's music. Ever-evolving and continuous imaginative creation was, for Jennings, rather than revolution, the mainstream of history.

David Gascoyne's images of London, less literary than Jennings's, were no less objective, no less eloquent of the city's collective life:

At night I've often walked on the Embankment of the Thames
And seen the Power Station's brick cliffs dominate the scene
Over on the South Bank, and its twin pairs of giant stacks
Outpouring over London their perpetual offering
Of smoke in heavy swags fit for a sacrificial rite
Propitiating some brute Carthaginian deity;
And thought they stood like symbols for the worship of our age:
The pillars of a temple raised to man-made Power and Light

Mile after mile of tenements and terraces,
League after league of palaces and parks.
Here hover hazes of green sick-ward light,
And there red neon blurs flick on and off;
In fixed directions avenues stretch sleekly
To disappear in ultimate uncertainty
In regions where the bottom of the sky
Mingles with fumes that rise from the abyss

Fearful and wonderful, that sleepless monster
Sphinx among cities, Megalometropolis
Stuns with her grave immensity all eyes beholding her:
One's wonder gapes and quickly palls and falls into dismay
Knowing the roaring labyrinth deep sunk in Night below
Teems with noctambulists too multitudinous
For any now to fear the Minotaur

At once grander and more intimate than Eliot's depiction of

The Waste Land, without any trace of that irony with which lesser writers stave off grave reality, the poet does not observe with camera's-eye detachment, but senses the imaginative import of every image; he reads the signs like words in some human record, or indictment. London becomes, in *Night Thoughts*, England's Book of Judgment, whose images are words not to be denied; words the poet reads with the fluency of long familiarity with the *signatura rerum* (an expression he often used in conversation, from Jakob Boehme whose writings are among his sacred texts). Dante and Blake are the two poets with whom this poem invites comparison; if not in its comprehensiveness, in its quality, and its kind.

Night Thoughts (the title is taken from Young, one of the self-chosen ancestors of surrealism) is, according to Mr. Robin Skelton, 'David Gascoyne's most ambitious work to date, and his greatest single achievement'. This work, commissioned by Douglas Cleverdon (the B.B.C. producer who also elicited from Dylan Thomas *Under Milk Wood*, and who has made known the writings of David Jones), is cast in the dramatic form required for broadcasting. The boy who had trained himself to observe ('for future reference') every detail of his world; who, in London, used to go for long walks at night (as Humphrey Jennings in the light of day) in Hampstead, or in Chelsea where across the river the chimneys of the Battersea Power Station send out their swags of smoke, has in this poem experienced the city's life 'tuned up to one high level of supreme importance'. He once described to me what it was like to experience everything as if the experience of others was his own; 'my brain leaks', so he puts it, under the great pressure of a collective consciousness 'the strain of which no human mind could stand'.

At the same time, this pressure towards a dissolution of separate barriers, which imposes upon individual consciousness a strain so immense, the poet understands, rather, as a dawning universal awareness, among common mankind, of one another; an awareness which Mass-Observation and Surrealism, as well as Teilhard de Chardin had, in the inter-war years, intuitively divined:

> . . . what can be done
> For anyone, what can we do alone, alas, how can
> The lonely people without power, who hardly know
> How best to help neighbours they know, help those
> Who surely would be neighbours like themselves, if they but knew

How to break through the silence and the noise of the great night
Of all that is unknown to us, that weighs down between
One lonely human being and another?

Night Thoughts is the final expression of a theme the poet had
already attempted in two long poems, 'Phantasmagoria' before
1935, in his surrealist period, and 'Noctambules' (1938). In
'Phantasmagoria' the poet first begins to speak with his own
voice; and along with the fusion of 'the flagrant contradictions
that exist between dream and waking life, the "unreal" and the
"real", the unconscious and the conscious' (*A Short Survey of Surrealism*, p. x) we recognize the characteristic scope of the later
poem. *Phantasmagoria* is a townscape; a sea-side town, and, as
always, at night, as befits the world between dream and waking.
Already the poet has found his characteristic, nervous, rapid,
long, flexible line:

The thoroughfares of Evening swarm with rapid shifting scenes
And everywhere the lamps of lust and terror thrust their beams
To scour the countless cage-like haunts of men with scorching light
While waves of sound roll out across the rooftops overhead

In an image which suggests the Egyptian goddess Nut whose
body contains the stars, he personifies night with a novel freshness
the poet owes to his surrealist schooling, but whose quality of
apotheosis is already his own:

now that the cavernous yawn of the lonely female
Titan lying sleeping on the softly gleaming sands
has at last swallowed-up every starfish in sight
The livid wind once more begins to lift,
Stealthily weaving its fine-spun shawls and writhing swathes around
the radius of that small black seaside town
through which by now down each long soundless street
swarms of somnambulistic barefoot children creep
by slow degrees, still sealed in spell of dream,
towards where soon the spume-besilvered waves shall shine and see the
as a new Sun soars like a song out of the silence of the sea.

Such poetry is more than a promise: it is already an achievement of a noble and characteristic beauty.

In 'Noctambules' (dedicated to Djuna Barnes) he returned
some ten years later to the city-scape; Paris, this time. By now
the poet has shed his surrealist trappings; and we see yet another
manner of being attempted by the unformed poet, who was at all
times so sensitive to the style of contemporaries:

An English drunkard sits alone
In a small *bistro* in Les Halles
And keeps rehearsing the Lord's Prayer
In a mad high-pitched monotone
To the blue empty air.
And in a Left-bank café where
At about half-past four
Exiles are wont to bare
Their souls, a son-and-heir
Of riches and neurosis casts
His frail befuddled blonde
Brutally on the floor
And with despairing fists
Tries to blot out the gaze
Of her wet senseless eyes . . . .
One who has wandered long
Through labyrinths of his own brain
More solitary and obscure
Than any maze of stone
Pavements and lamplit walls
Now stops beside the Seine
And leaning down to peer
Into the swirling gloom
Of swollen waters, says:
What day can ever end
The night of those from whom
God turns away his face
Or what ray's finger pierce
The depths wherein they drown?

A period piece in the expatriate style of Eliot's early poetry; the voice is not quite his own, but, as with surrealism, with the objective 'reports' of Jennings, and as later with Hölderlin, the style is not the merely superficial imitation of a manner, but the adoption of an imaginative attitude: it is acquired from within.

The grounds David Gascoyne gave for his break with surrealism were political; influenced, perhaps, by the climate of literary thought in England in the thirties, he thought that he was about to move in the direction of a more explicit Marxism; but what had surely begun to dissatisfy him in surrealism was the inadequacy of a theory of inspiration which did not go beyond psychic autonomy.

Hölderlin's Madness was published in 1938 by Dent & Sons; and in Hölderlin he found a doctrine of poetic inspiration which was to transform at once his theory and his style. Indeed from this time traces of the surrealist manner and imagery almost entirely disappear from his work, to be superseded by a lyricism whose exaltation is reminiscent of Hölderlin; with whom, it seems (as formerly with Rimbaud) the poet now began for a time almost to identify himself, so close an affinity did he discover. This work is a series of 'free adaptations' from Hölderlin, linked by original poems and prefaced by an introduction which is in the nature of a new declaration of prophetic faith. The bridge by which he was able to pass so easily from surrealism to Hölderlin was the theme of 'madness'.

Breton had seen in 'madness' an extension of the frontiers of consciousness akin to this 'dark night' of poetry. With a touch of surrealist excess, David Gascoyne calls Hölderlin 'one of the most thorough-going of romantics, because he went mad, and madness is the logical development of romanticism', but with deeper insight he concludes the sentence: 'and he went beyond romanticism, because his poetry is stronger than despair and reaches into the future and the light' (p. 2–3).

We are reminded of Blake's attribution to Cowper of the cry, 'Oh, that I were mad always!' Both poets imply the incompatibility of imagination's vision of perfection with the conditions of earthly life; Mr. Gascoyne sees in Hölderlin a spirit broken by this incompatibility; unable to sustain himself always in the light, he yet refuses to forget what he has seen there.

Like Rimbaud, Hölderlin had seen poetry as an activity by means of which it was possible to attain to hitherto unknown degrees of consciousness:

What is, then, the secret world to which the poet penetrates, the world discovered by the poet-seer? 'The poet is he who sees', wrote André Gide. 'And what does he see? Paradise!' And in fact this is so, if by Paradise we mean a state of autonomous existence unsubjected to necessity, a state of perfect freedom, without time or age, and if the non-rational imagination of the poet is distinguished precisely by its ignorance of Necessity's irrevocable laws (p. 11).

The fragmented subliminal psyche has now given place to a vision of an imaginative wholeness towards which the poet had long been feeling his way. Of Hölderlin and the other German romantics Mr. Gascoyne writes that they are poets and philosophers of nostalgia and the night, whose paths lead far among forgotten things, mysterious dreams and madness. And yet a night that precedes the dawn and is full of longing for the sun. These poets look forward out of their night, and Hölderlin in his madness wrote always of sunlight and dazzling air, and the islands of the Mediterranean noon (p. 2).

He had indeed been intuitively aware of some whole which gives meaning to the parts even at the time when in his early novel he had reflected on Beardsley's fantastic domains. These were, he divined, a single country:

Somewhere hidden in the fantastic landscapes of the *Morte d'Arthur* is the mansion where *La Dame aux Camelias* surveys herself in an oval mirror, and in another room of this mansion the delicate ceremony of the Coiffing from *Savoy* takes place, while in an annexe the Scarlet Pastorale is being performed. The ornate balcony which is the scene of the Fruit-Bearers leads into the domains of Salome.

Continuing his meditation on Rimbaud and Beardsley (those creators of artificial paradises) he reflects that

the artist, the real poet, must be aware of a certain *mental substratum* which exists beyond all merely visible or temporal activity. Rimbaud, in order to write his poems, must have listened to a voice speaking from within, a voice most of us silence as soon as it begins. Beardsley must have closed his eyes in order to watch the strange forms that congregated there, behind his lids, of their own accord.

The surrealists had themselves speculated upon a mental substratum beyond the 'pure psychic automatism'; and in their second *Manifesto* (1929. *A Short Survey of Surrealism* p. 86) admit that

there is a hint . . . of a belief that there exists a certain spiritual plane on which life and death, the real and the imaginary, the past and the future, the communicable and the incommunicable, the high and the low, are not conceived of as opposites. It would therefore be vain to attribute to surrealism any other motive than to help to determine that plane, as it would be absurd to ascribe to it a purely destructive or constructive character: the point at issue being precisely this, that construction and destruction should no longer be flaunted against one another.

This 'crisis of consciousness' to which surrealism cannot be said to have attained, Hölderlin had actually undergone; the 'mental substratum' upon which all opposites are reconciled is the living and creative imagination itself; called by Blake (as later also by Yeats) 'Eden', and by Coleridge 'Paradise', whose milk is the food of the inspired poet.

'But is not freedom the knowledge of necessity?' (so continues the passage from the introduction to *Hölderlin's Madness* quoted above).

Yes, if we are speaking of human freedom, the only freedom, that is to say, which mortals can expect to attain here on earth. But the freedom towards which the poet aspires, the 'free' Freedom of Paradise, is, on the contrary, a state in which necessity does not exist. It is this aspiration that caused Novalis to proclaim: 'Life is a malady of the spirit', and Rimbaud to cry in his despair: 'La vraie vie est absente!' (p. 11).

'For who knows', as Plato wrote, 'whether to live be not to die, to die to live?' But what for the Platonists was an aspect of metaphysical knowledge was, for these poets, an existential despair; as it was for St. Teresa, whose 'I die because I cannot die' was the same cry of the soul who in her descent from ecstasy must taste the bitterness of the world.

With his progress from surrealism to Hölderlin, David Gascoyne passed once and for all beyond a view of the soul explicitly materialist, to the perennial doctrine:

Both these poets (Rimbaud and Hölderlin) belonged to the tradition of the *seer*. That is to say that their *ars poetica* was an offspring of the Platonic doctrine of inspiration. They believed the poet to be capable of penetrating a secret world and receiving the dictation of a transcendental inner voice (p. 10).

But in order to catch even so much as a glimpse of Paradise (so Mr. Gascoyne continues to reflect):

the poet has to pay the price; for his undertaking is an attempt to transgress the laws of man's universe. The gates of Paradise are barred against us by the angel with the flaming sword; and the poet-seer, in attempting to escape that terrible interdiction is guilty of a promethean crime (p. 12).

He invites, indeed, the damnation of madness – a madness not of darkness but of too much light. Even Blake, who claimed to be 'an inhabitant of that happy country' knew that on earth man cannot live 'in Paradise and liberty'. In the world of mortality, he said, we must suffer. But Rimbaud, Hölderlin, perhaps David Gascoyne himself, caught between heaven and earth, had not discovered the secret of enduring the mortal state.

The group of *Metaphysical Poems* in the volume of *Poems 1937–1942*[1] bear the evident mark of Hölderlin's influence; whose imaginative flights David Gascoyne from this time dared, finding in his own wings an eagle-strength upon which he outsoared, in sublimity, all his contemporaries.

There was one more step to be taken by the poet who was to write the religious (and specifically Christian) poems which are his enduring gift to the world. Already before the Second World War it was clear to imaginative people that catastrophe was inevitable; Hitler's persecution of the Jews had already begun. Among the multitudes to be put to death in the concentration camps, one was a close friend of the poet, who himself passionately embraced the Jewish cause. The crisis that brought the French surrealists who were most serious to political maturity, and swept away the rest, brought to David Gascoyne the spiritual maturity whose evidence is first seen in *Poems 1937–42*. Kierkegaard, Dostoevsky, Chestov, Berdiaiev superseded the 'sacred books' of his surrealist and romantic phases. The dedication of the noble 'Miserere' sequence is to the poet Pierre Jean Jouve (never a surrealist), whose wife (who had studied under Freud himself) had given psychological help as well as friendship to the young poet whose imaginative sensibility was already proving more than the human vehicle (still little more than a vulnerable adolescent) could stand. The eight poems of this series are in praise of the 'Eternal Christ'; the poet speaks from these depths into which the divine Presence has descended in order to redeem our fallen world, in a voice of sustained eloquence, as if at last the angel spoke. Anticlerical now no less than when he made common cause with Jarry and Péret, he is so now in the name of the divine principle itself, continually betrayed yet ever-present in and to mankind, to the end of the world. He has given expression to that world-long crucifixion to which the 'god within' has at all times been subjected. Not one of these poems falls below the level of that oracular speech which from this time possessed him. He often spoke of Joachim of Flora, first prophet of the 'age of the Holy Spirit' which, so he foretold, was to follow the 'age of the Son'. In that age, so David Gascoyne believed, we live; or are about to live, for he is, supremely, the poet of the

---

[1] Published, with illustrations by Graham Sutherland, by Tambimuttu, editor of *Poetry London*.

Entombment which must precede the Resurrection. The darkness in which Hölderlin and the romantics awaited the dawn had become for him that uttermost descent in which the *deus absconditus* (he used also the alchemical language, and spoke much of Jakob Boehme) redeems the souls from their darkest prisons. He prefaced the series of 'Metaphysical poems' with a quotation from the Egyptian *Book of the Dead*: 'Without cease and for ever is celebrated the Mystery of the Open Tomb, the Resurrection of Osiris-Ra, the Increated Light.' And in 'Lachrymae',

> Slow are the years of light
> > and more immense
> Than the imagination. And the years return
> Until the Unity is filled. And heavy are
> The lengths of Time with the slow weight of tears.
> Since Thou didst weep, on a remote hill-side
> Beneath the olive-trees, fires of unnumbered stars
> Have burnt the years away, until we see them now:
> Since thou didst weep, as many tears
> Have flowed like hourglass sand.
> Thy tears were all.
> And when our secret face
> Is blind because of the mysterious
> Surging of tears wrung by our most profound
> Presentiment of evil in man's fate, our cruellest wounds
> Become Thy stigmata. They are Thy tears that fall.

Blake had taken from Swedenborg the concept of 'the divine humanity', that portion of the Logos in every man; he also (taking from Boehme the definition of the Logos as 'the imagination of God') names the Eternal Christ 'Jesus the Imagination'; and such is David Gascoyne's 'Christ of Revolution and of Poetry'; the 'mental substratum' has revealed itself as (in Martin Buber's sense of the word) the 'person' of God.

Nihilism is revolution without imagination, as the 'bourgeoisie' is social order without imagination; no less revolutionary now than as a surrealist David Gascoyne finally proclaims himself not as a Marxist but, like Blake, a revolutionary in the cause of the 'Kingdom not of this world'. In his maturity he emerges as a prophet whose subversive message is what it has always been: to live by the truth of the imagination, the Holy Spirit in man.

It was the Messianic aspect of surrealism (and also of Marxism) which has most strongly appealed to David Gascoyne; to whom

E

it would no more occur to regard the tasks of the Imagination as 'literary' than to Blake or to Shelley. 'One can state quite simply that their actions and their painting belong to that vast enterprise of re-creating the universe to which both Lautréamont and Lenin gave themselves entirely' (*A Short Survey of Surrealism*, p. 81). David Gascoyne too gave himself entirely to that aim; the only possible human aim, as he would see it.

For similar reasons he admired – somewhat unexpectedly – Carlyle; on whom he wrote a pamphlet for the British Council, published in 1952: 'From early manhood to old age, Carlyle was aware of a vocation, a duty, and responsibility: to bear witness to the Divine nature of the true man, and to speak and write the Truth as far as it lay in him to do so, and thus to transmit the message of God to man in this generation' (p. 7). 'He is one of our great national prophets' (p. 8), the poet says; classing him with Ruskin, Whitman, Kierkegaard and Baudelaire. Carlyle's hero was, besides, 'the common man who was forced by his Puritan conscience to assume national leadership in defence of civil liberty *against* autocracy. . . . None of Carlyle's heroes . . . bears the slightest resemblance to any twentieth-century national political figure, with the possible exception of Mr. Winston Churchill' (p. 14) David Gascoyne has retained an unshakeable loyalty to the cause of the oppressed against all oppressors; thus his religious vision is in no way counter to the great political changes of his time, 'the century of the common man' and the proletarian revolution.

In writing of Carlyle's prophetic role he is at the same time declaring his own:

'Man among the dark Satanic mills of industrialism has lost his Soul, modern society is no longer bound together by the cement of living faith, human life, devoid of spirit is only death and sordid nightmare' (p. 17).

The function of 'the writer who may be called a prophet' is 'to diagnose and understand the spiritual malady of the age, and to interpret the age to itself, by articulating, and not shutting his lips from, the thoughts which other earnest men suppress or leave unuttered' (p. 18).

Carlyle's conception of literature, he says, 'is one that much needs reconsidering in these days'; it is in fact his own:

'Literature is but a branch of Religion, and always participates in its character: however, in our time, it is the only branch that

still shows any greenness; and, as some think, must one day become the main stem' (p. 22, *Characteristics*).

In this conclusion he has on his side Blake, who believed that
the New Age of 'the Divine Humanity' was to be 'the Reign of
Literature and the Arts'; and Yeats, who understood that modern
man 'makes his soul' rather with poetry and philosophy than by
religious rites and observances.

Above all he found in Carlyle a conception also shared with
Blake (and with Yeats) of the 'palingenesic nature of the present
age'. Both prophets saw in the French Revolution the first
rumours of the Last Judgment of the world:

> Louis-Claude de Saint-Martin referred to the French Revolution
> as 'an epitome of the Last Judgment', and if we take the French
> Revolution as the convulsive overture with which the whole Palin-
> genesic era began, then we may still have a little less than a hundred
> and fifty years more of *Sturm und Drang* and indeed of the all too
> realistically prophesied fire-consummation to look forward to before
> we find ourselves again in a Living Society (p. 19).

Blake's 'frowning babe' of that Second Coming, Yeats's 'rough
beast' is for David Gascoyne the 'Christ by Revolution'; he is on
the side of change because in a 'bourgeois' world he sees only
what is fit for destruction.

Such, in bare outline, has been the background against which
David Gascoyne's poetry has developed, from small beginnings
to an achieved, if briefly held, greatness. There are only five
volumes of verse, two of them juvenilia; of *Roman Balcony* (written
before the age of sixteen) I give Mr. Robin Skelton's judgment:
'Already in this book there is that interest in hallucinatory
obsessive symbolism which gave so many of his poems of the
later thirties their individual and disturbing quality.' His second
volume, *Man's Life is This Meat*, covers his surrealist period.
Dedications to Ernst, Dali, and Magritte are no less revealing
of his tastes at that time than the poems themselves. In *Phenomenon* we recognize the objective style of Humphrey Jennings's
Reports, the stately cadences and sharp 'scientific' images of that
early nineteenth-century prose reflected in Jennings's verbal
collages:

> Nothing could have been more baffling than the way in which the
> words rose from the places where they had been printed, hovered
> in the air at a distance of about six inches from my face and finally,

without having much more than disturbed my impression of their habitual immobility, dissolved into the growing darkness.

Soon he was, in such poems as 'Lowland', 'Mountains', 'World Without End', assimilating (with a quality only to be attained by an interior identification with an underlying vision) the style of Hölderlin, his pure inhuman landscapes, the Orphic voice. A stylist; so much one might have deduced with certainty from these early exercises, experiments not only in the use of language and image, but in the assumption of imaginative attitudes, points of view. His vocabulary was, even at seventeen, remarkably large, expressive and at the same time used with the ease and naturalness of speech. Of the influence of those English poets of the thirties Michael Roberts's *New Country* first made known, there is little trace; yet in the 'Farewell Chorus' to that decade which he dated 'New Year 1940' he for a moment catches the style of Auden (or perhaps of Louis MacNeice) in a poem which would seem a remarkable achievement if it were not that in his higher imaginative flights, he has reached not only a higher degree, but a higher kind, of poetry.

From the moment the poet first spoke with his own voice, his style is unmistakable; and in his fourth volume, *A Vagrant* (1943–50) though it contains nothing finer than the 'Miserere' or 'The Gravel-Pit Field' the high level of pure poetry, the perfect command of language, never falters; whatever earlier 'influences' formed the poet have been assimilated so completely that they cannot be detected. He is no longer searching or experimenting; no longer speaks 'in the voice of another'; of the imagery of surrealism, the landscape of Hölderlin, the colloquial idiom of the thirties, the Churchillian rhetoric of Jennings, no trace is now discernible; the voice, sublime, grave and beautiful, could be that of no other poet. His images are at the same time as objective as Jennings, as true to the dreaming as to the waking mind as surrealism; for the real world is 'one continued vision of imagination', yielding up its secrets to that lonely vagrant, the poet:

Evening again.
       The lurid flaming light
That red sky's smouldering alkali spread on reflecting stone
Façades of ageing buildings seeming now to slant and strain
Backwards against the leaden East, sheer haggard cliffs
Pitted with windows, baffles with its glare
Those gazing panes. They see nothing but the wrath

Of still prolonged and future conflagrations. With the stain
Of night arising stealthily behind them, fresh leaves shake
Back on their rigid branches, shudder brusquely back and show
How underneath their sparkling green profusion there are hung
Shadows, dull undertone of mourning. Die down, die
Away, brisk wind, let the lit leaves lie still.
Let them with tranquil glitter once more hide
Their secret. Heavy beneath all that is seen
Hangs the forgotten . . . .

Every image is here experienced, not with the intensity of mere
sense-perception, of the 'detached' camera-eye of the realist
'mirror dawdling down a lane'; imaginative vision receives the
qualitative mystery communicated by the ever-present signs
written in the sky – the light of the sun, at once the light of the
world and the ominous threat of the destroying fires. The
'smouldering alkali' and the 'fume' suggest the furnaces of an
industrial landscape whose threat of destruction merges with
that written in the heavens. Virgil has described, in an image
almost identical, the dreams that hang under each leaf of the elm
of Hades; yet there is no reason to think Gascoyne's leaf-lives
are taken from Virgil; for his symbolic resonances seem re-created
from his unusual insight into the intrinsic qualities of things both
human and cosmic. There are no 'surrealist objects', no search
for 'images', since all is raised to the same high degree of imaginative intensity, just as his long, elegiac lines sustain continuously
the exalted speech of prophecy. With such apparent ease are his
poems composed that only after repeated re-reading does it
become apparent that their lucidity is not that of glass but of
diamond. Such poetry achieves splendour without for a moment
being pretentious.

'The Sacred Hearth' is an idyll as perfect as that of Calvert
which the poem recalls:

                    . . .Most
Mysterious and unrecapturable moment, when I stood
There staring back at the dark white nocturnal house,
And saw gleam through the lattices a light more pure than gold
Made sanguine with crushed roses, from the firelight that all night
Stayed flickering about the sacred hearth. As long as dawn
Hung fire behind the branch-hid sky, the strong
Magic of rustic slumber held unbroken; yet a song
Sprang wordless from inertia in my heart, to see how near
A neighbour strangeness ever stands to home . . . .

Again there is nothing 'literary'; yet because the poet has pondered over Calvert's *Chamber Idyll*, has assimilated the imaginative essence of that and countless other works of art and music and poetry, his own consciousness has been so formed and attuned to the significant detail that (as he wrote so many years before his prodigious reading and consumption of every kind of art) 'All this dream-spun beauty' has become a part of him. His poems need no learned notes: for his culture has been more deeply absorbed than that of Pound. Steeped in the great currents of consciousness as imagination has revealed and discovered itself in works of art and in ways of life, in cities, in all expressions of civilization, David Gascoyne's culture is not (like that of so much merely academic education) extraneous to himself; its enrichment is not of memory but of imaginative consciousness – qualitative, and therefore perceptible only qualitatively. His style is, so to say, seamless, and apparently (and really) original, unique. Yet no poet has so fully exposed himself to, or so fully absorbed, all the important currents of the thought of his time, whether in the arts, in politics, or in philosophy.

David Gascoyne, under that 'strain which no human mind can stand' has, like Hölderlin, endured for many years the 'quasi-dereliction' of the oracle deserted by the gods who at times possessed him. He has been silent for a decade; but, not yet fifty, he may perhaps write again. Yet what he has attempted and achieved is what only the greatest poets (who are, in attempting what is beyond unaided human skill, also the most humble) set themselves as a goal: absolute imaginative truth. 'Man', so he wrote in *Night Thoughts*, 'has become above all the most indefatigable mimic of all the ways of being man that have ever been thought striking.' But the poet's truth is never to be found where others have found it:

> Before I fall
> Down silent finally, I want to make
> One last attempt at utterance, and tell
> How my absurd desire was to compose
> A single poem with my mental eye
> Wide open, and without even one lapse
> From that most scrupulous Truth which I pursue
> When not pursuing Poetry – Perhaps
> Only the poem I can never write is *true*.
>
> *Apologia. Poems 1937–42*

Whatever the significance of the silence of this poet, the poems he has written are among the few of our times that bear such eloquent witness to that imaginative truth for which they speak.

1966

4

YEATS'S DEBT TO WILLIAM BLAKE

Blake was not only one of the earliest, but perhaps the most enduring of all the influences which formed his imaginative, intellectual and spiritual life. It seems that Blake was already revered by Yeats's father; for in *The Trembling of the Veil* Yeats writes of how his father had told him about Rossetti and Blake, and given him their poetry to read when he was fifteen or sixteen. That would have been about 1880; seventeen years after the publication of Alexander Gilchrist's *Life of William Blake,* in which many of his writings were published for the first time. This book was a great event in the Pre-Raphaelite circle in which the elder Yeats moved when in London. Dante Gabriel and his brother William Michael Rossetti had completed the work left undone at Gilchrist's death; and Swinburne's critical essay, published five years later, no doubt reflects an enthusiasm, amounting almost to a cult, shared by the group as a whole. Thus the name of Blake must have been a magical one heard by Yeats in his childhood; the name of a poet of supreme genius, who was more than a poet, a sage, a visionary; but who was as yet almost unknown outside the world into which Yeats himself had been born. He must early have felt himself, therefore, in a line of direct descent from the prophet; and he later tells how, when with Edwin Ellis he set to work on their joint edition of Blake's 'Prophetic Books', 'we took it almost as a sign of Blake's personal help when we discovered that the spring of 1889 when we first joined our knowledge, was one hundred years from the publication of *The Book of Thel.*' Yeats's eager acceptance of a doubtful tradition that Blake's father had been an Irishman named O'Neill proves mainly his wish to make the kinship nearer still. But if Blake and the Pre-Raphaelites were his earliest passion, Blake alone remained as an inexhaustible source into his poetic maturity. In 1915 he named as his chief mystical authorities Blake and his two teachers Boehme and Swedenborg; and to the end, when Yeats had exhausted or outgrown works of lesser genius and challenged Plato himself, he continued to write of Blake as a disciple writes of his master. In 'An Acre of Grass', one of his last poems, he was still striving to be more like Blake:

> Myself I must remake
> Till I am Timon and Lear
> Or that William Blake
> Who beat upon the wall
> Till Truth obeyed his call.

Every generation discovers in Blake that aspect of truth or error for which it is looking; thus, Swinburne found in that saintly man an advocate of 'evil'; the twenties of this century acclaimed him as an apostle of 'free love' (Yeats was almost alone in understanding why for Blake 'sexual love' was 'spiritual hate'); the Marxists (forgetting his later declaration that he was 'a Platonist in politics'), of revolution. The innovators of Eliot's day saw him as a pioneer of free verse and 'sprung' rhythm, the Surrealists as a prophet of the 'irrational'. Robert Graves has praised him as the author of the burlesque *An Island on the Moon*, which Yeats considered 'doggerel and scribble'. What, then, did the Pre-Raphaelites chiefly find in Blake? For them he was the prophet of the religion of art, and we find him strangely companioned among the apostles of 'art for art's sake'; with Wilde and de l'Isle Adam, and the author of 'that wicked book' *A Rebours*, whose superficial aestheticism demoralized Dorian Gray. 'He announced the religion of Art', Yeats wrote in his essay 'William Blake and the Imagination', 'of which no man dreamed in the world about him; and he understood it more perfectly than the thousands of subtle spirits who have received its baptism in the world about us'; that was in 1908. Yet the exaltation of art did provide a bridge between otherwise irreconcilable philosophies; and the young Yeats could quote, on the one hand, 'as for living, our servants can do that for us', and, on the other hand, Blake's gospel of 'Jesus the Imagination'. 'In his time', Yeats wrote in the same essay, 'educated people believed that they amused themselves with books of imagination, but that they 'made their souls' by listening to sermons and by doing or not doing certain things. . . . In our time we are agreed that we "make our souls" out of some of the great poets of ancient times,

or out of Shelley or Wordsworth or Goethe or Balzac.' The
sentence that follows is a fine amalgam of Blake and aestheticism:
'No matter what we believe with our lips, we believe with our
hearts that beautiful things, as Browning said in his one prose
essay that was not in verse, have "lain burningly on the Divine
hand, and that when time has begun to wither, the Divine
hand will fall heavily on bad taste and vulgarity".' Blake
certainly thought so too; for him the Last Judgment itself was
a destruction of bad art and a vindication of works of the
imagination.

Yeats was right in saying that it seems to have been from
Boehme that Blake took his identification of Jesus (as the Logos)
with the 'imagination' of God; and, as Yeats says, 'he drew the
deduction which they [Boehme and the Alchemists] did not
draw, that the imaginative arts were therefore the greatest of
Divine revelations'. In the same essay Yeats quotes at length
nearly all Blake's prose passages on the nature of the imagination: 'Christ's apostles were all artists, and Christianity is art,
and the whole business of man is the arts.' Perhaps in the nineties
this seemed to mean that life did not matter, only art; whereas
Blake meant that to live by the imagination was itself the supreme
art – as Yeats certainly came to realize later, when in *A Vision*
he wrote of living our thought. But he early took for his credo
Blake's words, 'I know of no other Christianity and of no other
Gospel than the liberty, both of body and mind, to exercise the
divine arts of imagination.' Blake's Los, the prophetic genius in
man, laboured at his 'furnaces to create forms of art in which
to clothe the soul of mankind', and it is, surely, those same furnaces Yeats invokes in 'Byzantium', to stem, by the creation of
sculpture and dance and the other arts, the tide of 'formless
spawning fury':

> . . . the smithies break the flood,
> The golden smithies of the Emperor!

It was natural, at the outset, for Yeats to be imaginatively
held by the great prophet of a New Age which, more than a
hundred years after his birth, had not yet begun; for Blake's
writings had remained a sealed treasury of wisdom and beauty,
awaiting the chosen disciple. No sooner, therefore, had Yeats
grown up, than he sought out Edwin Ellis, an older man who was,
like Yeats himself, interested in a kind of knowledge not taught

in the schools, and 'asked to have Blake explained. Very little' –
so writes Ellis – 'could be given him to satisfy so large a demand,
but with his eye for symbolic systems, he needed no more to
enable him to perceive that here was a myth as well worth studying as any that has been offered to the world.' He saw, too – so
Ellis records – 'that it was no mere freak of an eccentric mind,
but an eddy of that flood-tide of symbolism, which attained its
tide-mark in the magic of the Middle Ages'. Yeats's own account
explains that the Ellis and Yeats commentary

requires an exact knowledge for its pursuit and that traces the con-
nection between his system and that of Swedenborg and Boehme.
I recognized certain attributions, from what is sometimes called the
Christian Cabala, of which Ellis had never heard, and with this
proof that his interpretation was more than fantasy, he and I began
our four years' work upon the 'Prophetic Books' of William Blake.

Yeats thought such statements by Blake's biographer

as that, perhaps, the attempt to methodize Blake's many seemingly
contradictory utterances into a system is so much labour lost, and
the absurd idea of Gilchrist that the key to the wild and strange
rhapsodies Blake would utter can be supplied by love, but not by
intellect, have done great harm in discouraging a serious treatment
of his mystic system.

'Exact knowledge' means different things to different people;
it depends at what level we are attempting to be exact. To the
pedant, exactness means a textual or historical accuracy of dates
or punctuation of a text; for which neither Yeats nor Blake cared
at all. Such pedants may rightly point out that in quoting Blake,
Yeats nearly always misquotes; but far from proving that he did
not therefore know Blake as well as the quoters of chapter and
verse, it in fact proves that he knew him so well that he trusted
his memory, so full of Blake that he could at all times draw upon
it: he did not feel the need to look up passages which had become
as part of his own thought. Blake did not quote accurately
either, and for the same reason. Both poets wrote from the fullness of their thought, and not from books of reference.

The knowledge which Yeats calls 'exact' is, on the other hand,
of a kind which the verbal critics ignore altogether. There is a
learning unknown to textual scholars and literary historians no
less exact than theirs; and this learning of the imagination (from
his studies of theosophy, the Cabala, and Swedenborg he already

possessed the key) Yeats instantly recognized in Blake. Blake commentators have since wasted much labour in the invention of interpretations, more or less ingenious, but irrelevant once it is granted that there is an universal language of symbolic discourse, age-old and world wide, but inseparable from the kind of knowledge which it embodies. The present difficulty in understanding this language – or even in divining its presence – arises from the denial, by current philosophies coloured by positivism, of the reality of a spiritual order. In Europe spiritual knowledge is embodied and transmitted principally within that tradition which descended through Orphism to Plato, to the neo-Platonists and the Gnostic sects, and to their successors both within Christendom (Dionysius the Areopagite and Dante were of them) and outside it. It is the language of Alchemy and of the Cabala, and of all allied ways of thought whose foundation is what Blake calls 'the language of divine analogy', the teaching of the Smaragdine Table of Hermes, 'as above, so below'. The created world is, at every level, a manifestation (and therefore a symbol) of anterior causes. It is the language also of all symbolic art; or one might rather say that symbolic art is the natural language of such thought. The measure of its exactness is its conformity to the spiritual knowledge of the Perennial Philosophy. Just as the terms of mathematics must remain meaningless to those who do not comprehend number, so this symbolic language must remain forever hidden from those for whom its universe of discourse is as if nonexistent. It might be called 'occult' or 'esoteric' since it is hidden from all but initiates; yet it is so hidden only in so far as its terms are incomprehensible except in the light of knowledge of a certain kind. To those who, like Yeats, are both by natural bent and by a fortunate environment, capable of discerning its traces, it is everywhere apparent throughout the entire range of imaginative art. Yet Yeats is right in saying (in his essay on Blake's illustrations to the *Divine Comedy*) that Blake was 'the first writer in modern times to preach the indissoluble marriage of all great art with symbol'. The title of a book Yeats had studied, *The Lost Language of Symbolism*, by Harold Bayley (1912) truly describes the situation of symbolic thought at the end of the nineteenth century.

Yeats was only twenty-two or three when he set to work on Blake. He already knew the language, but not so well as he did later; for he 'set his soul to study in a learned school' on Blake.

Since one of the characteristics of this symbolic language is its universality (for the philosophy it accompanies is 'perennial') the pinning-down of allusions to this or that particular source is not, as in textual or historical scholarship, the measure of exactness. Such questions as whether Blake (or Yeats, for that matter) learned the symbol of the world-cave from Plato or from Porphyry, or the watery looking glass of Nature from the *Hermetica* or Jakob Boehme, are of no importance comparable with the one great question (which no textual source-hunting will answer): is the poet speaking the symbolic language of tradition, or is he not? Such symbols (like the Christian Cross or the Virgin Birth) are, within a whole cultural context, a common language. Thus, in terms of academic pedantry it may be 'inexact' to ascribe no particular source for such symbols; whereas, in Yeats's sense of the word, to point to this or that symbol as 'traditional' is to give sufficient indication, to those who share a certain context of thought, of its meaning; it may even be more, not less 'exact' to call such symbols as mirror cave or gyre 'traditional' than to narrow a poet's indebtedness to some single source; for such symbols gather their richness from the many contexts in which they have been used. The cultural whole within which this language is current is not confined to any one historical period, and there has never been a century in which it has not found expression. Yeats had discovered its traces in his own world, not only in the confused thought and more confused writings of H. P. Blavatski, but in the more scholarly works of G. R. S. Meade, W. Wynn Westcott, and the translations from Indian and other Far Eastern scriptures which were, at the end of the nineteenth century, for the first time making an impact on English thought.

There is a stubborn conspiracy of ignorance which pretends that, as a field of exact discourse, such a symbolic language does not exist; for to admit the language might admit many ideas subversive to the self-imposed limitations of academic discussions of poetry. When I was a student at Cambridge in the late twenties it was fashionable to scoff at Yeats on account of his mystical studies. Considering the ridiculous nature of his thought, it was often said, the merit of some of his poems was quite surprising; (a merit judged rather by style than content). But as he himself wrote to John O'Leary, mysticism 'has enabled me to make out Blake's prophetic books, at any rate'. For mysticism is not synonymous with vagueness, subjectivity, and emotion; it is, on the contrary (as Yeats points out in his introduction to *A Vision*), characterized by an 'arbitrary, harsh, and difficult' symbolism; 'Yet such', he continues, 'has almost always accompanied expression that unites the sleeping and waking mind. One remembers the six wings of Daniel's angels, the Pythagorean numbers, a venerated book of the Cabala where the beard of God winds in and out among the stars, its hairs all numbered.' His list ends with Blake (whose obscurity, as all know who have tried to interpret his work, is not vague, but of a sphinxlike concreteness) and one of Blake's master-books, Law's *Boehme*. It may seem a surprising conclusion, yet I believe it is true, that the common characteristic of Yeats's thought and Blake's is neither image nor mythology, but precisely its diagrammatic character. No other poet writing in English (unless Milton, a third with them also in the sublimity of his vision) has this character, and among European poets Dante alone has a comparable diagrammatic complexity of structure. Perhaps in European poetry spiritual vision is less often expressed than in the Oriental civilizations; Ezekiel, Daniel, and the Apocalypse of St. John find their counterpart in the mandalas of Tibetan Buddhist paintings, or the four-faced gods of Indian sculpture. 'We can' – so Yeats concludes his appeal to tradition in support of such structures – '(those hard symbolic bones under the skin) substitute for a treatise on logic the *Divine Comedy*, or some little song about a rose, or be content to live our thought.' Can we doubt that the 'little song about a rose' was by Blake?

A recent bibliography dismisses Ellis's and Yeats's commentaries on Blake as of historical interest only, and their method as 'hit or miss'. The second at all events is far from the truth, though it might strike in that way a pedant ignorant of the 'exact knowledge' of symbolic tradition. But because he was a learner of that great discourse of which he was later to become a master, Yeats often failed to recognize clues which, had he known more of the literature of such thought, would have been plain to him; some traces of neo-Platonism, for example, and the writings of Plotinus. At other times he followed false clues with misleading results, attempting to force upon Blake symbolic patterns which did not fit. Himself interested in astrology, he felt that the Zodiac must come into Blake's system, and attempted to impose what he called 'the rotation of the Zoas' – who do not, in fact, rotate.

It is perhaps more surprising that the eclectic Blake seems not to have been interested in astrological symbolism than that Yeats tried to discover it. He attempted, also, to impose on the Zoas a system of triads of 'head heart and loins', no doubt based upon the Orphic triads of Being, Life, Intelligence, or preservative, creative, and regenerative principles, known to Ellis and Yeats probably from their theosophical studies (G. R. S. Meade's *Orpheus*, perhaps). These defects notwithstanding Ellis's and Yeats's work comes near to the underlying principle and intention of Blake's symbolic thought. Blake would have condoned its mistakes, and probably set about adding to his all-embracing mythology whatever in Ellis and Yeats is not already there.

We know that it was Yeats who wrote the essay in Volume I 'On the Necessity of Symbolism'. He wrote to Katharine Tynan in July 1891 that he considered it a very important essay; as it is, no less for the understanding of Blake's symbolist thought than of Yeats's own. He begins by asking what a symbol can communicate which the dialectics of modern philosophy cannot? The answer lies, he says, in the Swedenborgian doctrine of 'correspondence', the 'as above, so below' of the Smaragdine Table, to which doctrine Blake had also made his appeal before him. 'Sense impressions may indeed be used in poetry and prophecy as a key to unlock religious truths, but "correspondence", as Swedenborg called the symbolic relation of outer and inner, is itself no product of nature or natural reason, beginning as it does with a perception of something different from natural things with which they are to be compared.' Since this very ground of all symbolic art is denied by the positivist philosophy which has created the climate of thought from which most academic critics write at the present time, it is not surprising that so many commentators, both on Blake and on Yeats, seem more exercised in explaining away than in explaining the meaning of symbols which imply, one might say by definition, a spiritual world.

This 'absolute difference may be described as the first postulate of all mystics', Yeats continues; and already in this essay he had realized that 'the chief difference between the metaphors of poetry and the symbols of mysticism is that the latter are woven together into a complete system'.

Edwin Muir, a poet who came to this world by natural gift rather than by study, was no doubt right in saying that no mythology could ever be complete; yet he too wrote – and I think came increasingly to use traditional myths as the support of vision – that some parts are known of those archetypal symbolic themes which form the common ground of the human imagination. Such knowledge is embodied in the myths which, in any traditional society, are a symbolic language shared by all its members.

In antiquity no poet invented his own myths; and Yeats, living, as Blake had already lived, in a society which has, as a whole, broken with tradition, knew how impossible it is to build up, from a series of intuitive flashes, that wholeness of context which great poetry requires. Is not the particular relevance of Blake to our own situation the way in which he set about the resolution of this problem? In his early studies of Blake Yeats had already realized that 'even the "Little Black Boy" cannot be understood unless it be taken as part of the general mystical manifesto that runs through all the work'. Later we find in his own poetry, as we do in any poem of Blake's, or in any single episode of Dante's *Commedia*, the whole order of the cosmos implicit. Neither Yeats, Blake, Shelley, nor any other poet of like stature, is at one time writing in symbolic terms, at another descriptive; for as Yeats wrote in a later essay, 'True art is expressive and symbolic, and makes every form, every sound, a signature of some unanalysable imaginative essence.' Blake too wrote that 'to the Eyes of the Man of Imagination, Nature is Imagination itself'.

At this point it may be of interest to notice what Yeats might well have borrowed from Blake but did not. To most readers Blake's pantheon is more striking then the formal structure of his myth. If myth be dynamic symbol, symbol in transformation, myths must be considered as wholes of which the symbolic figures and elements are parts. A myth is no more constructed from these elements than a living body from its component organs. Mythological thought is therefore the highest and most complete form of symbolic imagination; as it is also the rarest. Neither Milton, Spenser, Shelley, nor Coleridge equal Blake in the completeness, complexity, and energy of his mythological figures and configurations. Yeats, though he attempted the evocation, by magic and ritual, of such living symbols, is not the equal, in this respect, of any of the poets named; he handles single symbols or single figures rather than those complex embodiments of uncurbed energy in which Blake's writings and paintings abound. Whereas Blake's mind was essentially dyna-

mic, and all his myth alive with energy, action, transformation,
Yeats tends towards Platonic ideal forms, a sculptural stillness,
'a marble or a bronze repose'. Yet in his search for a pantheon
he did at one time seek to evoke the Zoas, whose life seems inde-
pendent of their creator, as both poets believed; he tells of Orc
appearing as 'a wolf in armour', or his face black instead of burning. Yet he never introduced these figures into his own poetry,
feeling perhaps a temperamental difference between himself and
his volcanic master; or perhaps simply discovering that he did
not possess the gift of visionary imagination to the same degree.
For of Blake's myths he wrote (in the essay 'On the Necessity
of Symbolism' already quoted),

The surface is perpetually as it were giving way before one, and
revealing another surface below it, and that again dissolves when we
try to study it. The making of religions melts into the making of the
earth, and that fades away into some allegory of the rising and setting of the sun. It is all like a great cloud full of stars and shapes
through which the eye seeks a boundary in vain. When we seem to
have explored the remotest division some new spirit floats by mut-
tering wisdom.

Even then Yeats was seeking for a more static and mathematical
paradigm, 'a stylistic arrangement of experience', the Pythagorean numbers 'that move, or seem to move, in marble or in
bronze', or the geometric order of *A Vision*. We do not find him,
like Blake, 'walking among the fires of hell, delighted with the
enjoyments of genius, which to Angels look like torment and
insanity'. In *A Vision* he places Blake in a phase characterized by
'a violent scattering energy', of 'mere rushing out into the dis-
ordered and unbounded', of the search for symbols to express
'the overflowing and bursting of the mind. There is always an
element of frenzy.'

Yet in another respect in not following Blake's example he
was following his precept. Blake was, above all else, a national
prophet; and Yeats could not so easily have re-christened his
essentially English pantheon as he renamed its author O'Neill.
For the world of prophetic vision is not a private world; and
Yeats believed, as did Blake, that the 'visions' of *anima mundi*
(or the Collective Unconscious, if we prefer to call it so) may be
seen 'by the imaginative eye of everyone according to the situation he holds', even though 'to different People it appears differently as everything else does'. 'The blessed spirits must be

F

sought within the self which is common to all', Yeats wrote in
A Vision. The prophetic imagination is no longer bound in by the
particular experience of the individual memory; 'He who has
thus passed into the impersonal portion of his own mind perceives that it is not a mind but all minds.' Prophets and prophetic
poets are oracles of their race. Yeats invokes Swedenborg in
support of the view that in the Bible, 'the historic books while
dealing with facts which occurred, treated them as symbols'.
This follows from the law of correspondence; for an outward
event is an externalization of what is felt and thought inwardly.
'Blake, weaving historical incidents and names into mystical
poetry, did so under the belief that he was following the highest
example, and that "prophecy" was the right term for literature
so conceived.' He was recounting the interior drama of the collective mind of the English nation, and of his own city:

> So spoke London, immortal Guardian! I heard in Lambeth's
>   shades,

Blake wrote,

> In Felpham I heard and saw the Visions of Albion.
> I write in South Molton Street what I both see and hear
> In regions of Humanity, in London's opening streets.
> I see thee, awful Parent Land in light, behold I see
> Verulam! Canterbury! venerable parent of men,
> Generous immortal Guardian, golden clad! for Cities
> Are Men, fathers of multitudes, and Rivers and Mountains
> Are also Men. . . .

Yeats tells in his *Autobiographies* how all his Blake studies arose
from Edwin Ellis 'putting into my hands a scrap of notepaper
on which he had written an interpretation of the poem that
begins

> The fields from Islington to Marybone,
>   To Primrose Hill and Saint John's Wood,
> Were builded over with pillars of gold,
>   And there Jerusalem's pillars stood.

Blake truly had the prophetic gift of speaking to, and from, the
collective mind of his nation; and Yeats would have liked to
have that gift, and to be a prophet of Ireland, perhaps, as well
as her greatest poet. He too believed, 'Nations, cultures, schools
of thought may have their Daimons. These Daimons may move

through the Great Year like individual men and women.' He tells how he had hoped to found an Order, whose purpose was the guardianship, so to say, of the imagination of the Irish nation:

I had an unshakeable conviction . . . that invisible gates would open as they opened for Blake, as they opened for Swedenborg, as they opened for Boehme, and that this philosophy would find its manuals of devotion in all imaginative literature, and set before Irishmen, for special manual, an Irish literature which, though made by many minds, would seem the work of a single mind and turn our places of beauty or legendary association into symbols.

But if Yeats wedded his poetry to Ireland it was not, as he had hoped, by prophetic vision, but by the labour of conscious artistry.

Day after day I have sat in my chair turning a symbol over in my mind, exploring all its details, defining and again defining its elements, testing my convictions and those of others by its unity, attempting to substitute particulars for an abstraction like that of algebra.

In his essay 'William Blake and the Imagination', written more than a decade after those magical invocations of Orc and Los and Ololon, Yeats had come to see Blake less as a supreme maker of new myths, than as himself suffering from lack of a traditional form: 'He was a man crying out for a mythology, and trying to make one because he could not find one to his hand. Had he been a Catholic of Dante's time he would have been well content with Mary and the angels'; but the question for Yeats was, rather, what Blake would have done in his own time? What would William O'Neill have advised William Butler Yeats to do? He answers his own question as he thinks Blake would have answered it, 'chosen for his symbols the sacred mountains, along whose sides the peasant still sees enchanted fires, and the divinities which have not faded from the belief, if they have faded from the prayers of simple hearts'.

In the end Yeats discovered that he could not limit himself in this way. Christianity was also a part of the Irish heritage, and so were the myths of Greece, and, through Yeats and his own friends, new streams still flowed in, from Indian philosophy, from that Byzantium whose Emperor lived already in those Irish fairy tales which stem (as does the intricate patterning of the Holy Books and the stone crosses of Ireland) from an ancient communication with eastern Christendom. Heroes and oratorst and writers, Emmet and Burke and Swift and Berkeley and Goldsmith and Parnell and Roger Casement, Yeats discovered, were no less part of the symbolic theme than Cuchulainn and Fergus. He did as Blake did, using all that came to hand, as Blake had used King Arthur and the Druids, Pitt and Nelson, Snowdon and Avebury, Tyburn and Lambeth and South Molton Street, where his own lodgings were. Thus in following Blake's example, and dressing his themes in imagery of Ireland, it be-came impossible for Yeats to borrow his symbolic imagery from English Blake.

What he took was the doctrine; the religion of art, he gave its grand and final expression in his symbolic Byzantium; a symbol appropriate to Ireland though no less so elsewhere; chosen because

in early Byzantium, maybe never before or since in recorded history, religious, aesthetic and practical life were at one ... the painter, the mosaic worker, the worker in gold and silver, the illuminator of sacred books, were almost impersonal, almost perhaps without the consciousness of individual design, absorbed in their subject matter and that the vision of a whole people.

The symbol of Byzantium, a city both Hellenic and Christian, is an image more splendidly poetic, as well as more intellectually and historically inclusive, than Blake's purely Biblical Jerusalem; but the thought – the city of the imagination – is Blake's, and the artificers of Yeats's Byzantium are Blake's 'golden builders' who laboured to make London that 'city coming down from heaven'. Yeats had learned from Blake that the Last Judgement is the coming of the kingdom of imagination and the triumph of true over false art, and that

> . . . none could pass Heaven's door
> That loved inferior art.

Such symbols as Yeats shared with Blake were generally of that traditional kind to which no single poet can lay claim. In Yeats his imagery of the mirror, the 'bitter glass', or 'mirror-resembling dream', Boehme's 'vegetable glass of nature', the 'watery image' of the *Hermetica*, Plotinus on the myth of Narcissus, are all implicit, along with Blake's 'looking-glass of Enitharmon' (who is space). So with

A tree there is, that from its topmost bough
Is half all glittering flame and half all green,
Abounding foliage moistened with the dew.

Yeats uses these symbols with the same exactness as Blake; for
both poets 'dew' is the neo-Platonic symbol of the hylic envelope
which is attracted to generating souls: Nature, the 'tree of life',
with 'parts kindling, parts going out' is also the Herakleitean
fire. No doubt, together with other sources, Yeats recalls, in this
fine image, Blake's Vision of the Last Judgement, where an
allegorical figure of 'Mystery' (elsewhere in his writings 'the
tree of Mystery' is a symbolic synonym for 'the Goddess Nature')
is burned with fire; 'it represents Eternal Consummation of
Vegetable Life & Death with its Lusts'. The wreathed torches
in the hands of the figures who set fire to the Mystery 'represent
eternal Fire which is the fire of Generation or Vegetation; it is
an Eternal Consummation'. These archaic symbols are at once
simple and splendid, and their content seems inexhaustible.
Used, as Blake and Yeats use them, with a learned exactness,
they continue to yield meaning whose clarity and depth we
come the more to appreciate as we ourselves come to know more
of the traditional language they speak and the kind of knowledge
they embody and communicate.

Very few such symbols in Yeats seem taken from Blake and
Blake alone, for this is not in their nature. One such is perhaps
the 'dragon reason' of 'Her Triumph', who may be Blake's
Urizen; for the 'half-dead dragon' is not a usual symbol for
rational thinking, though it was certainly Blake's. Another is that
most characteristic image of Yeats's, the superhuman cry, cock
crow, hound voice, shriek of a bird, the sexual cry of the lovers,
'For ever and for ever', which for him symbolized some supernatural utterance, at once terrible and expressive of an immortal
joy; a voice from beyond reason, the utterance of life itself.
Blake's Spectre of Tharmas, a strange figure of the divine principle 'distributed', like the alchemical *deus absconditus*, and im-
mersed in matter, is heard 'harsh shrieking', with the 'voice
unutterable' of nature; a striking image in the *Hermetica* which
both poets probably knew. Yeats quotes at length (in his essay
'William Blake and the Imagination') the marriage song of
Enitharmon; thus did Blake's

> The deep lifts up his rugged head
> And lost in infinite hovering wings vanishes with a cry.
> The fading cry is ever dying,
> The living voice is ever living in its innermost joy

give Yeats his curlew cry –

> . . . a curlew cried and in the luminous wind
> A curlew answered; and suddenly thereupon I thought
> That on the lonely height where all are in God's eye,
> There cannot be, confusion of our sound forgot,
> A single soul that lacks a sweet crystalline cry.

or

> She sings as the moon sings:
> 'I am I, am I;
> The greater grows my light
> The further that I fly.'
> All creation shivers
> With that sweet cry.

I have left until last the most important symbolic theme for which Yeats was profoundly and confessedly indebted to his master. I have written elsewhere upon the symbolism of Blake's 'A Mental Traveller',[1] in those elucidations I followed clues which confirmed Yeats's belief that he alone had understood the poem; but since this theme leads to the very heart of Yeats's 'system', I must summarize what I have written in another context.

'A Mental Traveller' is a poem upon the cyclic nature of history, and the Great Year of the ancients. Blake's symbolic figures have misled literal-minded interpreters for the poem opens with an infant male child, who is no sooner born than he is bound down, Prometheus-like, upon a rock, by 'a woman old'. The identity of the Babe with Christ is established by the image of the crown of thorns; and with Dionysus by the tearing of the heart out of his side by the 'woman old'; as Juno commanded the Titans to tear the heart out of the side of the child Dionysus. The babe grows to manhood and breaks his manacles, binding down in turn the woman, who has meanwhile grown younger. The reversal continues until the man, old and exhausted, 'wanders away', and his place is taken by 'a little female babe', who in her turn begins to grow up, is pursued by the now rejuvenated

---

[1] *Blake and Tradition*, Andrew Mellor Lectures, 1962, Bollinger Series no. 35. See also *The Huntington Library Quarterly*, 21, 1957, and *The Sewanee Review*, Summer 1962.

male principle, ages, and becomes 'a woman old'. Again comes the reversal, with the only difference that the male babe who in his first appearance was 'smiling' is now 'frowning'; as if at some Second Coming the Christ child were to appear not in meekness but in wrath. This Blake probably believed to be so in the time of social revolutions in which he lived, which heralded, as he supposed, a New Age. The thought, though in another guise, is repeated in Yeats's

> And what rough beast, its hour come round at last,
> Slouches towards Bethlehem to be born.

Swedenborg had announced the beginning of a New Age in the year 1757, the year of Blake's birth; and Blake's *The Marriage of Heaven and Hell* proclaims the birth of fiery Orc, the Messiah of 'evil, or energy'. But the source of the structure of 'A Mental Traveller' is Plato's myth of the Great Year, as told in the *Laws*. The god Saturn (ruler of the Golden Age) at one time conducts the world and its revolutions, at another relinquishes it, leaving it to unwind its gyrations like a coiled spring released. In the reign of Saturn, the myth says, men do not grow, as now, from youth to age, but from age to youth, as does Blake's babe. The slaying of the god Dionysus was associated, in his cult, with the beginning of a new cycle; and Blake (who knew the Dionysus legend from Thomas Taylor's *Dissertation on the Mysteries of Eleusis and Dionysus* – a book Yeats also came to know) quite correctly bases the myth of this 'babe', who undergoes the process of sacrificial 'descent' into the time-world, and all that follows, upon the theme of the child-Dionysus who was regenerated from the living heart, preserved by the goddess Athena. The 'female babe' is Blake's personification of the material principle (traditionally always female) whose dominance alternates with the male, and mental, principle. Blake's female is both Juno the destroyer and Athena the preserver of the heart of the god.

Ellis and Yeats had attempted an interpretation of this poem, without success; it is evident that they did not know Blake's sources and were merely guessing. But after many years of reflection, and with greater knowledge of symbolic themes, Yeats made Blake's thought so much his own that it was he rather than Blake who gave its final and most poetic expression in many of his greatest poems, in *A Vision*, and in his play *The Resurrection*, to the gyres of history.

It was in 1917 that Yeats, immediately after his marriage, began to receive, in the form of automatic scripts, profound intuitions upon the structural principles of the cosmos; just such a unifying symbol as he had looked to Blake for, at the end of his boyhood. Shortly before this he had written to Lady Gregory that he was reading Blake again; and it is likely that many of Blake's themes, which had long lain dormant in his imagination, now again rose to the surface, along with much else that he had since learned. Writing, in the first edition of *A Vision*, of his early Blake studies, he admits that at the time he and Ellis had

no understanding of this poem: we had explained its details, for they occur elsewhere in his verse or his pictures, but not the poem as a whole, not the myth, the perpetual return to the same thing; not that which certainly moved Blake to write it; but when I understood the double cones, I understood it also. The woman and the man are two competing gyres growing at one another's expense.

Yeats's use of the term 'gyres' proves that he was now in possession of the key to Blake's symbol. He seems not to have read the *Laws*; for in writing of his own gyres, he refers to the vortex of Empedocles, and the alternating gyres of Concord and Discord; to St. Thomas Aquinas, to Swedenborg, Flaubert, Vico; but of Plato only the *Timaeus*. He nowhere refers to Blake's theme of growing from youth to age, age to youth, to its source, which would have been obvious to him had he read the *Laws*. But he had certainly found his way to the Dionysus myth possibly, as Blake had before him, in Thomas Taylor's *Dissertation* (or possibly in G. R. S. Meade's *Orpheus*, where Taylor's version is also given), and knew of its symbolic association with the Great Year. In the opening poem of *The Resurrection* the beginning of the Christian 'year' is proclaimed under the symbolism of the sacrifice of Dionysus, and in images identical with those Blake had used in the opening verses of 'A Mental Traveller'; only Yeats describes the goddess under the aspect rather of Athena than of Juno; though it was the 'woman old' who in the classical myth brought about the sacrifice:

> I saw a staring virgin stand
> Where holy Dionysus died,
> And tear the heart out of his side,
> And lay the heart upon her hand,
> And bear that beating heart away;

and then did all the Muses sing
Of Magnus Annus at the spring,
As though God's death were but a play.

The beating heart, in the play itself, is felt, by a disciple, in the resurrected body of Christ, the symbolic figure of the Divine principle of the Year about to begin.

The Muses are especially associated, in Orphic theology, with Dionysus, each of whose nine epithets (according to the planetary spheres) is linked with one of the Muses; as Yeats no doubt knew, whether from Taylor or from Meade.

From these lines we could deduce only that Yeats was drawing upon the same symbolic context as Blake. It is he himself who repeatedly, in *A Vision*, refers to Blake's poem as a source; and the verse which ends the play is a superb restatement of the essence of Blake's thought on history, with its continuous and inevitable succession of changes in never-ending cycle. This aspect of the poem Yeats had understood when in the Ellis and Yeats commentary – he or Ellis – had written (of the male principle) 'As he grows old the wealth of his soul consists of the accumulation of his own smiles and tears. But he is male, and mental, and these things make the joy of others when he "teaches in song", as the overworked phrase has it, what he "learned in suffering".' In *A Vision* Yeats summarized this idea in the phrase, 'no civilization can spend what it has not earned'. In *The Resurrection* he has given dramatic and poetic form to the thought he learned from 'A Mental Traveller':

Everything that man esteems
Endures a moment or a day:
Love's pleasure drives his love away,
The painter's brush consumes his dreams,
The herald's cry, the soldier's tread
Consumes his glory and his might:
whatever flames upon the night
Man's own resinous heart has fed.

– the heart again: 'resinous', for is not a sacred emblem of Dionysus the fir cone?

Blake's poem was continually present to Yeats's imagination in all his writings on the theme of the gyres. At the second coming of Blake's male child,

They cry, 'The Babe! the Babe is Born!'
And flee away on Every side.

– and Yeats relates that cry to the beginning of the Christian era: 'Meanwhile the irrational force that would create confusion and uproar as with the cry "the Babe! the Babe is born" – the women speaking unknown tongues, the barbers and weavers expounding divine revelation with all the vulgarity of their servitude.' (The barbers are from Gibbon, in whose great panorama of a declining civilization Yeats, and Blake before him, had found food for their thought about the rise and fall of civilizations.) The Babe, like Byzantium, is a symbol which unites the Christian with the Hellenic Mysteries; for the Babe (Brimo) is Dionysus born to the Kore, in the Mysteries of Eleusis, as well as the Christian Babe born of a Virgin.

Blake's poem describes continual flux and change in symbols essentially dynamic; as the metre of 'A Mental Traveller' also is rapid and energetic. But Yeats's more static and diagrammatic mind saw the same process in terms of a succession of twenty-eight phases; which he relates to Blake's poem. He believed *A Vision* to be, in some sense, an extended clarification of 'A Mental Traveller'; for in a footnote to an explanation of his two pairs of opposite principles, *Celestial Body* and *Passionate Body*, which move in 'a double opposition to *Will* and *Creative Mind*', he refers to that poem, repeating that neither Edwin Ellis nor himself nor any commentator had explained it; but that 'the student of *A Vision* will understand at once'. His own system, he claimed, 'perhaps explains better than any I have used, Blake's "Mental Traveller" '. He might have added that the opposite is also true; but either way this might seem to an uninstructed reader to explain the obscure by the more obscure!

The young Yeats had not been altogether wrong in supposing that there must, somewhere in Blake's system, be a cyclic symbol; and although his 'rotation of the Zoas' was imaginary, the chapter 'The Covering Cherub' shows that Ellis and Yeats had lighted upon an 'arbitrary, harsh and difficult' symbol which certainly helped to form Yeats's later thought on the twenty-eight phases of the Moon. The 'covering cherub' comprises the succession throughout history of 'the twenty-seven Heavens and their Churches', a theme (together with the terms 'heavens' and 'churches' as here used), which Blake borrowed from Swedenborg; and which, although he twice repeats the list of these churches, he seems to leave rather in mid-air, unintegrated with

other themes of his mythology. One has the impression that
Blake himself had only half assimilated this material.

Yeats seems to have known Swedenborg even before he knew
Blake; and his own system is in some ways closer to their common teacher than it is to Blake himself. In brief, Swedenborg
taught that in every manifestation (whether of organic or human
life, or of a 'church') the original impulse is a spiritual energy
which spends itself, passing from pure energy to dead and rigid
form. Thus, for Swedenborg no less than for the two poets whom
he so deeply influenced, everything, however perfect, 'endures
a moment or a day', but cannot in its nature continue in stability.
'Churches', in Swedenborg's terms, represent new spiritual ideas
or attitudes; or what Blake calls 'states'; and 'there have been on
this earth several Churches, all of which in process of time have
come to their consummation, and then have been succeeded by
new ones, and so on to the present time; the consummation of
the church comes to pass when there remains no divine truth but
what is falsified or rejected'. Swedenborg goes on to announce
the consummation of the present Christian Church and the
beginning of a New Age, announced to him in 'the heavens', or
inner world. Can it be doubted that Yeats was deeply influenced
by both Blake and Swedenborg?

Of Blake's twenty-seven churches the general pattern is taken
from Swedenborg; but the first seven names of these point to yet
another version of the phases of history, that of Boehme; who
taught that 'there are seven Times appointed', which bear the
names, and take their character from the first patriarchs, from
Adam to Methuselah. His own lifetime Blake took to fall within
Boehme's Age of Enoch, which is to be followed by the Age of
Methuselah, the last age of the world, after which comes the
Deluge (Noah's symbol) the end of time, the coming of Christ's
kingdom, and the return of Adam to Paradise. The Age of
Enoch Boehme calls the age of the 'prophetical mouth', when
the mysteries are to be revealed openly; and for Blake prophecy
is poetry. In a letter to Flaxman (who like himself was at one time
a Swedenborgian) Blake wrote – as one initiate to another – of
the New Age, 'The Reign of Literature & the Arts Commences'.
He also made an engraving of Enoch, the prophet of this reign,
accompanied by allegorical figures bearing emblems of painting,
music, and poetry.

There is nothing to suggest that Boehme deviated from the

orthodox Christian view of the time process, which is linear and not cyclic. Swedenborg implies a cycle by analogy with the other cyclic processes he describes; he likens, for example, the variations in the spiritual state of the angels to the succession of morning, noon, evening, and night, or to the seasons of the year. A cyclic view of history is, however, incompatible with Christian orthodoxy; as Yeats knew, for he quotes Nemesius, who denounced 'certain Christians' who 'would have us consider the Resurrection linked to the restoration of the world' (as it is in Yeats's play) 'but they deceive themselves strangely, for it is proved by the words of Christ that the Resurrection could not happen more than once, that it came not from a periodical revolution but from the will of God'. The doctrine reappeared, however (Yeats goes on to say), as a recognized heresy until the thirteenth century; and, whether under Swedenborgian influence or no, it reappeared in Blake; who, strangely enough, expressed the cyclic view of history not only implicitly in 'A Mental Traveller' (a poem written from Platonic sources, though it contains Biblical elements and Christian overtones), but in his account of the twenty-seven churches; for after listing the names and the main phases into which these fall, he concludes

Thus are the Heavens form'd by Los within the Mundane Shell[1]
And where Luther ends Adam begins in Eternal Circle.

If Blake did not feel bound by the Christian linear view of time, Yeats was still less so; for if Blake's eclecticism included other traditions within a Christian framework, Yeats includes the Christian tradition within an eclectic framework, rather Indian and neo-Platonic than Christian in structure. In both these paradigms the cyclic recurrence is continual, Magnus Annus revolving through its four seasons, or ages, from spring to winter, from gold to iron; or, as the Hindu myth figures the process, the world is breathed out by Brahma, who after a certain time breathes it into himself again.

But enough has been said to show the affinity of thought between the two great symbolist poets, master and disciple, who speak and answer one another across their centuries, and who bear witness with those other sages round God's holy fire, Plato and Plotinus, Boehme and Swedenborg, to the grandeur of traditional cosmology. This cosmology is implicit in all Yeats

---

[1] An Orphic image.

wrote, as it is in Blake's 'little song about a rose'. Did he, did
Blake, did Plato, believe in the actual existence of these circuits
and cycles? Perhaps the question is best answered, for all who
think in symbolic terms, in the words of one of Yeats's earliest
poems:

> The wandering earth herself may be
> Only a sudden flaming word
> In clanging space a moment heard,
> Troubling the endless reverie.

All is symbol; 'Mirror on mirror mirrored is all the show'.

'They have helped me', Yeats wrote of his own intellectual
paradigms, 'to hold in a single thought reality and justice.' It
is within the great scale and scope of this cosmology, and the
harmony of its symbolic order, that Yeats was able to write

> Conduct and work grow coarse, and coarse the soul,
> What matter? Those that Rocky Face holds dear,
> Lovers of horses and of women, shall,
> From marble of a broken sepulchre,
> Or dark betwixt the polecat and the owl,
> Or any rich, dark nothing disinter
> The workman, noble and saint, and all things run
> On that unfashionable gyre again.

1965

5

TRADITIONAL SYMBOLISM
IN 'KUBLA KHAN'

I can remember how as a child the mystery of this most magical
of all poems set vibrating a responsive chord in my imagination,
and now that I am old the magic has not faded nor the poem
grown to seem less wonderful or less mysterious. Like the rain-
bow's, its source will always prove to be, however far you may
follow it, just beyond you: Coleridge well knew that poetry
springs from an inaccessible source. It can never be elucidated,
or if it can, it was not poetry of the imagination in the first place;
for words exist only on the surface of experience; its depths lie
beyond their reach. We enjoy poetry most, he said, when it is
'generally but not perfectly understood'; and he goes on to say
how much more he had enjoyed some poem of Gray when – to
him as a boy – it had seemed full of mystery, than later when he
had understood its whole meaning. But with the greatest poetry
the mystery only increases with our knowledge.

All know the story of how the poem was written. Coleridge,
staying at a lonely farm-house on the borders of Exmoor, had
taken an anodyne, supposed to be opium. He fell into a charmed
sleep, in which a poem rose to his mind, of not less than two or
three hundred lines; 'the images rose up before him as *things*,
with a parallel production of the correspondent expressions,
without any sensation or consciousness of effort'. On waking he
began to write the poem, but he was interrupted by

a person on business from Porlock . . . and on his return to the room
found, to his no small surprise and mortification, that though he
still retained some vague and dim recollection of the general purport
of the vision, yet, with the exception of some eight or ten scattered
lines and images, all the rest had passed away like the images on the
surface of a stream into which a stone had been cast, but alas! without the after restoration of the latter. . . .

When Coleridge wrote these words little or nothing was known of the nature of dreams.

He was indeed one of the few men of his age to observe or consider the question; and his writings contain many noted observations on, for example, the way in which the dreaming mind will misinterpret some physical sensation, like the ticking of a clock, and weave it into one of those stories which in sleep we all have such a talent for inventing – so much so that we may well wonder whether our sleeping selves are not more remarkable than those masks we wear in waking life. However, to the nineteenth century the world of dreams was closed. Dreams were not considered to have any meaning at all, and to look for meaning in 'Kubla Khan' occurred to no one. Its magical power was attributed to sound and image, the subtle incantation of its changing metrical pattern, and the intrinsic beauty of the landscape of imagination Coleridge has painted, like a picture of a country that nowhere exists.

The whole question of 'Kubla Khan' was reopened by the American scholar Livingston Lowes, in a book that delighted my generation, *The Road to Xanadu*. Freud's discovery of what he calls 'dream-work', the linking together of memories and other images charged with strong emotional association in the construction of dreams, was in the air and doubtless suggested to Lowes his method. Coleridge himself (following Hartley's theory of association) had written of the 'hooks and eyes' of memory which link by association something read the day before with something remembered from childhood, or noticed on a journey, by way of some common feature; and Lowes made the attempt to follow, through clues given in his writings, Coleridge's prodigious reading. We know – for he himself has told us so – that Coleridge, before he fell asleep, had been reading in a travel-book, *Purchas's Pilgrimage*, the sentence which had stirred his imagination so deeply as to set in motion the dream-work of the poem; we shall later consider why this was so.

In Xanadu did Cublai Can build a stately Palace, encompassing sixteene miles of plaineground with a wall, wherein are fertile Meddowes, pleasant Springs, delightful Streames, and all sorts of beasts of chase and game, and in the middest thereof a sumptuous house of pleasure.

To this, many related themes from Coleridge's wide reading have become associated. The richness of Coleridge's knowledge, the vividness of his memory for the minute particulars of an image described or seen with his own eyes, Lowes abundantly demonstrated. But images do not associate themselves to one another, but to some theme which draws them towards itself, as a magnetic field attracts particles of iron; and what this imaginative field of force was, Lowes has not told us.

Robert Graves a few years later made the attempt – someone was bound to do so – to interpret the poem on Freudian lines, as a dream of suppressed sexual desires and frustrations and so forth; but that fashion gave place in due course to Jung's imaginatively richer discoveries of an innate conformation of archetypes which tend to appear in similar forms in the myths of all religions, and also in dreams and visions. We may recognize them – whether in myths which move us or in dreams of unusual power – by a certain sense of something already known, of recollection of something we had forgotten, an assent, a coming into our own; anamnesis, Plato calls this awakening of innate knowledge we did not know ourselves to possess.

Let us recognize that not even Jung has said the last word about those regions of the mind into which we sometimes stray. Those who have penetrated most deeply into these mysteries are the least inclined to be dogmatic; but images of power like those which rose before Coleridge's mind are known to all imaginative poets in some degree, are perhaps the very essence of poetry, and of its power to move us. Yeats wrote that revelation is not from the human personality but from 'that age-long memoried self, that shapes the elaborate shell of the mollusc and the child in the womb, that teaches the birds to make their nests'; and that 'genius is a crisis that joins the buried self for certain moments to the trivial daily mind'. He used not opium but the techniques of magic to evoke this 'other mind'. (This expression was used by Beryl de Zoete in her writings on Balinese dancers, who, possessed by that mind, dance, as Yeats has written, 'on deathless feet'.) In his *Autobiographies* Yeats tells how persons sent into a trance perceive marvellous things which, upon waking, they, like Coleridge, quickly forget. Edwin Muir spoke of the theme of a Paradise lost by the Fall as a part of 'the Fable' which he saw in waking vision; and Yeats, too, relates, in his *Autobiographies*, how one man, in a trance, described 'a walled garden on the top of a high mountain, and in the middle of it a tree with great birds in the branches, and fruit out of which, if you held the fruit to your ear, came the sound of fighting'; and a young girl, sent to the same 'garden', heard in the tree 'the continual clashing of swords'. 'Whence came that fine thought of 'music-making swords, the image of the garden, and many like images and thoughts?' Yeats ventures upon no dogmatic answer, but knew himself 'face to face with the Anima Mundi described by the Platonic philosophers'. In parenthesis I may say that on one occasion many years ago I myself saw a tree loaded with blood-red fruit, with a blackbird singing in its branches, and its roots watered by streams that rose from darkness; and at the foot of the tree a figure was sleeping. The vision was of a quality unforgettable. There seem to be certain typical features of the Paradise archetype – the tree, the river, the wall, the singing birds, the clash of swords, the serpent, the fruit – of which no single vision has all. As Blake says of such visions, which to him were a matter of daily experience, 'to everyone it appears differently, as everything else does'.

It is easy to see resemblances between Yeats's descriptions of Paradise and the images of 'Kubla Khan': a walled garden on a high mountain, marvellous trees; the sound of discord in the apple, the presence of the principle of conflict, of Good and Evil, like Coleridge's 'Ancestral voices prophesying war'. Coleridge had visited that same garden. Purchas's description of the Khan's walled garden, with its fertile meadows and flowing streams and every kind of beast, had stirred in him the archetype of Paradise as described in *Genesis*, with 'every tree that is pleasant to the sight, and good for food; the tree of life also in the midst of the garden, and the tree of knowledge of good and evil. And a river went out of Eden to water the garden; and from thence it was parted, and became into four heads.'

In *Paradise Lost* Milton describes Eden in symbols which in the course of Christian art have become traditional; and it is easy to see that Coleridge's dreaming mind has drawn upon Milton.

> Southward through *Eden* went a River large,
> Nor chang'd his course, but through the shaggie hill
> Pass'd underneath ingulft. . . .
> (*Paradise Lost*, IV, 223–5)

There is a 'fresh Fountain' that

> . . . with many a rill
> Watered the Garden; thence united fell
> Down the steep glade, and met the neather Flood. . . .

G

The subtle magical atmosphere of Milton's Paradise, those

Groves, whose rich Trees wept odorous Gumms and Balme . . .

and

> . . . the crisped Brooks,
> Rowling on Orient Pearl and sands of Gold,
> With mazie error under pendant shades
> Ran Nectar, visiting each plant, and fed
> Flours worthy of Paradise. . . .

has left its trace on 'Kubla Khan':

> And there were gardens bright with sinuous rills
> Where blossom'd many an incense-bearing tree;
> And here were forests ancient as the hills,
> Enfolding sunny spots of greenery.

Enough has been said to illustrate briefly an archetypal theme which could be traced both backwards and forwards throughout the whole history of European poetry and myth; for imaginative poetry, far from being 'subjective' and 'personal', tends to use and perpetuate traditional images in which 'the age-long memoried self' has been repeatedly embodied. It is poetry of the personality and of this world which, on the contrary, seeks for 'originality' in images as ephemeral as itself.

But there is also a learning of the imagination: a learning which becomes accessible only to those who know how to use it, through their own insights into the world of intelligible forms which that learning embodies and transmits. All poets, and all readers of poetry who pass beyond the writing or reading of poetry for merely descriptive purposes, cross a frontier from the personal world into the world of those experiences which lie beyond the reach of our everyday consciousness, but to which, in our moments of greatest vision, of expanded consciousness, we have occasional glimpses. In his poem 'Sailing to Byzantium', Yeats reminds us that we can learn of this order of experience only by studying those works of poetry and the other arts in which it is embodied:

> Nor is there singing school but studying
> Monuments of its own magnificence. . . .

Traditional art is at once the embodiment and the normal means of transmission of imaginative knowledge. But to this study of

those works which embody and transmit the hidden order of the
soul all great poets must come in their maturity; it is the secret
language of the initiates. Yeats tells in the introduction to his
philosophical essay *A Vision*, written at the beginning of the
richest phase of his poetic life, of the course of unusual studies
which he had undertaken, whose influence upon his work we
immediately recognize, even before we are aware of what wisdom
it is which lends such depths of resonance to Yeats's later poems.
Blake too offered that wisdom in terms misleadingly simple:

> I give you the end of a golden string,
> Only wind it into a ball
> It will lead you in to Heaven's gate
> Built in Jerusalem's wall.

Milton in 'Il Penseroso' wrote of the proper studies of the poet
who in 'some high lonely Towr'

> . . . may oft out-watch the *Bear*
> With thrice great *Hermes*, or unsphear
> The spirit of *Plato* to unfold
> What worlds, or what vast Regions hold
> The immortal mind that hath forsook
> Her mansion in this fleshly nook:
> And of those *Daemons* that are found
> In fire, air, flood, or under ground . . .

– a list that forms the canon of the imaginative tradition. In
Europe the symbolic language of tradition, woven and interwoven both within and outside Christianity, is basically Platonic
and neo-Platonic. Like an underground river that from time
to time sends up springs and fountains, Platonism emerges in
different centuries and different countries, and wherever its
fertilizing waters flow, there the arts are reborn and flourish.
For no renaissance has ever yet come of iconoclasm and rejection
of the past, but, on the century, from renewed contact with
tradition: as the Gothic architecture from a renewed study of the
Greek philosophy of numbers; the Florentine renaissance and
all that followed from Ficino's Latin editions of the Platonists;
or, in our own country, the Irish renaissance from a study of
those same works that Milton's poet read in his High Lonely
Tower, and which were also the 'darling studies' – so he tells us
and a friend in a letter – of Coleridge. For when Coleridge was
still a schoolboy at Christ's Hospital, the foundations of the great

poetry of the Romantic movement were being laid by the re-
warded labours of Thomas Taylor the Platonist, the first translator of Plato into the English language. Taylor also translated,
between 1780 and 1800, many of the Tractates of Plotinus, as
well as Porphyry, Iamblichus, Proclus, and the other later
Platonists; he wrote, besides, a number of remarkable essays on
the Orphic mythology and the neo-Platonic use of those ancient
myths as the natural language of metaphysical thought. Blake
and his friend Flaxman the sculptor knew Taylor; Coleridge as a
schoolboy devoured his works; Shelley owned his Plato, and it
is likely that Keats also learned from him the use of mythological
discourse. His writings crossed the Atlantic to inspire Emerson,
Bronson Alcott, and the other American transcendentalists.
Emerson called Taylor 'the best feeder of poets since Milton',
and Yeats's friend, the poet and mystic George Russell (AE)
spoke of him as 'the uncrowned king'; and so, for the poets of
the Irish renaissance, he was. For Taylor not only placed in the
hands of, first, the English Romantics, then the American
Transcendentalists, and in our own country the Irish poets, the
mythology and philosophy of the Orphic, Pythagorean, Platonic, and neo-Platonic tradition; he also taught them to use
that language.

We find only what we are qualified to see; the neglect of the
importance, to the Romantic poets, of the perennial wisdom in
its European guise of neo-Platonism is a reflection of the metaphysical ignorance of the post-Protestant West. The worst ignorance is not to know that we do not know; happily, with the
rediscovery, through psychology, of at least some part of that lost
wisdom, we are beginning to realize how little we have understood in works long familiar. Indeed, the entire European tradition of imaginative poetry, with all the rich variety of image in
which ancient and enduring themes have been dressed, in various
places and at different times, proves to be strung upon a single
thread. To find this thread in one poet is to hold a clue to all;
Yeats and Shelley, Blake and Milton, Dante, Virgil, Ovid,
Spenser, and Coleridge all speak with the same symbolic language and discourse of the immemorial world of the imagination.
Far from introducing obscurity and confusion, a knowledge of
these themes draws aside a veil, so that we read familiar works
with a new clarity and depth of understanding; read, as it were
for the first time, the poems the poets themselves were writing,

and not some fantasy of our own which often barely approximates to the original conception.

In the literature of Tradition – the learning of the imagination – Coleridge was deeply versed. When he was a schoolboy he was already reading the Neoplatonists in Thomas Taylor's translations; and shortly before he wrote 'Kubla Khan' in the summer of 1797 he had written to his friend Thelwall (on 17 November 1796) in London, asking him to send him a number of the neo-Platonic texts in the original Greek. It was of these themes that his mind was full at the time he wrote the poem. Details of the imagery are of course added, as Livingston Lowes discerned, from personal associations or recent reading, by 'the hooks and eyes of memory'; but the thread upon which these images are strung is the common symbolic language employed by poets and painters of the European tradition, strictly or, as C. S. Lewis puts it, 'grammatically' used. For, as Lewis says, 'Giants, dragons, paradises, gods and the like, are themselves the expression of certain basic elements in man's spiritual experience. In that sense they are more like words – the words of a language which speaks of the mere unspeakable.'

'Alph, the sacred river' is one such theme, upon which I can only suggest a few of the associated strands which Coleridge has condensed into the phrase. The Jewish mystical tradition of the Cabala is based upon the great symbol of 'the tree of God', a symbol, like Yggdrasill and other sacred trees, of the whole of manifested being. The Tree is sometimes also conceived as a river through which the creative power flows down from the unmanifested source, the divine origin, symbolized by the letter Aleph, or Alpha; and the river of life descends perpetually from above down to the lowest plane of manifestation, matter: the 'sunless sea'. Burnet, whom Coleridge quotes at the beginning of 'The Ancient Mariner', and Robert Fludd, Christian Cabalists, both give accounts of this symbol. Moslem mysticism likewise regards the first letter of the alphabet in much the same way as the Pythagoreans regard the number one, and the geometrical point as the dimensionless *punctum* through which all manifestation issues from the unmanifest. A river that flows from a hidden fountain is found in many Greek myths. Psyche, in Apuleius's legend of Cupid and Psyche, is sent to draw water from the unapproachable source of the Styx; and the Orphic Hymn to the Fates (Thomas Taylor had translated it) describes those weavers of destiny as dwelling in a dark cave from whose depths the sacred river flows. Porphyry's *De Antro Nympharum* (On the Cave of the Nymphs) is a symbolic description of the cave (Plato's symbol of this world) from whose darkness, 'Through caverns measureless to man', issues the river of generation.

'The sunless sea' into which the river flows is a symbol no less universal; *hyle*, or matter, is invariably symbolized by water, on account of its continual flux. It is interesting to remember, in passing, that Taylor in several of his works has written of the use made by the Neoplatonists of the sea-voyage of Odysseus as a symbol of man's crossing of the stormy sea of life – a symbol retained in the Christian rite of baptism; and Coleridge's 'Ancient Mariner', as Mr. John Beer has mentioned in his book *Coleridge the Visionary*, derives in part from that old voyager. If we assume that Coleridge is following tradition, the sea into which his river descends is called 'sunless' because it is the farthest point from the source, the divine light; like 'the wat'ry shore' where Blake's Earth sits in the darkness of the world of Experience. To Coleridge the image of ceaseless flux, Herakleitus' Πάντα ῥεῖ is made terrible and concrete by the image of rocks, the most solid of all things, dancing like chaff in the ever-flowing fountain:

> Huge fragments vaulted like rebounding hail,
> Or chaffy grain beneath the thresher's flail:
> And 'mid these dancing rocks at once and ever
> It flung up momently the sacred river.

In such powerful images does the dreaming mind clothe our thoughts. The earth, that Plato calls an 'immortal animal' in whose life all individual lives are but momentary, breathes in 'fast thick pants' as the torrent of existence flows away.

But on the waves of 'the sunless sea' the 'pleasure-dome' is reflected – an image used by Coleridge when he described the fleeting of the idea of the poem itself, 'like the images on the surface of the stream'. Again the symbol is one common to all the Platonic philosophers. Proclus uses the image of a tree reflected in a river; Plotinus and the *Hermetica* (Milton's Thrice-Great Hermes) abound in images of the temporal world as a reflection, in water, of the eternal forms; and Plato himself in the *Timaeus* calls this world a moving image of eternity'; and eternity a sphere, the domed vault of heaven; the same dome which was retained in the symbolic architecture of the Byzantine basilica, itself a product of Platonism.

All knowledge, Plato says, is remembrance, anamnesis – not memory of events of time or of the individual life, but remembrance in time, and by the individual, of permanent intellectual realities: as of number and geometry, and the harmonious order which underlies all things. 'Kubla Khan' both is, and is about, remembrance; its theme is the imaginative experience itself, written in that exaltation of wonder which invariably accompanies moments of insight into the mystery upon whose surface we live. Coleridge likens the arising of remembrance to a woman singing:

> A damsel with a dulcimer
> In a vision once I saw:
> It was an Abyssinian maid
> And on her dulcimer she played
> Singing of Mount Abora.

The song and the singer come from 'Abyssinia', the country of the long-undiscovered source of the Nile, which so long remained a symbol of the inaccessible source of the river of life; Abyssinia, the high source where the gods dwell on their mountain-top – Olympus, Meru, Carmel, Zion, the Holy Mountain under whatever name; the mountain summit of Paradise where the Garden is traditionally situated. (The Fall is itself, according to Platonists and Cabalists, a 'forgetting' of eternity, and the 'mountain-top' the summit of human consciousness, the unfallen state lost with the lapse into the 'fallen' state of amnesia.) Abyssinia is also the Abyss, the depths perhaps of darkness as of light, Blake's 'distant deeps or skies' which underlie creation. From this source of mystery the damsel herself comes; for the beauty of the beloved person evokes, as Plato taught in the *Phaedrus*, recollection. She does not speak or instruct, but sings, to a dulcimer; for music, highest of the arts, springs from a source deeper than words, and nearer to the innate order of the soul, whose harmony, as the Greeks supposed, is that of number.

The dulcimer itself is a one-stringed instrument, the monochord; and upon the monochord Pythagoras worked out the mathematical proportions of three and four, the intervals of the diatonic scale. These intervals, as the Greek philosophers were well aware, can be expressed or discovered in other media besides that of sound: in architecture, sculpture, astronomy. By the Pythagoreans and their successors, it was held that the universe is itself built upon that scale, which was not so much invented as discovered. Kepler himself demonstrated that the relative distances of the planets from the sun correspond to these intervals. The Lyre of Apollo, an instrument seven-stringed like the diatonic scale itself, was also, according to Thomas Taylor, regarded as a symbol of the underlying numerical harmony of the whole universe – a symbol Keats has so splendidly used in his Hyperion fragments. When, therefore, Coleridge made his damsel play, not a violin, clavichord, lute, or flute but, specifically, a dulcimer, it was with intent; she plays upon the chords of harmony which underlie all creation. There could be no fitter symbol of the power of beauty and love to evoke the soul's deepest knowledge.

We may compare Coleridge's Abyssinian maid to Wordsworth's Highland girl in 'The Solitary Reaper':

> Will no one tell me what she sings? –
> Perhaps the plaintive numbers flow
> For old, unhappy, far-off things,
> And battles long ago. . . .

The image is closer to this world – or more clothed in this world – than Coleridge's, but far from mere realism; for her song too stirs recollection through 'numbers', and here too ancestral voices tell of far-off things, and, like the clashing of swords in Yeats's apple, of wars and battles foreknown in Paradise itself; that element of evil of which the Biblical serpent is another symbol.

Keats in the Hyperion fragments also describes some such initiatory anamnesis as Coleridge so dramatically underwent, though his symbolism is that of Greek mythology and not of dream. The first version opens with the god Saturn, removed from the world and sunk in sleep; a symbolic landscape whose every image evokes the state of Platonic amnesis, forgetfulness, the unconscious. Saturn, as Keats certainly knew, was the god of the legendary Golden Age, now lost to mankind; the Classical equivalent of Paradise, that fabled land we each carry within ourselves, forgotten.

> Deep in the shady sadness of a vale,
> Far sunken from the healthy breath of morn.

There the banished gods in counsel decide to send a messenger to the world that has forgotten them – Mnemosyne – memory; or, as she is called in the later fragment, Moneta: the meaning of her name is the same. She is the same figure as Wordsworth's singer, as Blake's Jerusalem, as Coleridge's Abyssinian Maid; Jung would have called her the *anima*, whose nature it is to mediate between the world of consciousness and the unconscious. The poet addresses her as someone he has formerly known and half remembers:

> How camest thou over the unfooted sea

(the sea is in every tradition – as in the Christian service of Baptism, the voyages of Odysseus and of the Ancient Mariner, or Blake's 'sea of time and space' a symbol of the material world and its flux). The figure of Recollection has crossed the forgetful waters; and the poet becomes aware that she has been there all the time, that she is deeply familiar:

> Or hath that antique mien and robed form
> Moved in these vales invisible till now?
> Sure I have heard those vestments sweeping o'er
> The fallen leaves, when I have sat alone
> In cool mid forest. Surely I have traced
> The rustle of those ample skirts about
> These grassy solitudes, and seen the flowers
> Lift up their heads, as still the whisper pass'd.
> Goddess! I have beheld those eyes before,
> And their eternal calm, and all that face,
> Or I have dream'd. . . .

Memory, at once strange and familiar, comes with 'antique mien', from 'the age-long memoried self', as if belonging to some immemorial past. The goddess replies that, like Coleridge's Abyssinian Maid, she has visited him in dreams;

> Thou hast dream'd of me; and awaking up
> Didst find a lyre all golden by thy side
> Whose strings touch'd by thy fingers, all the vast
> Unwearied ear of the whole universe
> Listen'd in pain and pleasure at the birth
> Of such new tuneful wonder.

Apollo's lyre, Coleridge's dulcimer, the instrument on which the poet plays the harmony of the universe, is placed in his hands by the goddess from the high lost mountain-top of Eden, or from Saturn's golden world. He has only to contemplate her silent form – for beauty comes from beyond the conscious mind whose communications are in words – in order himself to become eloquent:

> Mute thou remainest – Mute? yet I can read
> A wondrous lesson in thy *silent* face;
> Knowledge enormous makes a god of me

– and the poet then tells how he will banish the sorrows of the
world by telling what he knows from the silent goddess. As Yeats
says, 'Man can embody truth, but he cannot know it'.

Coleridge's Abyssinian Maid is a figure more rich in mystery,
a more complete expression than Moneta of the poet's relation
to the inspiring Muse; for she stands nearer to the mystery of
love, and shows, like the 'waning moon', a demonaspect which
is no less a face of her divinity than Moneta's tranquil beauty.
In all these female figures the truth is implicit that love (as also
for Dante) is the initiator. Yet her song is of 'Mount Abora', the
heights of the soul; and the poet's recollection arises from within
himself:

> Could I revive within me
> Her symphony and song,
> To such a deep delight 'twould win me,
> That with music loud and long,
> I would build that dome in air. . . .

He has but to *remember* in order to recreate in his poetry an image
of the sphere and harmony of heaven. Keats and Coleridge had
both looked into the source and understood that the poem is a
gift brought from beyond the poet's personality; he is possessed
by a knowledge not his own, a divine frenzy:

> And all shall cry, Beware! Beware!
> His flashing eyes, his floating hair!
> Weave a circle round him thrice,
> And close your eyes with holy dread. . . .

Like the Delphic Sybil or the Bacchantes he is literally possessed
by the god, so that his hair stands up; Shelley used the same
image in the same sense:

> Like the bright hair uplifted from the head
> Of some fierce Maenad, even from the dim verge
> Of the horizon to the zenith's height,
> The locks of the approaching storm. . . .

The 'approaching storm' is the possession of the poet by the god,
under the symbolic image of the cloud impelled by the West
Wind, the breath of the spirit – a meaning which the symbol of

wind and breath has in both Hebrew and Indo-European traditions. In *Job*, 'a spirit passed before my face; the hair of my head
stood up'. The overwhelming power of the god must be kept
within bounds by the drawing of the traditional circle with
which magicians draw round themselves a protecting *temenos*.

The invocation of the Inspirers was long customary among
poets; and now that the poetic Muse is no longer invoked under
that name, Yeats has written of his Instructors, and Edwin Muir,
'I have been taught by dreams and fantasies.' Blake wrote of the
Daughters of Inspiration as the muses of true poetry, and was
angry when the reality of such inspiration was questioned by
people who had never experienced anything of the kind; like
Joshua Reynolds, in whose margins he wrote that Plato and
Milton were 'in earnest' when they spoke of inspiration. Milton
(whom Blake took as the type of the inspired man) refused to
use the Classical symbol of the Muse for a figure whose sacred
aspect, for him, precluded the terms of Pagan mythology:

> Above the flight of Pegasean wing,
> The meaning, not the name, I call; for thou
> Nor of the Muses nine, nor on the top
> Of old Olympus dwell'st, but Heav'nlie borne
> Before the hills appear'd or fountains flow'd,
> Thou with Eternal wisdom didst converse,
> Wisdom thy Sister, and with her did'st play
> In presence of th'Almightie Father. . . .

Thus, in order to affirm more strongly her sacred nature Milton
translates the Classical into a Biblical symbol, relating the Muse
to the Divine Wisdom.

'Kubla Khan' is at once finished, and for ever unfinished; like
the Hyperion fragment, finished and unfinished likewise, and for
the same reason; for with the apotheosis of the poet through the
initiatory experience of anamnesis all has been said about the
nature of poetic initiation; and what remains to be written – that
to which the poet is at the end of the poem looking – is all the
poetry which might be drawn from the inexhaustible riches of
the world into which he has seen. Therefore at the end of the
poem the poet himself, and his reader, has the sense of standing at
a beginning, a threshold. It is not merely a threshold, but one
might say the Threshold itself of the archetypal world.

That to have undergone such an initiatory vision is the mark

of the true poet is recognized in the old Scottish ballad of Thomas
the Rhymer, initiated by the Queen of Elfland. Fairyland is, in
folk tradition (to quote from Y. Evans-Wentz's book *The Fairy
Faith in Celtic Countries*) 'the world of the subjective'. Thomas was
told to look at what he saw there, but to keep silence; as initiates
before the Mysteries in antiquity were vowed to silence. He was
shown a dark and awe-inspiring place, 'Far from the fiery noon,
and eve's one star', where the tides of human experience ebb and
flow for ever – powerful symbol of the collective mind upon which
the poet draws:

> It was a mirk, mirk night and there was nae stern light,
>   And they waded in red blude to the knee;
> For a' the blude that's shed on earth
>   Rins thro' the springs o' that countree.

We recognize the place to which they presently come:

> Syne they came on to a garden green,
>   And she pu'd an apple frae a tree:
> 'Take this for thy wages, True Thomas,
>   It will give the tongue that can never lee.'

– for the initiate of that world does not surmise its wisdom, but
knows it, and therefore speaks truth. The two stanzas which in
the *Oxford Book of Ballads* follow this (XVIII–XIX) are evi-
dently a later interpolation and have no bearing on the 'sacred
lore' of the ballad, with which they are no less out of key than
they would be in 'Kubla Khan' or Plato's *Ion*. The Queen of
Elfland has something of the ambiguous character of Coleridge's
Abyssinian Maid, with whom is associated the sinister aspect of
the 'waning moon' and 'Woman wailing for her demon lover'.
She who gives the poet the apple of immortal knowledge from
the Tree of Paradise is perhaps Lilith rather than Eve. 'The book
of the people' recognizes this ambivalent aspect of the *anima
mundi* and its images; and when in his admiration the poet calls
her the Queen of Heaven, she denies this, with perfect truth:

> I'm but the queen o' fair Elfland

– a place of numinous images, bearers of a profound wisdom;
the Muse may 'converse' with 'the Eternal Wisdom' but even
Milton does not quite venture to say that she is that Wisdom itself;
and Yeats knew that in that *Hodos Chameleontos* the poet must

keep his powers of discrimination, for the false is mixed with the true.

Plato tells the same story of poetic initiation almost in the form of a fairy-tale:

> For the authors of those great poems which we admire, do not attain to excellence through the rules of any art, but they utter their beautiful melodies of verse in a state of inspiration, and, as it were, possessed by a spirit not their own . . . like the Bacchantes, who, when possessed by the God, draw honey and milk from rivers in which when they come to their senses, they find nothing but simple water. For the souls of the poets, as poets tell us, flying like bees from flower to flower, wandering over the gardens and meadows, and honey-flowing fountains of the Muses, return to us laden with the sweetness of melody.

The last two lines of Coleridge's poem, which he brought back from those gardens in his state of divine intoxication, tell of the divine food in images which echo those of Plato, and evoke, for any reader who knows the *Ion*, Plato's dialogue on poetic inspiration, which doubtless was for Coleridge the supreme statement of the traditional role of the poet.

> For he on honey-dew hath fed,
> And drunk the milk of Paradise.

1964

NOTE

Ruthven Todd has made some interesting discoveries about hallucinogenic drugs known to antiquity and in the middle ages. Paracelsus refers to one of these by the name of *honeydew*, which Mr. Todd thinks was almost certainly an exudation of the mould *claviceps purpurea*, found in parasitic symbiosis on a number of plants. Coleridge, who had read everything, and who was, besides, interested in such things for more personal reasons also, doubtless knew this. This is a most interesting additional piece to be added to the Coleridge jigsaw-puzzle set up by Lowes. From the point of view of the present article honeydew, whatever it may be in nature, is a word in Coleridge's symbolic statement, and not the meaning of that statement or even the key to it. It does, however, provide a beautiful link between the 'honey' and the 'milk' which flow from the fountains of the Muses, and adds a suggestion of the sinister face of imagination, altogether in keeping with the ambiguous atmosphere of the poem. Poetic statements of this kind never have only one source or one sense, and the richness of association determines the poet's choice of this word rather than that. Honey is, in Greek mythology, the food of the gods, the infant Zeus himself having been fed by the bees on the honey of the Muses.

Mr. Todd's discoveries in this interesting and novel field have now been published in an article, 'Coleridge and Paracelsus—Honeydew and LSD', in *The London Magazine,* March 1967.

6

ON THE SYMBOL

It is difficult for us to realize wherein our own unspoken assumptions, the foundations upon which we build our world, differ from those of others; for this assumed ground is the very thing we cannot discuss, for we may not even know what it is, still less what it might be; we cannot imagine how the world might appear if we did not possess the groundwork of knowledge which we do possess; nor can we in the nature of things imagine how reality would appear in the light of knowledge which we do not possess. Yet we continue to assume that whatever theories we may construct upon it the primary experience of the world is the same for everyone; even when in theory we would admit that this cannot be so, we continue to imagine that we all live in the same apparent world through sheer inability to imagine otherwise. From time to time we receive a shock, when we are compelled to realize the immense divergence not of deductions and conclusions, but of the premises, the basic assumptions upon which these rest; and thus even of the primary experience itself, inseparable from the attitude of the consciousness which receives it.

I had assumed, when I reached that long-vanished Cambridge of the late twenties, that others who spoke of poetry and who wrote verse must understand it as I did; that those who claimed to be poets, and who acclaimed one another, must know (since they looked upon me as a naïve creature) not less but more about poetry than I. When I met these writers of my generation, some of whom have since become famous, I assumed that when they made pronouncements upon poetry that they and I were discussing the same thing. I did not like their poems any more than they liked mine (and they were more right than I, even though they would have disliked my work still more had it been better) but those of William Empson were of a brilliance I could not but admire; so that my own preference for Yeats (he was not fashionable at the time), for Keats and Shelley (who were despised) and even for Walter de la Mare I attributed to my ignorance, and kept very quiet.

Yet to me it seemed strange that a poem about love should begin 'And now she cleans her teeth into the lake'. What I found inappropriate in this image was its insistence upon a physical function belonging simply to the hygiene of the human animal, and not to the vision of the beautiful reflected in the person of the beloved. (William Empson's description of surface-tensions and so on which follows has an undeniable beauty, but the line in question creates the context; whatever inhuman and scientific beauty is introduced the 'human form divine' is, in such poetry, disintegrated). I had not read Plato, and so supposed I must be wrong to imagine a vision of spiritual perfection to be inseparable from the theme of love. I had not yet understood that those who adopt the new philosophy of positivism must forego such lines as

> She walks in beauty, like the night

or

> Had I the heaven's embroidered cloths

or even

> Yes, you, my dear, have the right human face

for these evocations rest upon foundations of another kind altogether, even Edwin Muir's concept of 'the human face', an immaterial expression which has nothing to do with surface tensions. The new physicality was consistent with premises which were 'in the air' rather than understood and examined. Russell and Wittgenstein were names I did not at the time associate with a taste in poetry which preferred Donne to Milton, and which Empson's poetry reflected with so much originality and intelligence. He was praised, in our circle, for his resemblance to Donne, and Donne too was admired for the very 'modern' physicality of his

> For Godsake hold your tongue, and let me love,
> Or chide my palsie, or my gout,

and

> Marke but this flea, and marke in this,
> How little that which thou deny'st me is;

If my imagination was dashed and bruised I did not dare to say so even to myself, but tried, rather, to school myself to the new ruthless exclusion of all which belonged to a scale of values condemned as 'meaningless' – that favourite word of the logical positivists – because immaterial. These I assumed, must have been understood and rejected, after a process of comparison, in favour of those which I saw supplanting them; that the new values represented a failure of perception did not occur to me until many years later. (The ignorant do not, in the nature of things, discuss those ideas or modes of experience of which they are ignorant, and this exclusion is misleading to the young, who are as yet unaware that these closed fields of knowledge even exist.) I had not read Plato, nor Plotinus, nor the Vedantic literature, nor Berkeley, nor *A Vision*, nor Coomaraswamy; nor any of the books I needed in order to discover the first principles of the kind of poetry I instinctively recognized as such; and Shelley's Platonism, in isolation from its context, was incomprehensible to me. I have since had to undergo the double process of discovering the underlying assumptions of the *avant-garde* in which at Cambridge I found myself; of discovering that I could not accept these (and that I need not, therefore, attempt an undue admiration which I did not feel for works expressing such attitudes) and then, after years of search, discovering the discredited and neglected writings which constitute the learning of the imagination.

What William Empson, in his subtle, brilliant, and influential critical writings gave his generation was a theory of poetry consistent with the positivist philosophy which flourished in Cambridge; the Cambridge of Darwin and the Cavendish Laboratory, of Russell and Wittgenstein and their successors. His theory of ambiguity lacks nothing in conceptual subtlety but dispenses with the imagination and disregards the metaphysical roots of poetic thought. I still admire the brilliance – though the brilliance is often perverse – of his theory of ambiguity and of complex words; yet I see now what then I only felt, wherein it fails as a full description of poetry; for all the complexities and ambiguities and relationships which he discerns are upon the same plane of the real. There is one type of complexity which he fails to consider, that resonance which may be present within an image of apparent simplicity, setting into vibration planes of reality and of consciousness other than that of the sensible world: the power of the symbol and symbolic discourse. Then, I thought (as we all did) that it was our outstanding intelligence which compelled us to forego beauty and lyricism at the bidding of intellect; but I have since come to understand that what such

H

theories as we then held, together with the kind of poetry we were bidden to admire, precisely lacked (in comparison, that is, with Spenser or Shelley, Milton or Yeats), is, in the metaphysical sense, intellectuality.

The language of symbolic analogy is only possible upon the assumption that these multiple planes do in fact exist. Those for whom the material world is the only plane of the real are unable to understand that the symbol – and poetry in the full sense is symbolic discourse, discourse by analogy – has as its primary purpose the evocation of one plane in terms of another; they must find other uses for poetry or honestly admit that they have no use for it. The description of sense impressions or personal emotions, or the evocation of group emotions is assumed, by many writers at the present time, to be the purpose of poetry; but those who subscribe to a materialist philosophy would, were they honest, admit that in their scheme of things poetry can be dispensed with altogether (there is in fact a school of writing whose explicit purpose is to affirm the 'meaningless' nature of life); and in fact it has no place in the lives of the majority of the modern populace, who differ, in this respect, from their illiterate ancestors, in whose memories songs and ballads had their place. No phrase has been more misunderstood than Milton's statement that poetry should be simple, sensuous, and passionate. Milton would never have imagined that a generation would someday exist so ignorant as to suppose that the poet should confine himself to simple themes, sensible appearances and personal emotions. He surely had in mind rather the opposite thoughts: the themes of poetry being so high, so philosophic, it is necessary for the poet to embody them in imagery of perfect correspondence – thought and image must be one (simple), perfectly realized in the image (sensuous) and felt as living experience (passionate) and not merely conceptually apprehended. It is in this that the poet is distinguished from the philosopher; not in any difference in the nature of their themes but in the way of experiencing them: where philosophy makes distinctions, poetry brings together, creating always wholes and harmonies; the work of the poet is not analysis but synthesis. The symbol may be called the unit of poetic synthesis; as Coleridge in his famous definition implies:

A symbol is characterized by a translucence of the special in the Individual, or the General in the Especial or of the Universal in the

General. Above all by the translucence of the Eternal through and in the Temporal. It always partakes of the Reality which it renders intelligible; and while it enunciates the whole, abides itself as a living part in that Unity of which it is representative.

Thus the poem is able to create in the reader a sense of the wholeness and harmony its symbols and its rhythmic unity both realize and affirm. The language of analogy at once presupposes and establishes relations between the different orders of the real, an orientation towards a source and a centre. The idea of the metaphysical is thus implicit in the very figures of symbolic discourse.

There has been among poets of my generation and those a little younger a rejection of metaphor as a poetic figure: only direct description or at most simile is tolerated. This rejection of the characteristic poetic figures of metaphor, symbol, personification, and, at the apex, myth, is not arbitrary, it is logical and honest, for it represents a rejection of affirmations implicit in these linguistic figures. For as we ascend the scale we are asked to make increasingly animistic assumptions about the world. Those poets who allow themselves to describe only sensible appearances, or to compare these one with another (simile) have understood that this is demanded by the materialist view of reality. They could not (for example) subscribe to the demands made by Shakespeare when he writes

> Hark, hark, the lark
> At heaven's gate sings,
> And Phoebus 'gins arise,
> His steeds to water
> At those springs
> On chaliced flowers that lies,
> And winking mary-buds begin
> To ope their golden eyes.

For these metaphors make profound assertions about the nature of things which no materialist could possibly accept; and to which, even by a 'suspension of disbelief' he could never fully respond, because the world they are designed to open is one which he cannot experience by so negative an act. What the poem affirms is that the world is, in its whole and in its parts, living and conscious; it also affirms that there is a hidden source ('heaven') from whose 'gate' visible things issue from invisible. The sun is not called Phoebus, as Fred Hoyle's fiery bodies in space are called 'red giants', but because the poet's sun is really conceived as a living god. He travels on an animate vehicle (steeds) and the marigolds are likewise living and therefore open 'eyes' to greet the sun. The identity of their nature with that of the maidens whose name they bear (Mary-buds) is double – flowers are alive like maidens, girls are like flowers opening to the sun. The marigold (and by analogy the maiden) is itself a sun in microcosm, bearing the solar 'signature' and partaking of the solar (and therefore, in terms of the symbol) the divine nature. The alchemical and magical doctrine of 'signatures' would have been as familiar to Shakespeare's audience as some scientific axiom at the present time. The new poets are quite right in dismissing such language from their own work; only fools would write in such a way and at the same time assent to the scientific materialist view of nature. Only many years later, through my study of the sources of William Blake, was I led to discover the almost obliterated traces of the mode of thought which is, implicitly or explicitly, the foundation of all supreme imaginative art, even of its most light-hearted songs.

In England it is above all the poets who have kept the knowledge of this perennial wisdom when this has been all but lost alike by churches and by philosophers; and their language has at all times been (not because these invented the truths they perceived or formulated, but because in Europe Platonism has been the mainstream of such thought) that of Plato and Plotinus and their predecessors and followers. The final authority of a perennial wisdom (in other civilizations differently expressed) rests not with those authors who discourse upon it, but in the nature of things, verified and re-experienced again and again; just as in the material order any other age whose scientists might investigate the laws of matter as exhaustively as our own have done, could verify their discoveries. So it is with the intelligible world, by whatever name we may choose to call it; all deities reside, now as always, 'in the human breast'.

Indeed a revival of the learning of the imagination, and especially of the works of Plato and the neo-Platonists, has been the inspiration not only of the Florentine renaissance and all that followed (in England as elsewhere) but of every subsequent renaissance. Spenser laid the aesthetic foundations of all English poetry since, in his four Hymns, of which one is to the earthly, another to the heavenly beauty. To speak only of the English language, the Romantic revival, the Transcendentalist move-

ment in America, the Irish renaissance, all have followed a return
to the same source. Yet as our culture as a whole has drifted
farther and farther away from its old roots, both within the
Christian religion and the Platonic philosophy, it has come to
seem almost as though the poets speak a secret language. Their
meaning is no longer understood – as we may see from the writings of contemporary critics upon such poets as Milton, Blake,
Shelley and Yeats, who are read with sheer incomprehension for
want of the knowledge out of which they themselves were writing.
In so little respect is this knowledge held that it seems to be
assumed by many critics that what the poets meant scarcely
matters, and that their poetry can be read without such knowledge or in terms of some entirely different system of ideas; although why, if this were so, it should be read at all is hard to see.

Recent popular discussion by Anglican bishops of the Christian
symbols has revealed the extent to which, even among professed
believers in the Christian revelation, the use of the language of
analogy, the capacity for thinking in symbols, has been lost. It
is perhaps conceivable that materialists should believe that
Christians when they speak of heaven being 'above' should
imagine it to be situated in physical space, since they are themselves limited by the terms of quantitative discourse; but that
there should be bishops who imagine – or who know – that this
view is held by professed believers in a spiritual order is almost
incredible. To a materialist such terms as 'above' and 'below'
refer solely to position in physical space; a quantitative mentality
Blake associated with Newtonian science, and wrote in a letter
'God keep me . . . from supposing Up and Down to be the same
Thing as all experimentalists must suppose'. In symbolic discourse above and below are qualitative, not quantitative; light
and darkness, the tree of life, the bird of the soul, voyage and
road and river and cave and house, mirror, sword, cup and
garment, rose and lotus, sun, moon and stars, are terms of symbolic discourse, the only language we have in which to express
not merely the appearances but the content, the quality of
experience.

Fortunately, while literalism has invaded poetry and religion,
science has itself been reaching the end of its tether, and approaching the realization that the world of appearances is itself
only a kind of symbol of anterior causes. When this point is
reached it is inevitable that we should again turn from physics

to metaphysics. According to the metaphysician René Guénon the law of correspondence operates throughout the cosmos.

By virtue of this law, each thing, proceeding as it does from a metaphysical principle from which it derives all its reality, translates or expresses that principle in its own fashion and in accordance with its own order of existence, so that from one order to another all things are linked together and correspond in such a way as to contribute to the universal and total harmony, which, in the multiplicity of manifestation, can be likened to a manifestation of the principial unity itself. For this reason the laws of a lower domain can always be taken to symbolize realities of a higher order, wherein resides their own profoundest cause, which is at once their principle and their end.

Of modern naturalistic interpretations of this ancient doctrine Guénon points out that these 'purely and simply reverse the hierarchy of relationships between the different orders of reality'. This is true, obviously, in the field of natural sciences whose phenomena, he writes, 'by the very fact that they are derived from higher and transcendent principles, truly serve to symbolize those principles'. In the special field of the arts the reversal of hierarchies, by denying the dependence of the present world upon higher causes, expresses a vision of things emptied of the values and dignity which they can only possess by virtue of such dependence. We see this clearly in the modern treatment of sex, and of the human body. The most 'real' has come to mean the sordid, the carnal, the plebeian; this is not accidental, since the natural world owes any qualities of the sacramental, the noble, or the sublime which it may possess precisely to its relation to higher causes. The loss of the vision of informing beauty follows of necessity from a closing of consciousness to these causes. Since matter and material objects are informed from a mental world, a materialist art is doomed to loss of form, such as we see in abstract impressionist painting and its literary equivalent, a fragmented outpouring of physical (and often obscene) images and sense-impressions, divorced from any qualitative context. No doubt such art owes its vogue to the accuracy with which it reflects a widespread mentality; but to reflect ignorance, however accurately, is not to embody truth. Believing as I do that the purpose and justification of poetry is to embody and reflect truth – or the real – or beauty – they are all the same – I cannot admire works which flatter or reflect (however accurately) ignorance, but which lack any transforming power. Nor can it be admitted that there is a 'real' world, which such art reflects, which imaginative art disregards in order to depict another, which has no reality in physical existence; on the contrary, imagination alone sees things as they 'really' are, since it sees them in relation to their causes and qualitative natures; the imagination does not see different things, but sees things differently. Herbert Read has long believed, or hoped, that the arts might save our society; but most that goes by the name at the present time (one need but read the pages of the *Evergreen Review* and the like) is no more than the mirror in which the disease is reflected.

There have been attempts to reduce symbolism to the terms of a materialist philosophy. Freud, it is true, made the first step on the road of return when he proved to an astonished world that the dreaming mind thinks in images, employing these, and not words, as its language; but the symbols he discovered in dreams, and in the arts, he understood as the mere disguise of repressed and mainly sexual content. To this theory (being a logical and passionate man) he was prepared to sacrifice the values of civilization, to see in the pearl nothing but a disease of the oyster, to reduce all art to terms of sexual fantasy, as one might reduce a picture to its component pigment and canvas. The Surrealists, inspired by Freud's theories, used their so-called symbols in a vivid and striking way; but these were not in truth symbols at all, lacking as they do Coleridge's essential mark of the symbol, 'the Translucence of the Eternal in and through the Temporal'. They do not relate one order of reality to another, still less are they oriented to any source or principle. They are only a code-language, in which both terms of their metaphors apply to the same order of reality, and are so disguised only (as in time of war) to evade the censor. Surrealism is just as much a materialist art as is Social Realism; as its exponents, seeking recognition from the Marxists with whom they wished to make common cause (a recognition they were not accorded) explicitly claimed. Its symbols, released by 'pure psychic automatism', provide no bridge or ladder from which contemplation may pass from effect to cause, from lower to higher. In contrast with this view Réne Guénon defines that of tradition:

A consequence of this law of correspondence is the plurality of meanings contained in the symbol. Anything and everything can in

fact be regarded as representing not only the metaphysical principles, but also realities of all orders higher than its own, even if still
contingent, for these realities, on which it also more or less directly
depends, play the part of 'secondary causes' in respect of it. These
multiple and hierarchically superimposed symbolic meanings are
not in any way mutually exclusive. On the contrary, they are perfectly concordant, because they express the application of one and
the same principle to different orders; thus they complete and cor-
roborate one another, while being integrated in the harmony of the
total synthesis. This, moreover, is what makes symbolism a far less
narrowly limited language than ordinary speech, and renders it best
fitted to convey certain truths. The possibilities of conception it
opens up are truly limitless, and it is for this reason that it constitutes
the initiatory language *par excellence*, the indispensable vehicle of all
traditional teaching.

In the ancient systems of magic and alchemy, based upon an
elaborate system of 'correspondence' or 'signature' (often perhaps in an arbitrary and unimaginative sense at least in popular
application) all things were symbolic; and such initiates as
Jakob Boehme saw the whole world as imprinted, in its whole
and in its parts, with the signature of the Source. To call this
'poetic' is to beg the question; for either this is a way of apprehending the real, or it is not poetic, but merely fanciful. It is,
however, the poetic mode of thought. David Jones, whose
'sacramental' view of nature comes near to the *signatura rerum* of
alchemy (even while lacking its symbolic precision), illustrates
in the refinement and beauty of his depictions and descriptions
of the natural world, and also of man-made (but not machine-
made) objects – ships and garments and all 'the gear and tackle
and trim' of craftsmen, the truth that the primary experience
of perception is itself, in its kind and quality, determined by what
the artist believes to be the qualitative nature of the things perceived.

Jung came nearer than did Freud to the traditional doctrine,
as taught by those alchemists, Gnostics and neo-Platonists whom
he himself took for masters; for he realized that dreams do not
so much conceal as embody meaning, and that this comes from
sources within the psyche – or beyond it – normally inaccessible
to the waking mind. Not all dreams come from the same level;
and besides the personal elements recognized by Freud, Jung
was led to believe in what he calls a 'collective unconscious'
because it is so as a rule, though at times accessible to conscious-

ness. This is the ancient *anima mundi*, the soul of the world, whose images at times, waking or in dreams, we behold with amazement, so beautiful and so fraught with meaning do these appear. Because this world is not personal but common to all, its symbols are intrinsically intelligible as Freud's symbols from the personal unconscious are not. To Edwin Muir that world seemed to open spontaneously, as it did to AE; Yeats sought by magical evocation, as others have attempted by prayer and invocation, to pierce the veil. Others again have recognized these forms, as Wordsworth did (and perhaps every poet who in describing the natural order has discovered beauty and meaning) embodied in mountain or waterfall or lake or tree; or like Dante in the beauty of some beloved person; an inexplicable magical power which illuminates from within. In whatever guise they appear, in dream, waking vision, contemplation, or reflected in the forms of nature or of art, it is characteristic of these symbolic images they they seem to communicate essential meaning; they mean what they are, are what they mean, embodiments at once of truth and of beauty, since they are informed by the real which we recognize as at once and inseparably true and beautiful; this is necessarily so since it is the ground of our own being, at once answering and calling to that which we also are and embody.

The symbolic images come, of necessity, from the perceptible world; for this world is, in the nature of things, and unalterably, the 'given', inseparable from our human nature as incarnate beings; all the knowledge of the soul must come to it in terms of this world of embodiment – that is to say in symbolic form. Truly understood the entire world is one great symbol, imparting, in a sacramental manner, by outward and visible signature, an inward and spiritual essence.

Every poet and painter has some one, or some few symbolic themes which for him live in an especial way. For Milton, the Garden of Eden and the Fall; for Shelley, cave and river and boat and sea-voyage; for Yeats, not the soul's voyage but its migration, under images of swan and dolphin; certain cosmic myths, the Great Year, the Mundane egg; and not Eden (the origin), but Byzantium, city of man's creation. For Edwin Muir it was above all Eden (the timeless world), time and the journey through time, with horse as symbol of the vehicle which carries the soul on its journey; the angel, being that enters time from beyond time, breaking the inexorable pattern by what seems a miracle but is in fact the touching of another plane of the real. None of these, surely, were deliberately chosen by the poets, but, rather, chose them; they come, not as allegory in which the poet searches for an apt symbol for some abstract idea – the sword of justice or the scales of equity – but rather as epiphanies, awe-inspiring glimpses that move us deeply and inexplicably. These images seem put into our hands like clues which we are invited to follow back and back, for they draw us irresistibly as by magic; and this is no less so when we encounter them in nature than in dreams of vision. By their numinous nature we recognize them; and not with academic curiosity do we pursue them to their mysterious source, but as we follow the beloved person, unable to keep away, or watch all night before a closed door hoping for a glimpse or a sign. We live under the power of their compulsion: for they do not present themselves, like academic problems, from outside, as tasks to be taken up by will-power, to which we must drive ourselves. They arise, rather, as living impulses, urges of our own being and therefore compelling. We cannot rest until we have followed them to their source, or as far as our understanding allows.

These haunting symbols seldom take the form of single, separate images only; more often they come as complex themes, constellated. Blake, most experienced of all English poets in these insights, made many attempts to explain to an uncomprehending world the nature of the archetypes. One which was vividly present to him was the Last Judgement. To Blake there was no question as to whether there ever would, or would not be, a Last Judgement: to him it was an ever-present archetypal reality.

The Last Judgement [he wrote] is not a fable or allegory, but vision. Fable or allegory are a totally distinct and inferior kind of poetry. Vision or imagination is a representation of what eternally exists, really and unchangeably. Fable or allegory is formed by the daughters of memory. Imagination is surrounded by the daughters of inspiration. . . . Fable is allegory, but what the critics call fable is vision itself.

The Last Judgement, he goes on to say, 'is one of these stupendous visions: I have represented it as I saw it – to different people it appears differently, as everything else does'. Yet, clothed in form however different, Kafka (for example of a modern writer on the same theme) and Blake would have recognized the essential identity of the theme they so differently treat.

When I was young, I looked for, and constantly discovered, the numinous in and through nature; and only in middle life did I first experience in an overwhelming degree one of these archetypal epiphanies. The vision was of the Tree of Life, with many associated symbols, all suddenly and clearly and simultaneously presented to my mind. For a long time I lived on that vision, to which I could return, so I discovered, not with the same overwhelming awe as the first time, but clearly enough, at any time, to contemplate aspects of it which I had not at first seen, or had forgotten. Others have come since, some in dream, some not. The place of my vision was neither more nor less paradisal than Wordsworth's 'tree, of many, one / A single field which I have look'd upon' which to him appeared 'Apparell'd in celestial light'; but we may see, with the physical eye, without the experience being numinous; physical perception may sometimes be the vehicle of imaginative vision, but is not necessarily so, though William Blake claimed that 'To Me This World is all One continued Vision of Fancy or Imagination', as it has been for many poets. A tree, a light over the sea, a mountain or a garden or animal or bird or human face may seem to speak to us from beyond itself; yet the 'visionary gleam', as Wordsworth himself discovered, may be entirely absent from the sensible world. But it is impossible to experience some interior and archetypal vision without at the same time experiencing it qualitatively, as an epiphany of knowledge, for these images are themselves the vehicles of that knowledge; only as such do they arise and exist. Their meaning is their only reality, the only content of their forms.

A recent fashion has been to define the poem as 'the words on the page'; how that can be so I fail to see, since a word is itself no more than a sign, a meeting-point of associated ideas often of the most complex kind. A word is not, like the natural creation, intrinsically meaningful and intelligible, and cannot, like these, become an object of contemplation which will yield infinite meaning. To the symbolist the written poem is only a part – perhaps a small part – of the whole organism, the living unity of interplaying patterns as the words and images set one another vibrating to produce some chord or dissonance whose ripples travel through our thought. It continues, like the resonance of a note after the key is struck, or like the statement beyond Edwin Muir's semicolon.

A young poet who visited me to talk about his proposed work on Edwin Muir said 'I do not believe in *anima mundi*; I know you do'. I assured him there was no question of belief, only of experience. Not to believe in the creatures of the mind (in their own plane of the real) is like not believing in the amphioxus; or the giant squid might be a better example, perhaps, since the little fish swim in and out of all our dreams. However, this poet had the humility to admit that he had not understood Muir and proposed to wait until he did before writing about him. The more usual academic mentality is undeterred by any such doubts, as we see in book after book in which ignorance passes judgement upon knowledge. In the academic world there are all kinds of theories of symbols, and, as in Plato's Cave, all these are given equal weight and attention. Indeed the more wrong the first principles the more ingenious the theories have to be; an ingenuity which commands more respect, in some quarters, than does the higher faculty of immediate perception of intelligibles. But those who know do not theorize, they merely bear witness to what they have seen and experienced.

In the past, the mythology and metaphysics of some total culture whose foundations are metaphysical and whose expression informs and orientates every aspect of life has been the foundation of all the arts, and provided its symbolic language; as even now in India the forms of the gods may be expressed equally in dance, sculpture, song and epic poem. It is not 'the words on the page' which create the god in question, but the reverse; and the same intelligible principle (an 'airy nothing' until it is embodied) can be recognized as alike in any and all these varied manifestations. Iconoclastic Protestantism largely destroyed, in England, the images which had always been, and must normally be, the natural language of spiritual knowledge; and one hears that religious symbols have 'lost their meaning'; but since the only meaning symbols can be said to possess lies in their power to evoke, all symbols, ancient or modern, religious or poetic, must be equally meaningless in a climate of positivism; since the function of orientation which they are designed to perform is precluded by the denial of all planes of the real other than the quantitative and the sensational. In the present situation, and within a society which as a whole has lost that unity of culture which belonged to Christendom (which included and perpetuated the earlier Classical tradition) symbolic discourse is inevitably (or must appear to be) a private, lyrical language; and not, as it normally has been, a shared and collective expression. Yet compared with the mythologies of any great religion our private revelations, vivid as these may be, are necessarily fragmentary. These myths, with their great ramification of interrelated symbols, have in the past constituted a body of imaginative traditional knowledge. To those alive to the order of reality which they embody, the old symbols will live again; it is not they, but we who are dead. The myths of all races are ageless, since their symbolic language is based upon the permanent and unchanging elements of the world we inhabit.

It is precisely the visionary poets who best know how to make use of the traditional language of symbols. The great gulf lies not between tradition and the visionary, but between tradition and vision on the one hand, and positivism in all its manifestations, whether academic or revolutionary. Shelley used the Aeschylean and Platonic myths, and nature was for him a vocabulary which he used with so much sensuous beauty that he has been misread as a nature-poet by critics ignorant of the exactness with which he employs such terms as sea and wind, dew and bees and reflections and shadows. Living imagination alone has the key to the meaning of traditional symbols, and the greater our imaginative insight the greater our understanding of these is likely to become; all the greatest English poets have used with majestic ease the myths of their inheritence, Classical, Christian, Hebrew and native. Visionaries are not iconoclasts. It is immediately evident, to those who are familiar with the universal language of symbolic discourse, whether a poet (writing of sea or river, wind or garden or cave or bird) is using such terms as words within the universal language, or in a personal and imaginatively unlearned way; those who know the secret language immediately recognize it, or miss its presence; while those, on the contrary, who do not know it may read even Shelley's 'Ode to the West Wind' under the impression that its images are merely descriptive of natural appearances; to such there is no difference in kind between Shelley and Swinburne. Spenser's *Faerie*, Shelley's caverns and river-journeys in light-sailed boats, Milton's Paradise and Coleridge's sea-voyage; Blake's images of Judgement and transformation; Yeats's migrant bird-souls and world gyres, all speak the same language, evoke the same unseen world, whose riches are as inexhaustible as those of nature. We shall do wrong if we think of symbols as single poetic images, used to obtain some literary effect; rather symbol is a language in each of whose parts a whole is implied, and each symbol in some measure makes known to us that whole, as a whole, and in its wholeness. Professor I. A. Richards, an instructed Platonist, in a remarkable exposition of the 'Ode to the West Wind' described the knowledge Shelley communicates, or seeks to communicate (invoking the supreme metaphysical tradition) as *vedantic*. Hinduism is, besides, above all a mode of knowledge which embraces and comprises every aspect and expression of life and art: nothing is outside its informing influence, which orients all to the one centre; as does all symbolic art, within its own terms, acting at all times as a principle of unification and of orientation.

Jung in his autobiographical memoirs makes an observation which I believe most poets could endorse and which seems to throw light upon the diction of poetry as itself of a symbolic nature. Jung, who himself (so he says) very much disliked anything high-flown in speech or manner, found, to his own surprise, that when what he calls 'mana, daemons, gods or the unconscious' speaks in words, its utterances are in a high style, hieratic, often archaic, grandiose; as far removed as it is possible to be from the speech of that common man the everyday self. Willa Muir, in her book *Living with Ballads* speaks of the 'high style' in which the Scottish ballads were traditionally sung. The oral tradition of the ballads was the heritage of illiterate people, shepherds and crofters; but the singing of the ballads was by no means in common speech. It was extremely slow, dignified, and highly mannered. There are recordings of Jeannie Robertson, a tinker's daughter, singing such ballads as Lord Randall in this manner. Indeed nothing seems more unnatural, in the art of poetry, than 'natural' diction, common speech, the conversational tone. It is a mark of imaginative inspiration and content to write in a high and mannered style, removed from common speech; as it is of the absence of imaginative participation to write either in a conversational tone or in a deliberately vulgar idiom. Milton's verse is no more the common speech of an upper than it is of a lower social class; it is the speech of his 'Thrones, Dominations, Princedoms, Vertues, Powers', of the celestial hierarchies. The inspiring daemons speak in voices far removed from common speech; the voice of the gods is oracular, rhythmic, sibylline. Its resonance stirs in us a response, when in poetry we find it, from that same level within ourselves. The language of that world is no more naturalistic than its images are, but awe-inspiring and mysterious, a sacred not a profane language. Above all, the voice of true imagination is never ironic; that is the mark of a divided mind, whereas the imagination is above all at one with itself, the principle of unification and harmony.

Among the misconceptions (one for which the Marxist doctrine of social realism was responsible) of my generation was the notion, that to speak to the common man it was necessary to speak the common language and employ an imagery of the commonplace. Auden and Day Lewis first introduced a whole range of such images from the grim, grey realism of the modern city: the bar in Forty-Second Street, the United Dairies, the pylons, the tramlines, the cigarette-stubs and the litter defacing even churches and sanctuaries of the countryside. Philip Larkin and others of his generation have since adopted and extended this demotic imagery, with no doubt the same commendable intention as inspired the poets of the thirties. I believe the doctrine to be false, for it confuses class-distinction with imagination. Indian dancers, whose audience is largely the illiterate population of villages, impersonate gods, royal persons, and heroes. In watching such dancers one may almost see the daimon take over from the human individuality as if the god were really present. A Bengali friend, who sang, from memory, one evening, songs written by Tagore, tells me that all over Bengal these songs are known and sung by the common people; their themes are often religious, always on a level of refinement and depth of feeling. I myself know, in Scotland, road-menders and foresters who can recite long passages from *Paradise Lost*, and whose memories are stored with heroic ballads; for the common man is not what their philosophy supposes. The imaginative world is outside time, and transcends class. For the more sublime the work of poetry or art, the more do we feel that it expresses something already and always known, something deeply familiar and intimately our own. Few feel that we could have written Dryden's *Annus Mirabilis*, or Auden's *Nones*; but Spenser's or Milton's description of Paradise, or *King Lear*, or *Songs of Innocence*, or 'The Ancient Mariner', do we not feel that we ourselves already knew? Juvenal's Rome, Dryden's Restoration, Auden's Twenties were all modern once and are all dated now, and what was written for the sake of easy comprehension is precisely that part of poetry which becomes incomprehensible within a few years. Those who look to a timeless world are least likely to fall into archaisms of style, for the world of imagination is outside history altogether. Pope, Dryden and Auden are dated in a way that Dante, Milton, Coleridge, and Yeats, even when these embody in their imaginative world themes from history, can never be.

If it has become difficult to use Christian canonical symbolism, may it not be precisely in so far as the canonical symbols have come to participate in history, in the temporal, that they are unusable? In themselves they are inexhaustible in content, and they, no less than those given to us in dream or in vision, may be taken like buckets to an inexhaustible well. They will never be drawn up empty except by those who do not lower them to water-level.

1964

7

ON THE MYTHOLOGICAL

Myth (from Latin *mythus*) is defined, by the *Shorter Oxford Dictionary* as 'a purely fictitious narrative usually involving supernatural persons, actions or events, and embodying a popular idea concerning natural or historical phenomena. Often used vaguely to include any narrative having fictitious elements.' If we were to try to unravel all the questions begged by this definition we should be led into the fields of metaphysics, theology, history, psychology, anthropology and beyond. The first phrase, 'a purely fictitious narrative', presupposes that the real is material fact, all events physical events; a view of reality which bedevilled for the Victorians such questions as the truth of the narrative of creation in the Book of Genesis. Unless the story could be shown to be matter of fact, in the same sense as last week's news, faith must founder and Darwinian evolution replace the old cosmogony. This materialist assumption, as it immediately concerns the English, goes back to William Blake's threefold enemy, Bacon, Newton, and Locke; but before them to the Greek natural philosophers who established the enduring bias of the Western mentality.

The next phrase, 'usually involving supernatural persons, actions or events' implies, therefore, that such persons, actions and events are purely fictitious because they do not belong, by definition, to the natural order. This assumption underlies the argument that other religions, unlike Christianity, are not 'true' because the events described in their myths never 'really happened' (Leda and the Swan, the dismembering of Dionysus or the miraculous birth of the Buddha); an attempt to establish spiritual truth by natural fact, which cannot be done; for if we ask what 'really happened', we are thrown back again upon the intangible order of meanings and values. As a child I became a confirmed believer in the ancient gods simply because as between the reality of fact and the reality of myth, I chose myth. Only

I

after a life-time have I come to understand that even a real event may be the enactment of a myth, and from that take on supernatural meaning and power. In such cases myth is the truth of the fact, not fact the truth of the myth.

As for 'some popular idea concerning natural or historical phenomena', the implicit assumption here is euhemerism; so named from a Sicilian philosopher of the fourth century B.C. who maintained that the gods of Greek mythology were deified men and women. Euhemerism (again the *Shorter Oxford Dictionary*) is 'the method of interpretation which regards myths as traditional accounts of real incidents in human history'. This view finds favour at the present time because in harmony with the positivist climate of opinion which is our heritage from the Victorian view of fact. It is put forward by Robert Graves, for example, in his writings on Greek mythology.

This was not, however, the view of the civilizations which created and used the myths. The late Platonist Sallust, in his tractate *On the Gods and the World* gave natural meaning as one only of the levels of mythological discourse. Thus the story of Demeter and Persephone tells, upon the natural level, of the sowing and harvesting of corn; on the psychological level, of the death and resurrection of the individual soul, symbolized by Persephone, daughter of the divine reason, Demeter; and on the theological, of an aspect of the relation of the divine to the human world. Symbol and myth, it might be said, above all express relationship not between facts upon any one level of the real, but of the multiple levels one with another; a kind of relationship called by the alchemical philosophers *signature*; by Swedenborg *correspondence*, by Blake 'the body of divine analogy'. A symbol indeed both affirms and embodies such a harmonious order; and symbol and myth can scarcely be used, as poetic figures, within a culture which denies or disregards the multiple levels of being.

It seems that since 1884 natural and historical phenomena have come to seem less tangible, and myths, supernatural persons and events, correspondingly more so. Dr. Johnson's answer to the immaterialist philosopher Berkeley when he kicked the stone ('Thus I refute him') would strike a modern physicist, accustomed to dealing in those shudders of invisible forces which are the only terra firma on which we stand as no less naïve than it must appear to a poet vulgar. William Blake's out-and-out affirmation that we imagine even the visible world into its apparent existence no long seems perverse, but (bearing in mind those shudders and waves) a mere statement of plain fact, as it did to him:

> . . . in your own Bosoms you bear your Heaven
> And Earth & all you behold; tho' it appears Without, it is
>   within,
> In your Imagination. . . .

The visible world itself is but a scene in the mirror of consciousness and may be nothing more; and Blake's follower Yeats, writing of their common philosophic master, reminds us that there may be a common or collective dream:

> God-appointed Berkeley that proved all things a dream
> And that preposterous pragmatical pig of a world and all
>   its farrow that so solid seem
> Would vanish on an instant, should the mind but change
>   its theme.

We have, at all events, come to understand that there are what Coleridge called 'facts of mind': myth is no longer for us synonymous with the fictitious.

When my father was a student at Durham University in the 1890's, 'Kubla Khan' was held to be a poem of great beauty but utterly meaningless; but at the same time, how the Victorians turned to 'non-sense' as an escape from their self-inflicted mental limitations, producing in the realm of the 'purely fictitious' such masterpieces as *Alice in Wonderland*, the Nonsense of Edward Lear, Kingsley's *Water Babies*, the fantasies of George Macdonald, to be followed by Rider Haggard's *She*, David Lindsay's *A Voyage to Arcturus*, Barrie's *Peter Pan*, down to Tolkien's Hobbits and Mervyn Peake's more disturbing *Titus Groan*, which have continued the genre of fantasy into the present. All these are excursions into the mythological made possible on the pretext of make-believe; a limitation which perhaps precludes such writings from being taken seriously in the same way as those myths which take the whole of 'real' life within their scope.

From the same pre-psychological craving for regions of imagination officially declared non-existent came no doubt the Victorian urge to collect folk-lore and fairy-tales. On the Continent the brothers Grimm and Hans Andersen collected or wrote such stories; Douglas Hyde in Ireland; in Scotland Andrew Lang and

Campbell (collector of *Tales of the Western Highlands*), to be followed by many others who obeyed the same urge.

With the recognition of the psyche as a reality no less complex
than the physical world, myths and fantasies have again found
a context. C. G. Jung above all has made the *Shorter Oxford
Dictionary* definition obsolete. A Jungian writer defines myth as
'the expression of archetypal imagery'. Jung himself defines the
archetypes as the inherent foundations of the psyche, and the
images in which they present themselves to us as 'self-portraits
of the instincts'. We do not know what the soul (or psyche) is,
only that it is, and something of its inexhaustible riches; for it
is here that we discover what Jung calls 'the unending myth of
death and rebirth, and of the multitudinous figures who weave
in and out of this mystery'. To this order belong those supernatural persons, actions and events, and the story they tell is the
story of our inner experience. If the psyche reflects figures which
on another level contain theological and metaphysical meanings
(as Sallust and all traditional definitions would say, and as Jung
also would, in principle, allow) it remains true that the figures
themselves take form in the psyche; or perhaps in the collective
mind where poets say they encounter them.

Edwin Muir wrote continuously from that source. Once I
remember he asked me if I ever used my dreams as the material
of poems, and when I said never, he advised me to do so. Like
Yeats he believed that poetic inspiration is a joining of the sleeping self with the conscious mind. 'There are times', he wrote, 'in
every man's life when he seems to become for a little while part
of the fable, and to be recapitulating some legendary drama
which, as it has recurred a countless number of times in time, is
ageless.'

Of this story no single life can realize more than a part; but
beneath our individual lives is the pooled experience of our inheritance, Jung's 'collective unconscious' which discloses itself,
so he says, 'only through the medium of creative fantasy'. 'It
comes alive in the creative man, it reveals itself in the vision of
the artist, in the inspiration of the thinker, in the inner experience of the mystic.' The mythologies of all races are its embodiment; the psychologists are newcomers in a field long known to
the poets; a fact they are apt to forget.

Yeats too believed that, appearances notwithstanding, the
positive and anti-mythological trend is not at this time the most

significant, though it may be the most widespread: 'The mystical life is the centre of all that I do and all that I think and all that I write, and I have always considered myself a voice of what I believe to be a greater renaissance – the revolt of the soul against the intellect – now beginning in the world.' Now that the 'modern movement' has disintegrated into what Yeats called 'spawning formless fury', where else can we discover a principle of order but in the soul itself?

Dreams resemble myths in their personifications and symbolic forms and enactments; and the knowledge which myths and dreams alike mediate and embody is not conceptual knowledge; in symbols the soul can speak, but not the discursive reason. Explanations come afterwards and are far less fundamental; one has only to think of the countless expositions given of some myth, which always survives these attempts to throw light upon its mystery. But the sign of the initiate of the ancient Mysteries was the finger laid upon the lips, the sign of silence. The Mysteries cannot be divulged because they elude verbal formulation. As D. H. Lawrence wrote, reflecting upon the Etruscan tombs, 'Knowledge is an experience and not a formula'.

Shelley wrote (perhaps paraphrasing, and certainly alluding to neo-Platonic accounts of the Daimons) of spirits who people our consciousness and seem to bring us a knowledge from a world beyond that of our daily selves.

> From unremembered ages we
> Gentle guides and guardians be
> Of heaven-oppressed mortality;
> And we breathe and sicken not
> The atmosphere of human thought:
> Be it dim, and dank, and gray,
> Like a storm-extinguished day,
> Travelled o'er by dying gleams;
>   Be it bright as all between
> Cloudless skies and windless streams,
>   Silent, liquid and serene;
> As the birds within the wind,
>   As the fish within the wave,
> As the thoughts of man's own mind
>   Float thro' all above the grave;
> We make there our liquid lair,
> Voyaging cloudlike and unpent
> Thro' the boundless element.

These messengers come from regions of mind of which we are normally unconscious which the poet both compares and contrasts with 'the thoughts of man's own mind', the formulations of consciousness. To pursue them further would lead to metaphysical questions which do not directly concern us: the empirical reality of 'the gods' has at this time forced itself upon many who do not believe in 'God' – a reversal of the mentality of the last century.

It is from myths, fairy-lore, and imaginative poetry that we normally learn of those supernatural persons, actions, and events which inform our own interior worlds; and through these symbolic embodiments learn to know ourselves. The hunger of childhood for that world is natural; for it is before we set out that it is most necessary to learn in advance the map of the interior country through which we are about to travel; of the situations we shall encounter in our own re-enactment of the human experience of birth, love and death. From the mythological stories we may gain insight which is none the less self-knowledge because circumstances may never arise which call upon us to enact in the outer world every stage of the drama of the soul. If all our knowledge were to be gained from experience we should indeed possess only Blake's 'fortuitous concourse of memorys accumulated and lost', the fragmentary knowledge of a single life time. Through myth we can participate in the whole of which any single lifetime is but a part.

Every civilization – indeed every human society, civilized or no, except perhaps our own, has had its treasury of myths, told and re-told in the arts of painting, sculpture, dance, and poetry in a common language intelligible to all. In contrast with the authors of the *Shorter Oxford Dictionary* who speak so contemptuously of popular tradition we may consider a definition given by Coomaraswamy: 'Symbols are the universal language of art; an international language with merely dialectic variations, current once in all milieus and always intrinsically intelligible, though now no longer understood by educated men, and only to be seen or heard in the art of peasants.'

The traditional stories of each race have a peculiar fitness to the conditions of life of that particular society, enabling a people to adapt the inner life to external surroundings. Jung admired the imaginative adaptation of primitive peoples to their environment, in this sense. The country primitive man inhabits 'is at the same time the topography of his unconscious. In that stately tree dwells the thunder-god; this spring is haunted by the Old Woman; in that wood the legendary king is buried; near that rock no-one may light a fire because it is the abode of a demon; in yonder pile of stones dwell the ancestral spirits' – and so on. 'Thus does primitive man dwell in his land and at the same time in the land of his unconscious.' Greek colonies would name some local mountain 'Olympus', in order there to rediscover their gods. In all cults, including the Christian, depictions of the holy persons in temple or church fulfil the same imaginative purpose. Imagination peoples its shrines with the presences of the gods, and at the same time these embodiments serve to reawaken the imaginative reality. The process is the same whether the symbol be a holy mountain, a sculptured god or icon of a saint, or a poem folded between the pages of a book.

One may still find in remote parts of the west of Scotland, or in Ireland, the vanishing traces of an ancient culture once universal, where the face of the land and sea and sky holds a meaning which those who live in its presence read continually every day and hour of their lives. Every bird has its own magical quality and significance; certain wells and springs are holy, and there are green mounds which no crofter would disturb because of the spirits who continue to inhabit them. England seems to have lost her supernatural population, for the most part, about the time of the Reformation; yet a few legends have kept their hold – the Arthurian cycle and the Grail have not even now ceased to haunt certain places, or to retain something of the magic they held for Tennyson and his readers. And did not Churchill's State funeral touch some archetypal myth in the national imagination? I heard at the time from several working-class people of London that they 'had not believed that Churchill would die': was our great champion the last avatar of the King who sleeps in some secret cave until his country's need awakens him? I offer this suggestion as 'a popular idea concerning a historical phenomenon'; and if such a projection has in fact been made, is it nothing more than a falsification of history? Is it not rather an imaginative transformation of a historic into an archetypal event?

Yeats hoped that in the new Ireland the national being would not lack this symbolic dimension, which was, as he understood, the norm: 'Have not all races had their first unity from a myth-

ology that marries them to rock and hill?' Yeats hoped that it
might be possible 'so to deepen the political passion of the nation
that all, artist and poet, craftsman and day-labourer, would
accept a common design'. Perhaps he had learned such thought
from Blake, who had peopled London with gods whose emblems
are not lyre and thunderbolt, but the hammer and furnaces of
industry, where Los the English sun-god labours, while his wife
Enitharmon, the moon-goddess, weaves the bodies of mankind
on her looms.

In England it is above all in poetry that the national imagination has expressed itself; and perhaps for this very reason (since
poetry, unlike the plastic arts, does not, by the very fact of its
composition, build cities) 'nature' has continued to provide most
of the symbolic terms of the national imagination. For English
civilization in its maturity, as for all primitive races, the 'characters in the great apocalypse' are mountain and waterfall, tree and
river and lake. The Lake District is for many a shrine more
numinous than St. Paul's; and indeed the English landscape
has remained, for painters no less than for poets, in every century, the setting of 'the good life'. When have the English not
dreamed of living in the earthly Paradise of Gainsborough and
Constable, Palmer and Calvert, recreated again and again by
Spenser and Shakespeare, Thomson and Cowper, Tennyson and
Hardy, Hopkins, and Dylan Thomas? But because 'nature' has
been the theme of so much poetry we have perhaps failed to
notice that it is not nature as such but nature transformed by
poetry and painting, that it is in fact the legendary Eden whose
reflected beauty we discern, which is the environment imagination inhabits. 'Mr. Wordsworth must know that what he Writes
Valuable is not to be found in Nature' was Blake's comment
upon what he regarded as Wordsworth's heresy; and were not
most of those who made the Lake District their shrine inhabiting
the poetry of William and the Journals of Dorothy Wordsworth,
without which those wet and birdless hills would have remained
as uncommunicative as they did to Thomas Gray?

The unfortunate converse of Wordsworth's doctrine may be
the inhuman ugliness of our cities, in which we seem scarcely to
expect or to miss the presence of those images which in the architecture, the sculpture and painting of the Mediterranean speak
back to the imagination and embody not Eden but the New
Jerusalem, built according to the imagination of man. We who

live in an environment created rather by the machine (an
expression of quantitative thought) than by the imagination go
to refresh ourselves in the old cities of France and Italy, or stray
into our own Gothic cathedrals like visitors from another world;
but in which environment do we feel more strange? In the profane and quantitative modern world we live like exiles from the
realities of our own imagination; to enter a beautiful building, a
city of art, is like a home-coming.

If a natural environment can reflect back to us imaginative
forms, and evoke these in us, the city is the embodiment of those
forms; what imagination creates is the city; which is, on that
account, and not the 'garden' the term of human history. A
city, symbolically understood, is the environment which imagination creates for itself, a work of all the arts, including (in this
sense) poetry and music. Blake called upon the English nation
to build Jerusalem; yet London seems farther than ever from
being the embodiment of the city 'coming down from Heaven'.

Yeats too is a poet not of Eden but of the city of the imagination, which he named Byzantium, an embodiment at once of
Plato's city and of the New Jerusalem. As such Byzantium was
conceived by the Emperor Constantine; and its realization was
perhaps the most perfect embodiment of the spiritual order
which has existed upon earth. Yeats believed, on good historical
grounds, that in early Byzantium religious aesthetic and practical life were one, the vision of a whole people embodied in the
work of architect and artificer, as never before or since. Like
Jerusalem Byzantium is called 'holy'; for all that comes from the
kingdom within (Shakespeare speaks of it as *Heaven*, as in the
Gospel) comes to us with the magical and compelling beauty of
the numinous. Byzantium existed for more than a thousand years
as a holy city; but like Plato's city and St. Augustine's *civitas dei*,
the eternal city is not primarily its visible embodiment; it is the
interior world the arts and poetry embody and express which the
imagination inhabits, 'unageing', as these are. First and last we
inhabit a myth: for what is civilization but the continual creation
of an environment of art, in which the imagination is mirrored
and embodied, and where it everywhere may discover images of
its own interior order?

In the absence of these forms it is hard for imagination to discover itself. Sacred mountain, holy well, tree of life and magic bird
are no longer (unless in dreams) every child's natural inherit-

ance; but the projection of the inner upon the outer must nevertheless go on, and childhood seems to possess the gift, too often and too early lost, of weaving into almost any environment, however naturally unreceptive of its forms, its delicate web of imagination. It was Hans Andersen's genius (as it is the genius of all folk-lore) to impart the life of that 'other' world to objects as common and unregarded as a darning-needle and an egg-shell floating down a gutter on a rainy day. Was not the unique gift of Walter de la Mare his power of projecting the magical upon a familiar environment? A door in a wall, an empty house, a neglected garden, is fraught with all the paradisal poignancy of Alain Fournier's lost domain. A small talent, certainly, as compared with the Irish poets, or with Kafka who mythologized bureaucracy itself; but then Joyce's imagination was formed by Catholic Ireland, and Kafka belonged to a sacred nation for whom history has at all times been conceived as the unfolding in time of a divine event. Perhaps it is impossible finally to create even a fairy-world when the idea of the sacred is entirely absent. Nothing, then, not even an egg-shell, can be transfigured, trans-substantiated, for the trans-substantiating principle is itself absent; and the soul then becomes the prisoner of an environment which offers no equivalence for its native numinosity. Perhaps this is the first society to build no environment of the arts for imagination to inhabit; and our cities have become all but imaginatively uninhabitable in the absence of those numinous presences. For if I were asked what contemporary English poetry most conspicuously lacks, I would say, the imaginative, and especially the mythological sense; and this no less so in the introspective and personal kind of poetry than in the social realist and other modes whose purpose is to report and describe the sensible world. The former is as claustrophobic as the latter, and for the same reason, an almost total absence of imaginative vision, the participation of the 'other' mind.

It seems that the poets have themselves been infected by the critics and by the anti-imaginative climate of the time. When I was a student at Cambridge mythological poetry was already out of favour. Milton was denigrated and we obediently preferred Donne, whose poems express personal feelings and conceptual wit, but which are totally lacking in the mythological sense. T. E. Hulme's theories of the poetic image set a fashion; we looked in poetry both past and present for fresh and striking images, much as the Augustans never tired of their search for the just adjective, the refined epithet. At the same time the politically 'engaged' left-wing writers were committed to, or strongly influenced by, the official Communist doctrine of social realism, a kind of poetry no less incompatible with the traditional function of the arts than the refined hedonism of the Imagists. Robert Graves, it is true, has made learned use of myths, but their language is no more for him than for Dryden and Pope a sacred speech. If the White Goddess is nevertheless numinous for Graves, it is because he draws his poetry from sources deeper than his theories. To another age this impoverishment of our own must be apparent.

Of the poetic figures myth is the most comprehensive, the unit and unity within each separate symbol or symbolic figure or symbolic enactment takes place. At a time when nearly all criticism takes the form of analysis, parts have come to seem more important than wholes and are studied as if they were themselves the units of poetry. Myth, if it is discussed at all, is in general regarded, not as the most complete and comprehensive of poetic figures but as something superadded; whereas the myth, in any work, is the principle of orientation within which all the parts are related.

The gift for the whole is rare at the present time; nevertheless – and necessarily among those poets alone who derive their work from an imaginative vision – there are some in whom it is to be found. Vernon Watkins has used Welsh Bardic myths; David Jones, most learned of the Welsh poets, has used Christian, Welsh, and Arthurian sacred and heroic lore as the epic and mythological setting of the common soldier fighting in the trenches of the First World War. By this means he places the anonymous and forgotten dead within heroic legend and the order of Christian redemption. Joyce imparted a mythological dimension and depth to the most obscure persons and events of a day and of a night in Dublin. Myth is more than a mere element in events; above all it is the context of events. In the absence of myth, events have no context, and poetry becomes a thing of parts, not wholes. One might, on another level, define myth as symbol in movement and transformation, for myths are essentially, like dreams, dynamic, undergo transformation and metamorphosis; they express processes, progressions of the imaginative life. In this respect 'The Ancient Mariner' contains all that a mythological poem should, though it is short; for a complete symbolic enactment takes place. Ovid's *Metamorphoses* contain more of this completeness than Virgil's epic, which is long and inclusive rather by its apparatus than by its organic unity. The work of some poets who have never written any in this sense complete mythological poem is nevertheless pervaded by a sense of mythological wholeness. Hölderlin is such a poet; even perhaps Poe, whose haunting images seem to imply a country of imagination from which they are inseparable; as David Gascoyne observed of the artificial paradises of Beardsley, each separate scene seeming to belong to some implicit whole. I find in the work of Edwin Muir a more continuous sense of a coherent underlying myth (using the word to describe that whole of which each symbolic unit is a part) than even in Yeats's. Horses and the road they travel, tower and labyrinth and the timeless fields of ancestral Eden, all belong to a single imaginative world which no poem fully describes but of which all communicate some aspect. This sense of an underlying unity may come from the fact that Muir took his symbols from his own unconscious, whose unity they therefore reflect; whereas Yeats, though he sometimes used dreams and visions as the matter of his poems, drew also on many myths, and perhaps therefore lacks the consistency either of what he himself called *unity of culture* or *unity of being*. The latter, he said, could not exist without the first; but if we may judge by Muir, we might say that in the absence of unity of culture unity of being alone can give any unity at all.

With Yeats each poem, though wrought with imaginative power, seems in some sense a new beginning, and his symbols, though magnificent, remain static, do not, as in the poetry of his masters Blake and Shelley, move into life, unfold a story, undergo transformation; or at most only to a limited extent:

> A shape with lion body and the head of a man,
> A gaze blank and pitiless as the sun,
> Is moving its slow thighs, while all about it
> Reel shadows of the indignant desert birds.
> The darkness drops again. . . .

So for Yeats the vision of what lies behind the trembling veil came in glimpses, seldom in whole symbolic episodes, still less in myths which unfold, like those of Blake, into a great epic drama enacted in an interior country within whose spaces we move freely. The unit of such poetry is not the symbol. Myths are not built by adding piece to piece, they are not the sum of symbolic parts. The unit of myth is the whole enactment, and all its figures; each symbol exists as a part within that imaginative unity, from which it is inseparable, and by which it is determined; as a sentence determines words, and is not merely their sum.

It is therefore foolish to try to describe or understand such poets as Blake, Milton or Spenser, or any mythological poet, in terms only or principally of the detail of their work, the verse, the language, or the separate images or symbols; for the royal gift of such poets is precisely their ability to create and embody a whole myth, as a whole. The recent inability to write or even to read such poetry aright (witness the preference of Donne to Milton, Hopkins to Shelley) may be compared to a taste which can apprehend only architectural detail but not the unity of a great building which determines the nature and quality even of the detail. Coleridge admired in Spenser his ability to create such a spacious country, to include the many characters and scenes of his poem within a unity less of structure than of imaginative ambience. Blake did not possess the gift of ordering, within his poems, his mythological material, as Milton or as Dante did; yet in every turbulent encounter with the mighty forms of his Zoas, we recognize parts within a great whole whose harmony is implicit. The ability to handle the units of myth – which might be defined as dynamic symbol, symbol in transformation – ought to be recognized as the supreme poetic gift. In such poetry the symbolic parts are inseparable from the imaginative configurations and constellations within which they appear. So naturally, in 'The Ancient Mariner', are sun and moon, albatross and ship, ice and ocean presented to us that we do not think of these as separate symbols but as parts of the world within which the poem moves, as we move in nature. Yet considered separately each symbol is used with the precision of words in a language of which the poet has perfect mastery.

I would be the last to suggest that the private symbols of dreams ever could, or should, replace the traditional and learned language of symbol which has given unity of culture to European civilization. In fact there is no conflict between the one and the other since both, ultimately, rest upon the intrinsic fitness of symbols derived from our relationship with the natural world. Collective myths, being the product of many minds, of experience renewed through many generations, and of perhaps some clearer revelation, are necessarily richer and more complete; and are the bearers, besides, of whatever cultural enrichment they have received from philosophers and artists of many periods. It is a necessary part of the *ars poetica* to transpose the personal vision into the common language, whatever that may at any time be. The paradox of the present time seems to be a reversal, by which the private language is the only comprehensible common language, the myths having lost their hold over the imagination, while dreams have become almost a new symbolic currency. Thus it may be that in order to make them understood a poet must clothe traditional themes in the vesture of dreams. I wrote such a poem a few years ago, in which symbols from a dream are combined with related Christian and Platonic iconography. The dream, which I had several years before the poem was written, was one which had that moving and significant quality which seems to characterize the 'other' mind. In the garden of a house I had just taken I discover a well, with 'the parallel production of the corresponding expression', *the ancestral fountain*. In the miraculously pure water of this well I was washing excrement from a new-born child. The dream pointed both backwards and forwards in time; for it resembled the well from which, as a child, I had daily drawn water; and a year or two later, in that garden, four generations of my family were gathered for the christening-party of my grandson. In the course of writing my book on Blake I had been working on a number of Greek myths in which the source of life is symbolized as a spring or stream flowing from an inaccessible source, guarded by women; but only after the christening did I realize, in a flash of understanding, that the Christian font, to be seen in every church, likewise symbolizes the same archetypal meaning as the Greek myths, and my own dreams. The dream for me had illuminated the symbol, but the traditional symbolism of the font proved to be far more complete and more profound than my own glimpse of the mystery. I remembered to have noticed, on the font of St. James's, Piccadilly, on the occasion of a service celebrating the centenary of Blake's death, some beautiful carved figures; and I therefore went to look more carefully at the font in which the poet had been christened. I now saw that the basin was supported by a group of Adam and Eve and the Tree of Life – the ancestors, the source of life. On one side of the basin is a remarkably Blake-like Ark riding the Flood, while a dove approaches with its olive-twig. The meaning contained in this symbol is almost inexhaustible – life as a sea-crossing of the mutable flux of material existence (in all mythologies matter is symbolized as water, or the sea – the 'unconscious waters' of the Rig Veda, the seas of Odysseus's voyage) The Virgin Mary is called the 'ark of the covenant' because the woman preserves and protects in her body the divine child on his way to birth; and she, too, is associated with the dove. Christ rises, on another face of the marble basin, from the baptismal waters; on a third is shown the cleansing of the leper, type of the spiritual condition of 'fallen' man, who in the Old Testament story bathed in the waters of Jordan. Christ walking on the waters and many more symbols ramify from the complex theme. Many minds (or one mind expressing itself through many minds) had created, in the traditional iconography, a statement far more perfect than my dream.

Yet – and any symbolist poet writing at the present time must encounter this paradox – it would have been useless for me to build my poem round the Christian iconography, which, as such, has very largely lost its power to evoke the numinous; more so perhaps for practising Christians than for persons who like myself have come full circle and rediscovered the power of the ancient symbols through a renewed contact with the source. Part of the trouble at the present time is the confusion of tongues. We know all myths but have none of our own; and (although there are still poets who are able to use the Christian symbols in a living way) it becomes increasingly difficult to know what is our own, still less to know what is communicable to readers no less eclectic than ourselves. In such uncertainty we can be certain only of what to other periods seemed the least certain of all symbols – those of our own dreams and visions. These, and not the cult, have become the touchstone of truth.

There can be no conflict between imagination and such traditional themes. On the contrary, the traditional symbols have at all times been at once the teachers of the imagination and the record of its insights. With every new insight there must be an accompanying discovery of the fitness and power of old symbols; such a discovery is the natural, the inevitable consequence of our own insights into the world they embody.

But the projection or interiorization of these forms must de-

pend upon culture and period, natural and personal tempera-
ment. At the present time, as the alternative to a demythologized
naturalism from which all the numinosity has been withdrawn,
I would expect any profound renewal of poetry to come from
an exploration of the interior, the anterior landscape of the
imagination. If the present use of symbolism can no longer be
in the form of the old religious myths, we must, knowing as we
now do that the mythological order is an interior order, follow
those figures who were at one time objectified in the cults of the
old religions, into their own country. Into that interior world
the figures of the gods and their myths have withdrawn, drawing
after them the old cults, there to renew their immortality by re-
immersion in the source: which has at all times been the only
source of the life of the cults themselves.

8

A DEFENCE OF SHELLEY'S POETRY

Shelley is at the present time perhaps the least understood of the major English poets. Reasons for this are not far to seek: the positivist philosophers who have so strongly influenced the climate of modern critical opinion are fond of applying to all that cannot (following the scientific method) be perceived by the senses or subjected to quantitative measurement the term 'meaningless'. But in fact their philosophy precludes the notion of meaning by definition, since meaning can never be 'positive', being precisely that in any word or image which communicates a mental, and therefore immeasurable, attribute. Shelley, most Platonic of poets, becomes, in such terms, the most open to the charge of being 'meaningless' precisely in so far as he is most rich in that quality. Emptied of meaning, poetic figures stand only for their physical terms; and Shelley's richly metaphorical poetry, read as merely descriptive, or 'imagist' verse, seems superficial precisely to those readers who have least understood it. The beauty of metrical form and symbolic image speak immediately to the imagination, or not at all; to the discursive reason 'meaningless', beauty is, to that higher faculty, meaning itself.

Not that Shelley was unlearned; quite the contrary. But his learning belongs to that old European civilization which has, in the course of a single generation, been all but submerged in the modern tide. One universe of knowledge has been replaced by another; and while this can be seen by those who work in the field of the sciences as an advance, we who belong to the other culture are aware of what has been lost. It is not among the scientists but, paradoxically, in the world of philosophy and the arts that the new barbarism is to be found; for these are the modes in which the old knowledge found its expression. It seems unlikely that in the new world which is replacing what C. S. Lewis called 'old western' civilization poetry will have any place at all; for poetry is a language of analogy whose terms establish rela-

K

tions of a mental character and within an immaterial order which is for the positivist mentality as if non-existent. Those poets who best survive the change of background are necessarily the least poetic, or those whose work contains the most alloy of the un-poetic – the passionate but unimaginative Donne with his con-ceptual 'conceits'; the Augustans; poets who are, or who appear to be, concerned chiefly with the image (fulfilling the shallow requirements of the poetic theory of T. E. Hulme, which met the needs of a generation who had lost the old values but who still wanted to keep poetry of a sort); the pious 'metaphysical' poets rather than metaphysical poetry. Even the relatively less learned and more sensuous Keats has suffered less than has Shelley by the disappearance of the universe of reference implicit in his poetry.

Shelley's work is poetry itself, as Mozart's is music itself; and the critic who does not recognize this can tell us nothing but his own inability to discern the very thing he pretends to evaluate. Between Milton and Yeats, Shelley is most perfectly the thing itself. Yeats, who devoted many years to the study of Blake, con-fessed that after all his greater poetic debt (Blake as a prophet is another matter) was to Shelley. He has taken, again and again, from Shelley, images, phrases, ideas essentially poetic in the sense in which certain themes and melodies are essentially musical. To say 'poetic' is not to say 'aesthetic'; for poetry is, for both these poets, a mode of thought, or even more a kind of consciousness, in whose expression mythological themes, images, ideas, language and music are indivisible; a synthesis perhaps more continuous and consistent in Shelley's work than in any other English poetry. In this lies the secret of his power to delight those who are able to respond with the whole of the mind and its 'quick elements, Will, Passion/Reason, Imagination'; and doubtless also of the inability of these critics to appreciate his genius whose thought is conceptual. Shelley is too 'difficult' for such readers, but in a way they themselves cannot recognize, because he calls not for a degree but for a kind of understanding they do not possess.

'Poetry in the general sense may be defined as the express-ion of the imagination', Shelley wrote in his *Defence of Poetry*; poetry

awakens and enlarges the mind itself by rendering it the receptacle of a thousand unapprehended combinations of thought. Poetry lifts the veil from the hidden beauty of the world, and makes familiar objects be as if they were not familiar. Poetry enlarges the circumference of the imagination by replenishing it with thoughts of ever new delight, which have the power of attracting and assimilating to their own nature all other thoughts, and which form new intervals and interstices whose void for ever craves fresh food.

To perceive these intervals and interstices (as with musical quarter-tones and unfamiliar harmonies) discursive thought cannot help us.

Such poetry, speaking as it does to 'minds extended and enlarged', supposes, however, an extremely high level of culture both in the poet and in those to whom he addresses himself. Shelley's command of the English and the two classical languages (besides French, German, Italian and Spanish) was the natural heritage of his class and his excellent education. To read in Greek the works of Homer and the Athenian dramatists, of Plato and Proclus and the neo-Platonists, was as natural to him as to Coleridge. He belonged to a world and a class in which a man of culture measured himself against the whole of knowledge – a knowledge still given its unity by the spiritual orientation of the civilization from which it had arisen. But culture is more than education, than learning. It consists also, and above all, in a certain refinement in the quality of response, something which cannot be defined or measured but which is, within any civilized society, wordlessly communicated. Shelley was, in this sense, the inheritor of the fine essence of that now almost extinct English culture of which an aristocratic class and the universities of Oxford and Cambridge were once the custodians.

Shelley's poetry can best be understood in terms of his own definitions and principles, as he sets these down in his *Defence of Poetry*. Not that this essay is more than an indication of the context, the universe of reference, of the poetry: it contains little or nothing which is 'original'; rather it is a recall to order, to the Platonic tradition, an eloquent descant upon those first principles also set forth by Coleridge in his *Biographia Literaria*. Shelley's emphasis is in some important respects different, especially perhaps in his closer adherence to Plato's view of the relation of the arts to politics.

First of all attributes of poetry Shelley names 'a certain rhythm or order' with which (following Plato) he associates 'mimetic representation'. This mimesis of the poet is the reverse of naturalistic imitation, for 'language and gesture, together with plastic or pictorial imitation, become the image of the combined effect of those objects and his apprehension of them'. Thus poetry is the expression at once of object and response; in the savage or the child, to natural objects, in the civilized man to 'higher objects'. Above all mimesis is an 'approximation to the beautiful', 'an echo of the eternal music'. A perception of the approximation to these originals Shelley calls 'taste', a term whose disappearance from the vocabulary of modern criticism is to be regretted.[1]

This rhythmic sense of form is his own most outstanding natural gift, and so seemingly spontaneous is his lyricism that it appears (like all supreme art) effortless; and an examination of his notebooks (upon which Neville Rodgers has written discerningly in his *Shelley at Work*) suggest that when he composed, lyric form often preceded words. We can see whole stanzas blocked out, like a musical score, with only a word or a phrase here and there, to be filled in later, as if in an instantaneous perception of the lyric form which is antecedent to the words, drawing them towards itself like particles of iron into a magnetic field. At other times no doubt words and metre came together. He wrote at astonishing speed, 'Laon and Cythna' in six months, 'The Witch of Atlas' in three days. He entrusted himself to that *enthusiasm* of which Plato speaks in the *Ion*, by whose inspiration the poets compose their lyrics 'which they could not do when in their sober minds'. Shelley himself wrote that 'Poets are the Hierophants of an unapprehended inspiration, compelled to serve the power which is seated in the throne of their own soul. . . . I appeal to the greatest poets of the present day, whether it is not an error to assert that the finest passages of poetry are produced by labour or study:' and he cites Milton's 'unpremeditated song', adding that 'Milton conceived the *Paradise Lost* as a whole before he executed its portions'. That this was so of his own work, the evidence of his manuscripts suggests. It is Plotinus (whose tractate *Concerning the Beautiful* Shelley certainly knew, probably in the original, and in any case in Thomas Taylor's translation, one of the seminal works of the Romantic movement) who most clearly has stated the Platonic view of the precedence of the idea, or whole, of any work, over its parts; instancing a building, whose

---

[1] The Japanese Nō plays, completely stylized as they are, are a perfect instance of mimesis in Shelley's sense.

form as a whole exists in the mind of the architect, the stones of which it is constructed being fitted to a pre-existing form. To those critics who know only of discursive thought such rapid composition appears to be something abnormal; yet it seems to be the normal mode of poets who write from the 'other' mind, from the imagination, abnormal only to those who laboriously imitate such spontaneous productions without what Plato in the *Ion* calls the inspiration of the Muses. We no longer speak of the Muse but the empirical fact remains, that true poets, when inspired, can accomplish what they could not accomplish, as Plato puts it 'in their sober minds'; works 'inspired' by the enthroned power of which Shelley speaks present themselves as wholes. Blake had written of poetic inspiration in similar terms, saying that portions of his *Milton* were written 'from immediate dictation, twelve or sometimes twenty or thirty lines at a time without Premeditation and even against my Will . . . and an immense Poem Exists, which seems to be the Labour of a Long Life, all produc'd without Labour or Study' – Shelley's very words. Yeats, a laborious composer, was perhaps a little envious of Shelley's virtuosity, for he wrote in *A Vision* 'he was subject to an automatism which he mistook for poetical invention, especially in his longer poems'. But most of these are juvenilia. It is on the work written after he was twenty-five that his reputation rests.

In thus entrusting himself to *enthusiasm*, he had himself experienced what Plato describes, that magical and apparently spontaneous generation of poetic form which comes about when the inspiring spirit descends upon the poet. Such spontaneity is at once the expression of the energizing of imaginative thought, and the evidence of it. Shelley was, at the same time, skilled in traditional prosody, using with apparently equal ease the Spenserian stanza, *terza rima*, the strophe and antistrophe of the Greek chorus, the structural elaboration of the Pindaric ode, besides a whole range of new and lovely lyric forms. That power enthroned in the poet's soul can, it seems, make use of whatever technical knowledge the poet has at his command. In this respect Shelley was a perfected instrument: not, however, through laborious imitation, but rather by ready imaginative assimilation of poetic forms of every kind, and his long and deep familiarity with the whole range of poetic literature.

Shelley has been most misunderstood by readers schooled in the positivist criticism of which T. E. Hulme's Imagism is an early expression, and which in Cambridge has found the kind of scorched earth upon which it thrives. Such readers look in Shelley's symbolic images for the kind of naturalistic description we find at its best in John Clare. A storm-cloud, it was proclaimed, does not resemble 'a Maenad's hair'; whereas Hopkins's 'silk-sack' is an image fit and worthy of the fullest admiration, because some clouds do look like silk sacks. John Holloway, who had looked at more kinds of cloud than one, and who had presumably also asked himself what happens to the hair of those 'possessed', has pointed out that Shelley's image is, even visually, exact: a thunder-cloud on the Mediterranean often does send out strange points and ragged fringes of vapour, 'the locks of the approaching storm'. Nature is a mirror that reflects back to the observer whatever he is capable of discerning or chooses to notice. Turner is not less a painter of 'nature' than is Stubbs, but of light not of animals; and Shelley's 'nature' is (following perhaps, as has been said by others, his interest in chemistry and allied sciences) seen rather in terms of light, flux and transmutation than of Dr. Johnson's stone, more apt to the boot than to the eye. 'Nature-poetry' is no less a convention than any other selection we may care to make from our environment; and has become, in England, an extremely meagre one; admirers who see in D. H. Lawrence's garden-tortoises a novel and expanded vision have seldom read (for example) St. John Perse's *Vents* or *Amers*. No poet has more beautifully described than has Shelley, in the volatile alchemy he shares with his contemporary Turner, landscapes real or imaginary; but even when this is so, his description is at all times a means not an end. Shelley's second mark of poetry is not vivid imagery, but a language 'vitally metaphorical; that is, it marks the before unapprehended relations of things, and perpetuates their apprehension'. When in the course of time these metaphors have ceased to be vital, and become mere abstractions and 'signs for portions or classes of thought' they cease to be poetic, and new poets must discover new relations, must extend and explore those 'intervals and interstices whose void ever craves fresh food'. Shelley was a Berkeleyan immaterialist; and there is already implicit in what might appear simple description the relationship, itself mysterious, 'between existence and perception'. He makes his Ahasuerus, embodiment of knowledge itself, declare that

                                    . . . Thought
Alone, and its quick elements, Will, Passion,
Reason, Imagination, cannot die;
They are what that which they regard appears,
The stuff whence mutability can weave
All that it hath dominion o'er, worlds, worms,
Empires and superstitions. . . .

To perceive is already to create; and there is, alike in Shelley's imaginary and his earthly paradises, that quality of primary reality we occasionally experience in dreams or waking visions, in which thought and its object (landscapes, figures, or enactments) seem one and indivisible. In 'that Elysian light' nature itself is perceived as if it were itself a region of imagination. Word and image have, in such poetry, that unity and correspondence Coleridge experienced when in writing 'Kubla Khan' 'all the images rose up before him as *things*, with the parallel production of their correspondent expressions', as if both alike from the same creative ground, the primary imagination itself. Those enchanted landscapes are not reflections of nature but immediate creations of that mental ground of which natural forms are themselves images, 'idle shadows/Of thought's eternal flight'. Therefore it is that in reading such poetry what we experience seems more real than reality; it comes from the source.

There is in Shelley's poetry a congruity between his lyricism and his themes. AE wrote of the inappropriateness of employing lyrical speech (which is the natural expression of the exalted imagination) for material of a discursive kind. Such poetry is factitious, an imitation of poetry more or less ingenious. But in Shelley both form and substance belong to the kind of thought, the level of consciousness to which lyrical rhythms and symbolic metaphor are alike native.

Besides the metaphorical essence diffused throughout Shelley's imaginative descriptive writing there are more complex symbolic figures. In his handling of mythological themes he stands with Spenser, Milton, Blake, Coleridge, and the Keats of 'Hyperion', above all English poets except Shakespeare. Yeats may be right in finding his figure of Prometheus lacking in life, a mouthpiece of propaganda; but those female soul-figures the Witch of Atlas and the Lady of the Sensitive Plant; Ahasuerus, mask of a Hermetic wisdom; or even those winged and living boats of the poet's interior journeys, and the rivers and seas on which they move, are informed with the life of the mystery in which they originate. In many passages (as in the last chorus of 'Hellas' the ancient doctrine of the Great Year) some theme of traditional symbolism is explicit; more often, as in the 'Ode to the West Wind' the metaphorical sense of his neo-Platonic symbolic language of wind, sea, seed, lyre, image and reflection, storm-inspired cloud, is all implicit, and unapparent to the untaught reader; but, yielding to our growing understanding, 'acts otherwise than in a lyre, and produces not melody alone, but harmony'.

Shelley must have known, besides the Platonic tradition in which he was learned, something of Indian, Cabalistic, and Hermetic works expressing the same metaphysical gnosis, found also in the plays of Calderón, whom he admired. He calls the truth of poetry 'eternal truth'; in either case the order of truth is metaphysical. This truth, he says, belongs not to the poet himself but to his inspirers: 'The persons in whom this power resides may often, as far as regards many portions of their nature, have little correspondence with the spirit of good of which they are the ministers' and may even be 'themselves perhaps the most sincerely astonished at its manifestations'. In this Shelley is nearer to Plato than was Blake, who blamed the philosopher who 'made Socrates say that Poets and Prophets do not know or Understand what they write or Utter; this is a most Pernicious Falsehood. If they do not, pray is an inferior kind to be call'd Knowing?' Shelley, like Yeats, believed that 'the poet may embody truth, but cannot know it'. This must be so, for those who understand that 'the deep truth is imageless'.

An example will illustrate Shelley's metaphorical richness; and I choose one of his most characteristic poems, the 'Ode to a Skylark' because, through its deceptive simplicity and the lightness of its vesture, the subtlety and strength of the internal structure of this poem has often been overlooked.

No poem is more suffused with 'the Elysian light' wherein nature is apprehended as a region of the imagination, nor is there in this poem any point at which we can draw a distinction between the physical and the metaphysical objects of the poet's discourse. The metaphorical character of the whole lies in the perfect fusion of the two terms of the metaphor, which because of its very perfection may pass unnoticed. This assimilation of object and apprehension is established in the first stanza when

the 'blithe spirit' of the singer is said not to be a bird; the source
of the song of which the bird is only the instrument is of a more
mysterious kind. Like the poet the bird is the 'hierophant of an
unapprehended inspiration'; for 'heaven or near it' is not a mere
synonym for the sky; like Shakespeare's lark who sings at
'heaven's gate' the bird's nearness to heaven lies in the immediacy
of the song's inspiration: the ground from which it springs is not
the material earth but 'thought and its quick elements'. The lark
is less a symbol of imaginative creation than itself an immediate
expression of 'the stuff whence mutability can weave'.

There is in the phrase 'unpremeditated art' used in the fifth
line of the poem an implicit allusion to Milton's 'unpremeditated
song'. Blake's lark too, which in his poem, *Milton*, 'leads the
choir of day' is equated with the poet who was, for Blake as for
Shelley, the type of the 'inspired man'. It is tempting to wonder
what of Blake's work Shelley might have seen; for Godwin, or
perhaps Mary Shelley herself (of whose mother Mary Wollstonecraft Blake had been a friend) might well have possessed
some of his illuminated books. Does the image of the eagle
struggling with a serpent, which Shelley uses in 'The Revolt of
Islam' as an image of revolution, bear only an accidental resemblance to the emblem used in the same sense, of *The Marriage
of Heaven and Hell*? Had Shelley read Blake's defence of free
love (written perhaps with Mary Wollstonecraft herself in mind)
the 'Visions of the Daughters of Albion'? Blake's Urizen and
that God-simulating Satan whose image his Milton casts down
is uncommonly like Shelley's Jupiter. Had he even met Blake
himself (who outlived Shelley by five years) in London? Shelley
is, whether he knew it or not, Blake's spiritual successor; and his
skylark has its prototype in Blake's whose 'Nest is at the Gate of
Los', spirit of prophecy. Perhaps both poets, supremely admiring
Milton, chose the lark as the bird who in 'L'Allegro' sings 'From
his watch-tower in the skies'. Shelley's skylark can, in any case,
be seen as his tribute to Milton as the defender and exemplar of
the Platonic doctrine of poetic inspiration.

Shelley's verse-form is itself a beautiful example of mimesis.
Anyone who has listened attentively to the soaring lark will
recognize in the delicate hesitant poise of each stanza upon its
prolonged floating last line, the lark-song with its extended trill.
The reiteration, too, of the verses has this mimetic quality; but in
content these lovely musical variations are not a mere series of

fragile images strung out on a slender thread. This reflection on the nature of inspiration owes its unity to the interior structure of the metaphysical idea which the images explore, each following from the last with the inevitability of a Socratic discourse.

First the poet seeks to identify the singer; the 'blithe spirit' who is not a bird is called, in the third verse, 'an unbodied joy', which 'floats and runs' with the freedom of its mental being, on the clouds, like one of Blake's bright forms who, likewise, are often vested in 'a cloud of fire', element of the spirit and of 'the enjoyments of genius'. A famous passage in the *Hermetica*, certainly known to Shelley, as it was to Blake and to Coleridge, describes this power of the soul to travel wherever it will, to be in those very places of which it thinks; a power which no body, however fine, can possess. 'Command it to fly into Heaven, and it will need no Wings, neither shall anything hinder it; not the fire of the Sun, nor the Aether, nor the turning of the Spheres, not the bodies of any of the other Stars. . . .'

The bird song which the sensual ear receives as sound, consciousness experiences, more intimately, as 'a joy'. To this theme of joy the poet returns until he has, not by statement but by repeated re-immersion in the experience of song, established the identity of song-spirit-joy; as the Hindu metaphysicians equate *sit-chit-ananda*, *being-life-joy*, the primary reality; making joy not an attribute of spirit, but its essential nature. The divine rapture exceeds any pleasures compassable in natural terms, those of love, or wine. Like the Vedantic definition of the divine principle by a series of negations the poet rejects all apprehensible objects, all desire for known or knowable satisfactions: the joy 'ignorant of pain' (and by implication the spirit itself) can only have its being in another principle than this world of duality, in an eternal order untouched by death. The poem ends, like the 'Ode to the West Wind', with an invocation – the poet aspires to draw his music from that immortal source which no human virtue, knowledge or art can approach.

A series of metaphors suggest what cannot be defined, the mystery of the emergence of the song, whether of art or of nature, from the 'blue deep' where the bird soars to 'heaven or near it'. The singer, bird or poet, is a minute centre through which the unmanifest issues into the temporal world. Again we think of Blake's timeless moment in which 'the poet's work is done', of his minute flower centres in which 'eternity expands', and of his

lark whose 'little throat labours with inspiration'. Shelley's metaphors are a star, in daylight invisible but nevertheless present;
the moon which from a 'lonely cloud' diffuses light which fills
all space; rain falling from the sky, as heaven nourishes earth.
Each image metaphorically embodies the idea the poet is exploring, the flowing of the created from the uncreated; as Blake,
again, describes how the work of creation flows forth 'like visible
out of the invisible'. Implicit in both poets is the teaching of the
Perennial Philosophy that every natural effect has a spiritual
cause.

'A poet hidden/In the light of thought' is a mediator, like bird
or star, between the seen and the unseen; here conceived as the
specifically human power of giving form to immaterial thought,
the 'higher objects' of poetic mimesis.

> What objects are the fountains
>   Of thy happy strain?
> What fields, or waves, or mountains?
>   What shapes of sky or plain?
> What love of thine own kind? What ignorance of pain?

Here the figure – in itself beautiful – of the bird which perceives
a world unlike the human, is the vesture of Shelley's deeper
thought on the higher, and invisible, objects of the poet; the
Platonic ideas, discovered perhaps in that Garden of the Muses
of whose 'fountains' Plato writes. Blake's lark too nests near a
'fountain', a nesting-place improbable in nature, but symbolically inevitable for the bird who, like the poet, 'winged, light and
volatile', visits Plato's heavenly gardens.

As the poet embodies thought, 'a high-born maiden/In a
palace tower' gives form to love. The maiden is called 'high-
born' in the same sense as in Michelangelo's sonnet (translated
by Wordsworth) the soul is called 'heaven-born':

> Heaven-born, the Soul a Heavenward course must hold.

Heaven-born love is, like thought, one of the channels through
which the eternal beauty may enter the world. With this introduction of the theme of love comes a change of key; the action
of the poem moves down from the 'blue deep' of the uncreated
to the 'dell of dew', the world of generation. Here the image of
light is not star but 'a glow-worm golden', a fallen star, a star
generated, as Plato describes the descent of souls as stars into
earthly life. As the souls descend into generation they become,

in Porphyry's words, 'drenched in moisture'. Blake too uses the symbolism of dew in this sense, and also 'dell' and 'valley' as the physical world. Yet even in the 'dell of dew' the light continues to shine as the poet, fallen child of Paradise, continues to scatter the 'aerial hue' of Elysium in the darkness of this world. As the glow-worm echoes the 'poet hidden', so the rose of love echoes the 'high-born maiden'; and again Shelley uses an image Blake had used before him in the same sense, and in the same passage of *Milton* as his lark:

> . . . the Flowers put forth their precious Odours
And none can tell how from so small a centre comes such sweets.

So the poem which to a superficial reading seems so slight proves to be, like the grace of Botticelli or Yeats's 'little song about a rose' the delicate veil of thought which soars towards the bounds of the knowable, evoked rather than defined by images of star and cloud and fragrance of rain on flower. As Edgar Wind has somewhere said, this lightness of touch is ever the mark of supreme artistry. Where beauty is greatest, there we should look also for the greatest depth of meaning.

The same richly metaphorical internal structure is to be found no less in poems whose outer vesture is occasional; as in the deceptively simple poem 'To Jane: the Recollection'. Here the little pool in a pine-forest in which reflections are interfused with 'an elysian glow' not perceptible in the real objects, is, like 'the waves' intenser day' of the 'Ode to the West Wind', the microcosm of imagination. In the 'intenser' medium of consciousness all that is reflected from nature becomes 'more than truth', transmuted into the higher mode of existence. Freed from every 'unwelcome thought' which effaces its images like the 'envious wind' that ruffles the surface of the woodland pool, consciousness itself manifests, in moments of peace and love, its radical nature as the mirror of paradise. The true poet, when he seems to be describing some experience purely personal, is never, in reality (as with so many modern writers of verse) doing so; the personal occasion is merely another image, or symbolic term, by whose means he is enabled to discover some aspect of the eternal harmony. West wind, skylark, or Shelley and Jane Williams walking in a pine-wood, may according to Coleridge's definition of the symbol, themselves 'abide as a living part in that Unity' of which they are representative, but never are themselves the subject of the poem, by definition an expression of the imagination, never of the personality.

Shelley's third mark of the poet is that of legislator or prophet; 'for he not only beholds intensely the present as it is, and discovers these laws according to which present things ought to be ordered, but he beholds the future in the present, and his thoughts are the germs of the flower and fruit of latest time'. Legislator more than prophet: for Shelley belonged to the ruling class, the class of Walpole and of Pitt, and in the natural course of things would have succeeded to his father's seat in Parliament. Even in exile the sense of political responsibility remained with Shelley, as it did with Byron (to whose genius the liberation of Greece is a monument perhaps more enduring than his poetry). A very high proportion of Shelley's early prose writings are on immediate political issues. That he was a liberal and a republican is not in any way surprising, though it is difficult now to sympathize with his enthusiasm for the ideas and ideals of Rousseau and Godwin and that contemporary ferment of atheist humanism whose nihilistic term our age has seen. But it would be difficult even for those who still might share his political faith to read without embarrassment his doctrinaire proclamations of the advent of Utopia as soon as those vaguely called 'tyrants' should be overthrown. Yeats wrote that 'the justice of "Prometheus Unbound" is a vague propagandist emotion and the women that await its coming are but clouds'; perhaps in 'The Triumph of Life' we see the beginnings of political maturity. But Shelley understood that the poet, whose politics are those of eternity, has for that very reason a responsibility towards the politics of time. His political concern is an aspect of his greatness. He was not a poet, as Keats was, of private feelings and introspective imaginings; even more than Coleridge and Wordsworth (spectators rather than actors in the politics of their time) he understood the responsibility Plato lays upon the poets for their moral influence in society. In terms which the present time might do well to consider he castigated obscenity, 'which is ever blasphemy against the divine beauty in life, which becomes, from the very vest which it assumes, more active if less disgusting: it is a monster for whom the corruption of society brings forth new food, which it devours in secret'. The connexion of poetry and public morals is more observable in drama than in any other form; 'And it is indisputable that the highest perfection of human society has ever corresponded with the highest dramatic excellence; and that the corruption or the extinction of the drama in a nation where it has once flourished is a mark of corruption of manners, and an extinction of the energies which sustain the soul of social life'. Prophet of freedom as he was he would have assumed as of course that in the good city censorship is necessary for the protection of society, indeed of freedom itself; for he believed (as Ireland and Russia at the present time believe but not, apparently, the Anglo-Saxon nations) that people are changed by what they read and see, 'become what they behold', and that its spiritual food can nourish or poison a nation.

Shelley gives a strange reason for holding poetry superior to the plastic arts: language only 'has relation to thoughts alone', 'to that imperial faculty whose throne is curtained within the invisible nature of man'. Language is 'a more direct representation of the actions and passions of our internal being, and is susceptible of more various and delicate combinations than colour, form or motion, and is more plastic and obedient to the control of that faculty of which it is the creation'. For Shelley (and of this his political sense was an aspect) man's thoughts were of all things the fittest subject of poetry. For what reason, at the present time, sensations or tenuous personal emotions are regarded as more 'poetic' than the more specifically human ideas of truth, justice, freedom, honour, and (in the spiritual sense) love, ideas of which humanity becomes capable only as a social being, it would be pointless here to discuss. Suffice it to recollect that these were the principal themes of the poetry of the Athenian dramatists not because the ancient Greeks had 'no sense of natural beauty' (an opinion whose untruth can be seen by any student who visits Delphi and Sounion and Epidaurus, the most beautiful natural sites in the world) but because to those same Greeks things of the mind were held to be of a higher order than things of the senses, as alone belonging to man's unique nature and creation, to the god-imposed 'know thyself' of Delphic Apollo. It is precisely in those energies of the mind which are at the present time so apathetically regarded, the 'ideas' which man alone is capable of conceiving, that the ancient Greeks found the highest degree of beauty. A poetry of ideas is the most aristocratic order of poetry; for only the educated man is capable of any distinct notion of ideas; and in a demotic society therefore not likely to flourish. At the same time such poetry has the greatest potential power of civilizing and transforming unbred mankind. Shelley's poetry of ideas (when not on the level of the 'vague propaganda' of his juvenilia) is, at its best, as impassioned, subtle and beautiful as that of Aeschylus; as in 'Epipsychidion', 'Adonais', 'Prometheus Unbound', or in 'Hellas'. 'Plato was essentially a poet', Shelley believed, 'the truth and splendour of his imagery and the melody of his language are the most intense it is possible to conceive'; but it is especially Plato's 'harmony in thought' which entitles him to be called a poet; a quality Shelley himself possessed in a high degree – it is this 'harmony in thought' which establishes the structural ordering of the 'Ode to a Skylark'. Conversely Shakespeare, Dante and Milton 'are philosophers of the very greatest power'. 'A poem is the very image of life expressed in its eternal truth', Shelley believed; and the 'deep truth' of imagination – 'imageless' likewise – is not different in kind from that of the traditional metaphysics, called in the ancient world philosophy.

Shelley, Yeats objected, 'lacked the vision of evil'. A child of Paradise, the mistakes of his own tragic young life were all made through this obliviousness. He was bedevilled, besides, by the mistaken notions of his time on the innate virtue of 'natural man'. Shelley had not yet learned, as Blake had, in the bitter world of experience, wherein lay the error of 'Paine and Voltaire with some of the Ancient Greeks' (all Shelley's false gods) who say 'we will live in Paradise and Liberty. You may do so in spirit, but not in the Mortal Body, as you pretend. . . . While we are in the world of Mortality we Must Suffer.' His mistakes were those of the same generosity, disinterestedness, and lack of self-knowledge which sent out young idealists of a later generation to be killed in the Spanish civil war in the name of an ideology insufficiently examined just because generous youth wants a cause to live and die for; an easier way, to be sure, than the long arduous way of perfection, or than to 'wither into truth' with those who have, in Yeats's phrase, 'awakened from the common dream'. Had he lived he must have applied to those current opinions too hastily assumed the critical discernment with which he wrote that 'Euripides, Lucan, Tasso, Spenser, have frequently affected a moral aim, and the effect of their poetry is diminished in exact proportion to the degree in which they compel us to admit to this purpose.' Of none of these is Shelley's criticism so true as of himself.

But if Shelley had not the Christian 'vision of evil' (as Blake had, and Shakespeare and Dante) and imagined Paradise to be more easily realizable 'on earth as it is in heaven' than it really is, he certainly had the Platonic vision of that golden country itself, and of the radical innocence and beauty, likewise, of all human souls, however disfigured by outward personality; as his Witch of Atlas could see

> Where in bright bowers immortal forms abide
> Beneath the weltering of the restless tide.

He is the poet of apokatastasis, of the restitution of all things to their essential perfection. In his belief that this possibility lies latent in man and in all creation, Shelley has the unanimous teaching of tradition, both pre-Christian and Christian, with him; besides the interior assent of every spirit not quite dead. Nor was he wrong in believing that love is the transforming principle which alone can bring this about, uniting what is divided, transforming ('And that with little change of shape or hue') the hateful into the beautiful. Perhaps Shelley's 'love' was too restricted, being, above all, that of lovers. But the glimpse of 'the Elysian light' given to those in love is not therefore illusory. In 'To Jane: the Recollection' it is the presence of the beloved which trans-substantiates the world:

> There seemed from the remotest seat
>   Of the white mountain waste,
> To the soft flower beneath our feet
>   A magic circle traced, –
> A spirit interfused around,
>   A thrilling silent life, –
> To momentary peace it bound
>   Our mortal nature's strife; –
> And still I felt the centre of
>   The magic circle there,
> Was one fair form that filled with love
>   The lifeless atmosphere.

Love is the agent of apokatastasis; a truth the Christian church itself acknowledges in the sacramental nature of marriage. His vision of the harmonious co-existence of all things in the state of Paradise (to which love, in whatever form, gives access) he has perhaps communicated (in 'Prometheus Unbound' especially) more perfectly than has any other English poet; as

C. S. Lewis wrote in an essay in which he contrasts (to the entire advantage of the former) Shelley with Dryden. We can no more object that such poetic evocation of the state of beatitude itself lacks 'the sense of evil' than we can make the objection to Mozart's D-minor quartet. It might be said that the arts exist, finally, for no other end than the holding before us of images of Paradise.

No stupider judgement was ever passed upon Shelley than by Arnold who called him an 'ineffectual angel'. There spoke the school-inspector who believes that 'good' is something done by busy people. Giving men material goods and material aid can not make them better, only better off; the effect of poetry is to change us permanently in our nature; a transmutation by no means ineffectual. It would be hard to name a poet whose political and social propaganda – to put it at its lowest – has more effectively changed public opinion and altered the course of history. More far-reaching is the transforming power of poetry itself. Only those lacking in all sensibility to a poetry which speaks to the soul in its own language and of its native place and state can read Shelley unchanged.

1967

9

THE USE OF THE BEAUTIFUL

What do we, at the present time, ask of poetry? I may be mistaken about precisely what is asked, but I think I am not mistaken in the conclusion that the present times does not ask – or receive – enough. Much verse published seems to set itself no goal beyond description, sometimes pleasing, but just as often of displeasing things seen or felt. I doubt if anything is to be learned from such descriptions or from the self-expression of the subjective states reflected in so much current verse. Far from expanding our consciousness, we have often, on the contrary, in order to understand such states to make ourselves smaller, like Alice, before we can get inside such mean rooms as are opened to us. Perhaps the poet gains by articulating and objectifying his neurosis (though I question whether that is the cure of souls it is said to be) but what the reader can hope to gain I fail to see. Does not the confusion at the present time come from the fact that many now writing, and writing about verse, are genuinely unaware that what they are writing and writing about, is not, properly speaking, poetry at all – not in any way related to, or comparable with, the art as practised and understood by those on whose account poets are, in all civilized societies, honoured? It would be absurd to say that there should be no such thing as satirical verse, or descriptive, narrative, or occasional verse; what is deplorable is the confusion of mind which has arisen, even among those who claim to be poets: an ignorance of the order of things to which their own work purports to belong, a forgetting, a deliberate turning away from the recognition that they share neither the ends, the means, nor the knowledge, of what I cannot but call the real poets.

There is one word for which we may look in vain in the writings of contemporary critics: the word beauty and the idea of the beautiful, has ceased to count for anything. Why is this? Has this age discovered something better or have we simply failed to understand a concept which to other civilizations has seemed inseparable from any consideration of the arts? I will not labour the obvious fact that this is a beautiless society. Does this matter? In losing beauty have we lost anything vital to our arts or indeed to our lives? No need to enumerate the material advantages of hygiene, transport, television, frozen vegetables and so on, not enjoyed by ages whose typical expressions were the sculptures and paintings, cathedrals and liturgy of the Christian religion; yet in terms of happiness, our exchange might be harder to defend, and in terms of the quality of our lives, harder still. George Russell, the Irish sage who wrote on the relation of what he called 'the politics of time' to 'the politics of eternity' observed that 'One of the very first symptoms of the loss of the soul is the loss of the sense of beauty'. Is what our society has lost perhaps its soul?

I am not calling in question the beauty, or want of it, in this or that school of modern poetry or art; the beautiful has taken, in the past, innumerable forms and styles. Dorothy Wordsworth thought some Indian sculptures she saw hideous idols, but we find no difficulty in recognizing the beauty of a dancing Shiva or Parvati, or of some work of Buddhist art. No, the question now is, whether certain fashionable schools, both of painting and of poetry, make beauty an end at all? William Empson does not consider it. For all his skill in the analysis of parts, he has no gift – and in this he is not alone – of perceiving wholes. Herbert Read, the chief apologist of the Modern Movement, as such, has said, if I remember aright, that the idea of beauty has been, for those involved in that movement, replaced by the idea of energy. It might certainly seem that revolution for its own sake, transformation as such, an instantaneous gesture which expresses finally nothing but its own instantaneity, process as such, has become the be-all and end-all of art; process so accelerated that all images have dissolved into the flux of continuous transformation, so much so that form, in such art, can no longer be said to exist.

A similar trend was introduced into literature with the 'stream of consciousness' and, again, all bounds of form seem to have been broken in some recent works. Not all the writers I have in mind are social realists; but a materialist philosophy precludes orders of reality and value other than the physical; and some sort of positivism or humanism is the inevitable tendency – the uncon-

scious drift, if not the conscious intention – of all who, whether
as a consciously held theory, or as an unconscious mental attitude, take their colour from the prevailing climate of opinion.
This is the cast of mind of those who do not consciously adopt
some other attitude, who do not think at all, or who feel that,
because they are drifting with the tide they are active agents in
the progress of evolution.

Social realism would presumably demand of any work of
literature a respect for the truth of things 'as they are'. To depict
the world otherwise than as it appears to the senses is to falsify
and sincerity demands that we look at the worst unflinchingly;
there is a kind of stoicism in this attitude, admirable perhaps in
its way; because things are such, we ought to look at them. But
since for positivism reality is situated (by definition) in the physical order only (a view consistent not only with Marxist economic
theory but with the exclusively quantitative criteria of science),
truth to the nature of things has come to mean truth to the
physical order – a fact which perhaps explains the apparently
inexhaustible current preoccupation with carnality. But in what
are these records more 'true to life', more 'real', than the thoughts
of Plato, St. Paul, Dante or Mozart? These too are human. This
question is not even asked; but if it were, it might be answered
that spirituality, abstract thought, and intellectual beauty, not
being quantitatively measurable or experienced by the senses,
have not, in terms of the positive, any reality at all. It is a question
of where, for a society, a caste, or a civilization, reality is situated.
In this respect there seems to have taken place a revolution,
which has reversed the normal hierarchy of values, situating the
physical and the quantitative above intellect and the spirit.

There has been talk of 'two cultures' and (leaving unasked the
question as to whether the absence of culture can be called
another kind of culture, ignorance another mode of knowledge)
it seems impossible that the rift between them can be mended by
good will, since the difference lies between two irreconcilable
philosophies. The one is an expression of quantitative science
and philosophic positivism; and since quantity is the proper
measure only of physical phenomena, it must in its nature reduce
the artist to some form of recording-apparatus. Upon the tele-
vision-screen, the typical 'cultural' expression of the quantitative
culture, we can see images from anywhere in space; but the difference in quality between the two sides of the screen is negligible.

Viewers and viewed could change places and nothing would be altered. The kitchens of the common man, in which all kinds of ignorant persons express themselves in a language indistinguishable from what such persons would use in real life are held before the 'viewer'; and 'true to life' has come to mean true to the lowest expression of the lowest intelligence – true to the life of the *bête humaine*.

'The men who created the communism of the masses' – to quote Yeats – 'believed that religion, art, philosophy, expresses economic change, that the shell secreted the fish'. But this implicit positivism is by no means confined to the Communist world: it is, and must necessarily be, the philosophy of the masses now everywhere rising to power, for whom the real is situated (as for material science, the philosophy inseparable from the ascendency of the proletariat) in the physical. But when Shakespeare wrote that poets hold a mirror up to 'nature', he used the word in another sense: not the physical 'nature' of science, but the nature of man, his soul and passions. To quote Yeats again, the mischief began at the end of the seventeenth century when man became passive before a mechanized nature; that lasted to our day with the exception of a brief period between Smart's *Song of David* and the death of Byron, wherein imprisoned man beat upon the door. Or I may dismiss all that ancient history and say it began when Flaubert described a masterpiece as 'a mirror dawdling down a lane'.

A mirror very different from Shakespeare's; the eye of the realist has become as passive as a camera-lens and the animal lusts are often all that distinguishes the records of man from those of his machines. On the other hand the art of 'abstract impressionism' has no ordering principle at all, and has at best the negative virtue of release from an imprisoning realism. These two extreme forms, different in appearance are alike in that which they lack. A true reflection of our civilization such work may be; but of what is that civilization itself a reflection? Nor should we forget that nature – human nature – mirrors the forms held up to it, and the man who keeps company with machines will, as Blake says, become what he beholds.

Flaubert's mirror can but reflect what is there, it is passive, it changes nothing: what, we must ask, does such art propose as its end? What can it do to us, or for us? How add to our knowledge or transform our consciousness when all it does is to reflect back

to us what we can see without its assistance, which the camera
can show us as well? The story of Cinderella, which recurs
in many forms in many parts of the world is an allegory of the
soul disfigured, as all are, by the dust and ashes of this world; she
toils in just such a kitchen as those whose sinks and dustbins and
ironing-boards are images which have set their mark on a decade.
One version (given by Harold E. Bayley in *The Lost Language of
Symbolism*, a book Yeats read) tells how the kitchen-maid found
a looking-glass in which she saw not her grimy self but a princess
of perfect beauty whose dress shone like the sun, moon and stars.
There are mirrors and mirrors; and a work of imagination is a
magic glass in which we may discover that nature to which
actuality is barely an approximation. Fairy-tales tell always of
royal and heroic (that is to say perfect or perfected) persons, or
of humbly born persons who become royal; as do the sacred
dances which in Indian villages are the culture of the illiterate;
not for economic, but for symbolic reasons. Yeats made of this
myth a poem whose images have a beguiling and deceptive lightness:

> If I make the lashes dark
> And the eyes more bright
> And the lips more scarlet
> And ask if all is right
> From mirror after mirror,
> No vanity's displayed,
> I'm looking for the face I had
> Before the world was made.

The woman who attempts to make herself more beautiful is an
imaginative artist seeking to make her actual appearance accord
with her (in the Platonic sense) real nature, to which her bodily
appearance is only a rough approximation. Demotic art ('paint
the warts') dwells on the blemishes which the eye sees; imaginative art reflects 'the true man', 'To which all lineaments tend and
seek with love and sympathy', as Blake said. Imaginative poetry
alone has a real function to perform; for the pseudo-arts of
realism perform no function beyond that of endlessly reporting
on the physical world; which quantitative science (whose proper
function it is) can do very much better. But true poetry has the
power of transforming consciousness itself by holding before us
icons, images of forms only partially and superficially realized in
'ordinary life'.

This, in part at least, is the immemorial truth which underlies
Keats's 'Beauty is truth, truth beauty'. The realists who hold the
contrary, that beauty is false because it does not correspond with
the imperfections of actuality, at once deprive poetry of any function whatsoever, and make of actuality a prison from which
there is no escape.

In a story by another precursor of social realism, Tolstoy,
there is a discernment of a kind of truth Flaubert's mirror cannot give. In *The Kreutzer Sonata* the hero, if hero he can be called,
is a sensual brute of an ordinary man, as intensely aware of all
to do with his own tortured animality as any modern could desire;
but this brute has an inexplicable – to himself inexplicable – love
of music; so unrelated is this love to all else in his life that the
beauty of Beethoven's music comes to him as a kind of torture,
outrage and fear:

That piece had a terrible effect on me: it was as if quite new feelings, new possibilities, of which I had till then been unaware, had
been revealed to me. 'That's how it is, not at all as I used to think
and live, but that way', something seemed to say within me. What
this new thing was that had been revealed to me I could not explain
to myself, but the consciousness of this new condition was very
joyous. All these same people, including my wife and him appeared
in a new light.

The human beast at that moment saw something by no means
reflected in the mirror of his outward life; and yet he knew it not
as less but as more true; 'not at all as I used to think and live'.
There is a truth, a reality, different from that of realism, which
the realist has recognized as more real. What had he seen? Plato
would say that the music had stirred in him a latent knowledge,
the anamnesis the soul has of an order inherent within it, a wholeness, a harmony to which the outer life is scarcely even an
approximation. If this order be real, then may we not call the
mundane reality less real – as the Platonic philosophers in fact
did, on the grounds that it is only a partial realization, a blurred
copy, a faint imprint. He had experienced beauty; and what he
saw he recognized as a harmony already and forever existing,
something he already possessed, but as lying away in the dark.
Plato and Plotinus would say that this experience was in no way
inexplicable; for this harmonious order is said to be an attribute,
a possession of the soul, and not at all alien to it. If this were not
so, the more perfect the beauty, the more foreign would it seem

to us; but the contrary of this is true – the greater the beauty, the more does it strike us not as strange but as deeply familiar; 'that's how it is'. Seen with the eyes of realism, that is not how it is at all; and in Tolstoy's terrible story, the glimpse of perfection was not sufficient to transform the man's life. His rejection of the music threw him back into the murderous fury in which his story reached its climax. Even so we may say that his momentary realization was a momentary self-knowledge; for, to quote Plotinus, 'we ourselves possess beauty when we are true to our own being; our ugliness is going over to another order'. Our deepest self-knowledge, that is to say, is a discovery of the beautiful. In self-ignorance we see the ugly, which is not a quality in itself but, precisely, the absence of quality, form, unity; or, as the philosophers say, reality. Of what use is Genet's *The Maids* or Wesker's *The Kitchen* to working girls? With the instinct of their sanity the Cinderellas prefer *Swan Lake*; as their young men, with the sense of the heroic still uncorrupted, prefer 'Westerns'. Their instinctive choice is not made from 'escapism' but is on the contrary a search for self-knowledge, the 'know thyself' of the Delphic Oracle. The Greek populace had Agamemnon and Achilles and the Elizabethan groundlings Shakespeare's long procession of kings; and in these the humanity they discovered was their own. Realism cannot show us what we are, but only our failures to become that to which the common man and the common woman inadequately, but continually, aspire and strive. The common people crave for the heroic and the beautiful; and when they cease to do so (under the influence of a nihilistic minority) can our civilization long survive? The ugly and the vulgar enable us not to feel, not to think, not to live; they save us from the anguish of living. Let us admit that our society as a whole has chosen death – death in small, painless doses. Fortunes are made by selling it.

The present decadence of the arts, and all the more or less ineffectual attempts to find other foundations upon which to rebuild them than those of tradition, arises quite simply from the disappearance of the idea of an intelligible world (to use Plato's phrase) a spiritual order, a world of the soul, whose existence is not that of the fleeting images of nature. Existentialism is a serious philosophic attempt to do away with the necessity for a distinction between existence and essence, body and soul, idea and embodiment. In France the necessity is at least recognized;

in England few trouble about such things, and our writers live, in matters of first principles, from hand to mouth; forgetting that even the aspect of the natural world and the quality of carnality itself depend upon what we believe to be the nature of these things.

Had Tolstoy's jealousy-tormented husband allowed the music to form him to its pattern, instead of rejecting it, as he did with his whole being, as an outrage, a violation of social decorum, he might have been saved. Tolstoy had understood, in a profound intuition, that music has a function, a transforming power. It exists to bring the human beast to anamnesis of another order which exists in him; knowledge of what was once called the soul; if we prefer now to call it the psyche, its reality remains the same. This use of poetry and the other arts has at this time been almost universally forgotten – as must be so if that other order is held to be non-existent. If there be no such function for them to perform I cannot see why anyone should trouble with the arts at all: as mere diversion, are they worth keeping alive? By reason of this transforming power their existence becomes not merely justified but indispensable to the civilizing process by which the human animal is transformed into something else; and what is man, if not the one creature in whom this possibility exists, upon whom this task falls?

Tolstoy's hero was a member of the old Russian aristocracy, a class by no means lacking in the means of living in comfort, luxury, affluence. These people had intelligence and feeling, and a terrifying insight into man's animal nature and the depths to which it may drag us down. What seems in the society Tolstoy describes to be lacking is precisely what is lacking in modern society: a culture adequate to its needs, of the kind which in some times and places has raised human societies as a whole to greater self-knowledge, a finer consciousness of what is in man. Italy has continued to produce, over many centuries (in painting and architecture especially, whose influence is enduring) a multitude of images, which in churches, cities and houses were continually before the eyes of people of all classes, and continue to this day to exert upon all who come into their presence, their transforming power. Edwin Muir, living in Rome, and finding himself everywhere surrounded by such images, found himself contrasting the Eternal City with Glasgow, where his youth had been spent. He was amazed to find everywhere emblems, icons of the divine mysteries; an environment created not only for the needs of the body, but above all for the needs of the soul. Do we not, in those cities where in architecture, sculpture and painting, the needs of the spirit are met, feel instantly at home, as if we could live there? And do we not, in such cities as Glasgow, or in the wastes of suburbia, seem as if exiles, living provisionally, but not as in our right place? Even when, in our modern cities and suburbs, the needs of the body are catered for, few are happy; for such an environment is intolerable, even to many who are unable to articulate the reasons for their profound unrest in the presence of the ugly – or to be more exact, in the absence of the beautiful. For, if Plotinus be right, 'the soul itself acts immediately, affirming the Beautiful where it finds something accordant with the ideal form within itself. . . . But let the soul fall in with the ugly and at once it shrinks within itself, denies the thing, turns away from it, not accordant, resenting it.' People may live a lifetime in beautiless cities, never losing the sense of exile, of alienation from something which they have never even known.

Yet no act of protest, or reiteration of the predicament as such, can give any release; for it does not provide the cure, but only describes the disease. Did not Dostoevsky say that our salvation can only be through the beautiful?

To the behaviourists, as to their predecessor Locke, nothing is in the mind which was not first in the senses, and consciousness is a mere *rasa tabula*, an empty recipient of impressions. For the Platonic philosophy, on the contrary, the soul is 'a plenitude of forms, an ever-written tablet, a vital intellectual energy'. The concept of the beautiful (from which it is inseparable) has for this philosophy a precise meaning, as what corresponds to an innate formal order. Whatever is congruent with the ground of our nature seems to us beautiful. The square, the circle, the laws of geometry and number are, in this sense, intrinsically satisfying to some sense of order which belongs to our nature. It is for this reason that Plato said that we learn by remembering; and shows us Socrates proving this by questioning an illiterate slave-boy in such a way that he 'saw' the solution of a problem of geometry; for the order of the soul, so understood, is not something 'personal' and 'subjective', but universal. Music is considered by the Platonic philosophers to be the highest of the arts because the nearest to the harmonious innate order of number, reflected in all the arts and in nature itself.

The order of which the arts have in the past been the expression does not cease to exist because it is no longer perceived; but
the arts, as these are practised and understood by a newly
literate, but still barbarous populace, are no longer its vehicle.
That works of poetry and the other arts which have survived
from more civilized times and places had intentions utterly different from those imputed to poets and artists in our own, has
been so largely forgotten that a book like Edgar Wind's *Pagan
Mysteries of the Renaissance* amazes us by its revelation of the intentions of the painters of pictures long familiar. Instead, the
arts have become the expression of the very incoherence and
ignorance from which they normally provide release. Some
would defend the modern movement on the grounds that the
task of the artist is to reflect any and every experience; an opinion
unimaginable in any culture which recognizes that not all experiences are of the same qualitative value. Tradition replies
that a true work of imagination reflects not the imperfect but
the perfect, not the disorder of failures and ignorance, but a perfection to which we are drawn; and if imperfection, only in the
context of such perfection, which alone gives meaning to the
process of becoming. When literature becomes merely a formulation of some state of ignorance or vulgarity, it is like a magnet
which has lost its power and become common iron like the rest.

Plotinus, more fully than Plato himself, has given expression
to the traditional philosophy of art. A statue, he said, is not
beautiful as stone; Phidias modelled his sculpture of Zeus not
upon things of sense but by 'apprehending what form Zeus must
take if he chose to become manifest to sight'. Blake had read
Plotinus on the Beautiful, and seems to be echoing his very
images when he answers those critics who objected to his representation of spiritual essences with real bodies that they 'would
do well to consider that the Venus, the Minerva, the Jupiter,
the Apollo, which they admire in Greek statues are all of them
representations of spiritual existences, of gods immortal to the
mortal and perishing organ of sight. And yet they are embodied
and organized in solid marble.' Plato, Plotinus and all who have
followed their doctrine have known that to copy from a mental
form, an idea, is to come nearer to perfection than to copy nature;
which is itself only a reflection, image or imprint of an anterior
pattern. The artist must look to the original, not to the copy.

This is not to say that nature is to be rejected in favour of abstract mental forms; for nature is itself informed by harmonious patternings of the same kind as the ideas of poet and artist. Since natural objects are themselves expressions of the formative principle, we must recognize that artists who work from nature, with knowledge of what these forms really are, give no bare reproduction of the thing seen, but go back to the principles from which nature itself derives. It is when the ideal forms of nature are themselves forgotten, and nature seen as mere opaque matter, that naturalism abandons the first principles of art. It is a paradox worth reflecting upon that in times and places where nature has been seen in terms of the traditional wisdom, depictions of bird, beast and flower and of the human body have been minute (though not necessarily in a visually literal way) in detail, impassioned and beautiful. In our own age, an exaltation of matter and a denial of spirit has led to a loss of the sense both of form and beauty in natural objects; a disintegration of form. Our modern realism no more refers to any principle of form than does its apparent opposite, abstract impressionism. It sees form and deformities alike, for without reference to any norm, the accidental and the malformation are just as 'true' as the ideal perfection – more so, it might be argued, because only these are to be found in the physical world. Even more is this so when man is depicted; if there is no innate moral perfection to which human conduct must tend and seek, all, again, is equal – the noble and the vile, the trivial and the significant; or rather all becomes trivial, and nothing significant, since there is no standard by which anything can be called worse or better. Blake warned us long ago of the formlessness which must inevitably result when instead of copying from the 'divine originals' artists copy accident and deformity, 'blots and blurs'. Then, he said, 'The line of the Almighty must be drawn again before man or beast can exist.'

Tolstoy's hero, listening to Beethoven's music, became dimly aware that the music meant something, represented some kind of knowledge which eluded him. 'That condition had a meaning for him [Beethoven] but for me – none at all. That is why music only agitates, doesn't lead to a conclusion.' The truth of course was that this man was too far off, too deeply sunk in sensuality to follow the music into, so to say, its own world; to such as him, beauty must perhaps always seem a kind of torture, forcing its demands beyond anything we can, in our low condition, answer to. I have often found myself wondering why the present age seems positively to shrink from beauty, to prefer the ugly, to feel safer, more at home with it; and I have come to realize that there is a reproach in the beautiful and the perfect; it passes its continual silent judgement and it requires perhaps a kind of courage to love what is perfect, since to do so is an implicit confession of our own imperfection. Can it be that the prevalence of the low and the sordid in contemporary writing is a kind of easy way, a form of sloth, an avoidance of that reproach which would call us, silently, to a self-perfection it would cost us too much to undertake? And yet it is in order to work upon us that transformation, that perfection, that works which embody the beautiful alone exist. That is their function, their justification in terms, one might almost say, of citizenship.

Strangest of all is the ease with which the vision is lost; consciousness contracts, we forget over and over again, until recollection is stirred by some icon of that beauty. Then we remember and wonder why we ever forgot. It is because of the continual downward drag of amnesia – for apathy and death are less exacting than life, they are the easy way of 'effortless barbarism' – that works of poetry and the other arts are necessary for our survival; survival, that is, as human beings; without, we tend to revert to what the Hindu philosophers called 'animal incarnations' – the *bête humaine*.

Indeed it may be said that it is because the beautiful is too troubling an experience to natural apathy that we avoid it; or one too painful to be endured in a world so out of tune with its order. It is certain that those who recollect most clearly the order of perfection find the life of the common world correspondingly painful, so far does it fall short. Yet, try as we may to come to terms with the ugly and the vulgar, they continue to shock, hurt and jar some intuitive sense of fitness of form and the truth of beauty. Images formless and deformed are continually being forced upon us, so that the shocks and 'kicks' which compel our attention, much as pain does, are even confused with the aesthetic experience itself; yet the formless and the deformed can only disintegrate and lacerate, whereas images of order unify and heal. There is implicit in any art which holds before us images of human perfection, the idea of perfectibility – again, a concept compatible only with a spiritual view of man.

The beautiful, then, is the active principle in any work of transforming power, summoning us to self-knowledge of the innate human norm to which we always tend, but from which we always deviate; and the greater the disparity between a sordid actuality, and the perfection of the beautiful, the greater, not the less, is the need for the 'truth' of beauty, to rectify and inform the formless reality – or unreality – of the everyday world. It is by images of perfection alone that poetry transforms consciousness. There are, among *avant-garde* writers, some who seem to use the ugly and the shocking in order to attract an attention to themselves which their work could not command on its merits. Plotinus also knew that sensations of the ugly and evil impress us more violently than those of what is agreeable; but they leave, he says, less mark; whereas sanity tranquilly present explains itself better; it takes first place, it is the natural thing, it belongs to our being; illness is alien, unnatural, and thus makes itself felt by its very incongruity. But what of our age in which the sick and the unnatural have become the norm?

In a normal society the soul finds everywhere in the arts, in myths, in religious symbols, in all that people make and use, images expressive of that order. Yeats saw in Byzantine civilization a nearly perfect expression of those ideal forms – a flowering of Plato's thought long after Athens. 'The painter, the mosaic worker, the worker in gold and silver, the illuminator of sacred books, were almost impersonal, almost perhaps without consciousness of individual design, absorbed in their subject-matter and that the vision of a whole people.' The work of many that seemed the work of one, that made building, picture, pattern, metal-work of rail or lamp, seem but a single image was, as he says, 'a proclamation of their invisible master', that most Platonic concept the Logos, 'the true man' or Imagination, according to Blake. Edwin Muir in his last series of lectures, *The Estate of Poetry*, spoke of our present world and its soul-destroying ills; but the most terrible, he said, is nothing which is there: it is, rather, what is lacking. We can no longer give a name to what we lack; it is precisely our forgetfulness, our amnesia, our want of orientation which ails us. Art is the normal environment of the soul, the normal means of anamnesis and orientation. Lacking this environment we starve in the midst of quantitative plenty. What is worse, we are everywhere invaded by images of a destructive – literally a soul-destroying – nature.

The ugly and the abnormal make a quick and easy impact upon attention, to which mass communication has accustomed us. But there is another influential minority who are no friends to the beautiful – those academic critics whose conceptual *apparatus criticus* the beautiful transcends and eludes. Such criticism is concerned with parts, the *ars poetica* with wholes which are more than the sum of parts, which on the contrary inform and determine the parts. The recognition of the beautiful is immediate and intuitive, but it is the response of a faculty higher than the discursive reason; with the Platonic *nous*, the higher reason, not with *dianoia* the *ratio*. But the *hybris* of those whose profession is discursive will never admit this, perhaps do not even know it, since the higher perceives the lower but the lower does not perceive the higher. The climate of critical opinion is indeed at this time increasingly plebeian and quantitative; for imperception may become articulate, may learn the terms of critical discourse, without ever discovering that those terms were never and never could have been the terms which enabled poet and artist to create those works on which they so complacently pronounce; to the satisfaction only of those (and these are inevitably a majority) who share their own limitations. They even appear to regard direct access to works of poetry as an infringement of their own territories (which some might say they have in any case usurped, as the rabble after the French Revolution parcelled out more concrete estates). The power to perceive the beautiful arises from a quality of consciousness: something for ever inaccessible to the *apparatus criticus*, which can be manipulated by persons who do not possess this quality at all. The cleansing of the doors of perception is a matter rather of culture than of education, and may be possessed by people in the academic sense unlearned; while it is possible to be a notorious critic and yet to be entirely without it.

We can learn about beauty only from beauty; and therefore Yeats called the sages of Byzantium (teachers of metaphysical and spiritual knowledge) and its artists, the singing-masters of the soul; for the school in which the soul must learn self-knowledge is not that of the conceptual critics but such works as awaken self-knowledge by Platonic recollection; and therefore works of art and not works of criticism; with the exception of the few such works as are themselves (like those of Ruskin or Pater or Proust) works of art.

> Nor is there singing-school but studying
> Monuments of its own magnificence. . . .

Like calls to like. At best scholarship, by placing in our hands knowledge which we should not otherwise possess, can fit us to read the works of the poets, to decipher what they have written. Yeats, a poet of this century, can no more be understood by those who do not possess the knowledge of the 'learned school' in which he himself studied, than can poets of other periods; and to such knowledge there is no critical short-cut: we have to acquire it, or remain in ignorance.

Yet the common people (within a traditional society, that is, in which illiterate men and women may possess, as even now in India, and perhaps still in Ireland, a culture) respond to the beautiful, which speaks to an intellectual order innate no less in the ignorant than in the learned. Indeed it is easier for those not educated at all to respond immediately to such forms than it is for those who are mis-educated; as all those are who are given false criteria. An aristocratic culture operates throughout society; and works made in knowledge communicate the quality of that knowledge (though not its learning) to 'the people'; and also to another group who may be called unlearned, to those in love; since these are (according to Plato's sense of the word love) oriented towards the beautiful as by a divine enchantment.

> Pythagoras planned it. Why did the people stare?
> His numbers, though they moved or seemed to move
> In marble or in bronze lacked character.
> But boys and girls, pale from the imagined loves
> Of solitary beds, knew what they were . . .

The mathematical proportions based upon Pythagorean number speak immediately to an innate sense of harmony; and Yeats goes on to consider those more mysterious ideas which evoke in the common man a response to conceptions of the heroic:

> When Pearse summoned Cuchulainn to his side
> What stalked through the Post Office? What intellect,
> What calculation, measurement, replied?

Painful as it may be to remember an order of perfection with which the common world is out of tune, it is even more painful not to remember – would indeed be spiritual death were it possible. We are haunted by the presence of an inaccessible knowledge, and by a sense as of estrangement from some place or state native to us; the Paradise of all mythologies, once and for ever known, but lost. Of this Paradise all are native, for it lies within ourselves, forgotten or half forgotten. Adam, according to the *Genesis* myth, fell into 'a deep sleep'. Plotinus describes mankind passing 'as it were from bed to bed, from sleep to sleep'. Plato tells in a fable that souls as they approach birth drink the forgetful waters of Lethe – matter. Some drink so deeply that they forget all they knew in eternity; some who drink less deeply have partial remembrance.

> The Soul that rises with us, our life's Star
> Hath elsewhere had its setting,
> And cometh from afar:
> Not in entire forgetfulness

– so Wordsworth paraphrases Plotinus. Or as Yeats wrote, those born

> must sleep, shriek, struggle to escape
> As recollection or the drug decide.

Jung is but returning to tradition in holding that beyond and behind our personal memories there lies a *terra incognita* which we have perhaps known, as Plato taught, in some former state; or which we have never known, but which, when we bring it to consciousness, has the familiarity (it being a part of ourselves) of something recollected. To speak of remembering (anamnesis) is something more than a figure of speech; superstructures of theology have been erected upon what remains, whether or not we accept the Orphic or the Christian theology, empirical fact. Poetry and the other arts exist in order to hold before us images which have the power to awaken recollection, anamnesis, of that virgin land, our native country because it is the ground of the psyche itself. That is why it comes to us as something deeply familiar. It is with no sense of surprise, no shock of strangeness that we listen to a fugue by Bach or follow with our eyes the meeting and flowing of Gothic arches, or attend to those profound realizations of *King Lear*, or read Milton's or Dante's descriptions of Paradise. The greatest art seems always like our own thoughts made conscious. We recognize in some Chinese or Italian landscape, in a Samuel Palmer or a Claude, in Shelley's 'little lawny islet, with anemone and violet like mosaic paven', or in the tapestries of *La Dame à la Licorne* a world we seem always and for ever to have known. To experience such art is, as when we contemplate the beauty of a Botticelli face, a figure drawn by Giotto, a homecoming, though the way from this world to that is long and we may well fear the journey.

M

To transmit, to raise to consciousness this hidden order which we call 'the beautiful' the arts have traditionally existed. Yeats indicted the modern movement in words both contemptuous and exact:

> Scorn the sort now growing up
> All out of shape from toe to top;
> Their unremembering hearts and heads
> Baseborn products of base beds.

Baseborn and unremembering: to be base-born is to be earth-born, the *bête humaine*.

'The sort now growing up' have not forgotten what they have learned in their text-books; they remember events of the physical order to the last sordid detail. What Yeats declares they do not remember is the order of beauty and wisdom, and the orientation of all things towards perfection. On Plotinus, 'beds' they are sunk in Blake's 'deadly sleep'. Lacking access to the ordering principle their works are 'all out of shape', and covered with warts. Art becomes formless when it becomes soulless. The Platonists spoke of the 'souls' of stones, plants and animals; the 'soul' of a crystal is the form – the mathematical formula – of the crystal; the soul of the plant, more complex, is the tendency towards a certain form of which time as well as space is a dimension. Soul, far from being a vague concept was, on the contrary, the principle of form and the formative principle; which in man is the imagination. According to Coomaraswamy 'Art is expression *informed* by ideal beauty'; 'My shaping spirit of imagination,' Coleridge wrote; and Yeats indicts the modern movement for its 'spawning *formless* fury' – the quantitative proliferation of anything and everything in the absence of a controlling formal principle; a kind of cultural cancer.

Spenser beautifully defines, in what amounts almost to a paraphrase of the Platonic doctrine, the poet's philosophy of the beautiful:

> What time this world's great workmaster did cast
>   To make all things, such as we now behold,
> It seems that he before his eyes had placed
>   A goodly pattern, to whose perfect mould
>   He fashioned them as comely as he could;
>   That now so fair and seemly they appear,
>   As nought may be amended anywhere.

That wondrous pattern, wheresoe'er it be,
    Whether in earth laid up in secret store,
Or else in heaven, that no man may it see
    With sinful eyes, for fear it to deflower,
    Is perfect Beauty, which all men adore.
        Whose face and feature doth so much excel
        All mortal sense, that none the same may tell.

Thereof as every earthly thing partakes,
    Or more or less by influence devine,
So it more fair accordingly it makes,
    And the gross matter of this earthly mine,
    Which closeth it, thereafter doth refine,
        Doing away the dross which dims the light
        Of that fair beam, which therein is empight.

The same philosophy runs through Shakespeare; but he, enchanted, like Plato's lovers, by a particular beauty, as it were
plays with the doctrine, pretending that the mortal exemplar is
really the heavenly original; by this inversion he pours out at the
feet of the one beloved all the riches of the immortal treasuries:

Describe Adonis and the counterfeit
Is poorly imitated after you;
On Helen's cheek all art of beauty set,
And you in Grecian times are painted new:
Speak of the spring and foison of the year,
The one doth shadow of your beauty show,
The other as your bounty doth appear;
And you in every blessed shape we know.

Shakespeare could not have written so if these originals had not,
for him, kept their place of honour in the order of perfect forms;
only because these divine originals may be invoked can he delight
in the play of hyperbole in praise of the beloved.

Spenser, Shakespeare, Milton, Herbert, Blake, Vaughan,
Coleridge, Keats, Shelley, Yeats, all these poets are strung upon
a single thread, all echo one another and the doctrine of poetry
in all is the same; so that examples might be multiplied endlessly,
as if a single mind spoke in all. Shelley in 'The Sensitive Plant'
describes the presence of beauty in this world in the form of an
allegory, of a lady who tends a garden, bringing to their perfection all its flowers; the theme is an old one – Venus in Spenser's
Garden of Adonis is the same figure, the 'goddess nature'. When
Shelley's divine lady dies, the garden decays, and weeds, rank-

ness and death alone are left. Yet the truth is the reverse of that which appears; the garden is

> this life
> Of error, ignorance, and strife
> Where nothing is, but all things seem

but truly understood

> That garden sweet, that Lady fair
> And all sweet shapes and odours there
> In truth have never passed away:
> 'Tis we, 'tis ours, are changed; not they.
> For love, and beauty, and delight
> There is no death nor change; their might
> Exceeds our organs, which endure
> No light, being themselves obscure.

Since the beautiful is an order of wholes, and of wholeness, a mark of its informing presence is the symmetry and pattern of verse. It is impossible to speak of beauty without speaking of form. Beauty is a unity, a unification; and lyric form, as all poets know, comes from something 'given', precisely when imaginative inspiration is strongest. Such forms can, of course, be imitated, but that is quite another matter; although it may be that such dead imitations for a time brought lyric form into disfavour. However, a deeper reason for the disappearance of lyric form between the two wars, and the use of a disjointed and broken 'free verse' had probably much more to do with precisely that loss of access to the 'other' mind which both occasioned and characterized the mood of 'the world of entre deux guerres', as Eliot himself called it. It is wholly consistent with his Platonic view of poetry that Yeats should adhere to formal verse; and with the nature of life that lyricism should have risen up with a rush in the poetry of Dylan Thomas. Contemporary critics have little to say of lyric form, just because it is impossible to discourse about it, to analyse its whole into parts. Is not Yeats the greatest poet of his time because, together with the learning of the imagination he possessed this natural gift, which no learning can command? James Joyce, with his natural ear for verbal music singled out as supremely beautiful the poem which begins

> Who will go ride with Fergus now,
> And pierce the deep wood's woven shade,
> And dance upon the level shore?

> Young man, lift up your russet brow,
> And lift your tender eyelids, maid,
> And brood on hopes and fear no more.

Paraphrased into discursive terms there is nothing there at all, nor in the verse that follows; which haunts like a phrase of music, and, like music, communicates a meaning and a knowledge not of fact but of quality. Why is it that those very poets who held to the Platonic doctrine can write perfect lyrics, whereas those who do not can produce only imitations of such forms, working by rules of prosody which are themselves merely deduced from spontaneous rhapsodic speech? Lyric form is itself the supreme embodiment of archetypal order, the nearest to music and number; it is beauty itself informing words in themselves ordinary; and it cannot, as Plato wrote in the *Ion*, be achieved by the poet writing from his mundane consciousness, but only in that divine madness in which he is possessed by the 'other' mind.

AE (George Russell) objected to the unfitness of marrying such forms to prosaic content, instancing Robert Graves, who with his great talent has no difficulty in producing any verse-form he likes. He instances a letter supposedly from a British officer, written in iambics; and goes on to say

the heart of love, in imagination, in meditation mounts at times to an ecstasy where its being becomes musical . . . the pattern of sound, the recurrent beat of verse echo that inner music. In all languages where poetry has been written there has been pattern, rhythm, echo, measure or recurrent beat, and what would be unreal if it was merely speech of lip or brain becomes most sincere when we feel it of intense spiritual or emotional life. We need not discuss the psychology of this, whether when the inner nature subdues the outer nature, whenever flesh is melted into soul, the soul imposes upon the body some image or echo of itself, as a ray of the logos, of the Mind which made music and harmony in the universe. We need not enter upon difficult or unprovable speculation. It is certain that metrics as a mode of speech correspond to something in the soul. But if we say this we are impelled to deny the fitness of verse as utterance of any feeling, imagination, or reverie which has not originated in the magic fountain.

1966

10

ST. JOHN PERSE, POET OF THE MARVELLOUS

In conversation the author of the poems published under the pseudonym St. John Perse once said to me what a pity it was that, whereas up to the beginning of the last war English and French poets knew one another's work as a matter of course, this was no longer so. The context of St. John Perse's poetry is by no means limited by the language in which he writes. His earliest master was Conrad, whom as a young man he knew intimately, and who introduced him also to W. H. Hudson and his writings; one of his earliest poems ('*Images à Crusoe*') is an evocation of Defoe's hero by a poet whose boyhood was lived in the tropical archipelago of the Antilles. He was associated, in the period between the two world wars, with the American-born Duchess of Sermoneta, Marguerite Caetáni (then Princess Bassiano), in the editing of the magazine *Commerce*; as was also Paul Valery. His latest – and finest – work has been written in America, in whose natural features and majestic scale he has found the correspondence of his characteristic themes. Alexis St. Léger Léger, one-time Permanent Secretary of the French Foreign Office, has lived in the United States ever since the destruction of the Third Republic; at which time he lost, with everything else he then possessed (including the manuscripts of several unpublished poems), his French citizenship. He has now once again a house in France, but (though no longer as an exile) continues to reside in America, where his work is known, and better understood by poets of the New World and the heirs of Whitman, than it is in England.

Like most of my generation I read *Anabase* because it was translated by T. S. Eliot, in 1930. Even in this early poem (first published in 1924) and indeed in the earlier *Eloges*, his inimitable style ('Innumerable the image, and the metre prodigal') was already formed. But I remember being puzzled where to fit this poet into the picture my generation was at that time building up of what modern poetry was and should be. Surrealism was easy to understand, being little more than *avant-gardism* as such; Joyce and Proust had obvious contemporary points of reference, but its very originality made the *Anabase* seem the more strange. Its theme – the setting-out of a nomadic prince on an expedition of conquest – was in no obvious way related to contemporary experience, even though the images (exotic in the style of Gauguin) were, as such, pleasurable. The great sweep of the rhythm had no obvious similarity (other than not being confined within any traditional metrical form) with the free verse of Pound or Eliot; it is in fact nearer to Claudel. It was not clear what affinity such poetry had with Eliot's own theory and practice as a poet; nor do I even now know the answer to that question.

Twenty years were to pass between the first publication of *Anabase* and the appearance of *Exil, Poème à l'Etrangère, Pluies* and *Neiges* in 1942. These poems were written in the United States, and first published in Buenos Aires, and in France on the presses of the Resistance, without the name of the author. During the intervening years the diplomat had kept 'his brother the poet' in abeyance. We shall never know (unless those lost manuscripts should be recovered) how St. John Perse developed from the author of the romantic epic *Anabase* into the poet of *Exil* and that greater poem of exile, *Vents*, written in the United States and published in 1946. With these poems, the poet and the times moved into conjunction; what had formerly been a personal voice became a voice of the age. If *Vents* is his greatest poem this is surely so in part because the vision of these 'very great winds over all the faces of this world',[1] whose storm tore down the edifice of European civilization and carried the poet into the New World was experienced so immediately by 'his brother the prince', Alexis Léger; as Dante, Milton, Byron and Yeats, whether as rulers or as exiles, played their part in and shared the suffering of their cities. No more than these is he a political poet; but like them political concern and knowledge is part of the structure of his thought, giving authority to his prophetic speech. There is no longer, in 1945, any question of how St. John Perse's poetry relates to the contemporary experience. The migrant tribe is ourselves, the country we must leave, our own past, and Western civilization; whether as conquerors or

---

[1] '. . . *de très grands vents sur toutes faces de ce monde*'. (*Vents*, I.)

exiles – and there is little difference – we must set forth again into that future open alike to all. 'All to be done again. All to be told again. And the scything glance to be swept across all man's heritage.'[1] The state of exile, in many cases physical, but above all spiritual exile, is the typical condition of poet and prince alike in the new dark age of barbarism and the reversal of the natural hierarchies with all their values; the state to be explored.

Claudel, writing of *Vents*, pointed out that whereas the *Odyssey* is an epic of home-coming, *Vents*, an epic description of the fall of the civilization whose beginnings Homer scarcely saw, is a poem of setting-out; as that other epic, *Finnegans Wake*, ends, like the *Götterdämmerung*, with a purification by re-immersion in the source. But for St. John Perse, this purification, re-immersion and setting-out is not cyclic, but at every moment to be enacted as life moves always into its future.

He chooses for his symbols those freely-moving elements which traverse and unite all times and spaces – seas, winds, birds, the perpetual setting-out of migrant swarms, flocks, human tribes; an 'open' poetry in which all spaces and times co-exist in a single present. No theme could be more true to one of the as yet unformulated experiences of this time. The scope of his poetry is coterminous with the earth in its single indivisible space-time.

The English reader may be alarmed by the initial difficulty of a poetry whose vocabulary is full of unfamiliar words, many of them not to be found in a dictionary, which in any case tells us little. The writings of Darwin, the paintings of Audubon, or a text-book on boat-building could tell us more, an acquaintance with the things themselves more still. Knowing that T. S. Eliot was interested in words and read largely in the *Oxford English Dictionary*, I asked if this was a meeting-point between the poet and his translator. He said this was not so; for Eliot's interest in words was literary and philological, whereas his own vocabulary comes from his knowledge of many skills, his travels in many places, his knowledge of plants and their products and uses, the flora and fauna of many coasts, the ethnography of outer Mongolia; of whatever mankind has made or valued, objects rather than myths, all that can be handled rather than what has been thought. His interests are not primarily literary, still less academic. A man of wide experience, he is able to create those astonishing syntheses and analogies which could occur only to a

[1] '*Tout à reprendre. Tout à redire. Et la faux du regard sur tout l'avoir menée!*' (*Vents*, I, 4.)

man of trained sensibility and many kinds of exact knowledge. Only if 'exotic' and 'tropical' are synonymous can even his early imagery be so described; but in so far as the word implies a certain artificiality (as in Beardsley) this is not so. Those immense random samples of the wonders of the world ('*La terre enfante des merveilles*'), miraculous drafts from that thalassic fecundity are all taken from the real, and the accessible. Modern mankind inhabits, as did no former generation, the earth as a whole, whose flora and fauna with all the regions they inhabit, have for the first time become a book open to all.

'All the land of trees, out there, its background of black vines, like a Bible of shadow and freshness in the unrolling of this world's most beautiful texts'; 'The land in its long lines, on its longest strophes, running, from sea to sea, to loftiest scriptures'; 'And this great winter prose that is, to the Old World's flocks, the wolf-lore of the New World'; 'Those flights of insects going off in clouds to lose themselves at sea, like fragments of sacred texts, like the tatters of errant prophecies and the recitations of genealogists and psalmists'.[1]

Our generation has become intellectually, but not imaginatively, habituated to the retrospect of natural evolution, to the new spacious simultaneity of the relativity of time and place. In reading the poetry of St. John Perse we experience this new freedom, familiar to the scientist, which poetry has been slow to enter. Plato called the world a happy and immortal animal, one immortal joy sweeping through its myriads of component lives; and all Perse's poems are (as one is entitled) praises, *éloges*, of this 'moving image of eternity'. His prodigality of image both illustrates and suggests the infinitely various and inexhaustible fecundity of one life in all.

When we come to examine those 'marvels' which are ever before the eyes of the poet, we recognize, with some astonishment, that they are such as are everywhere present but generally unheeded; the moon 'thin as the ergot on a white rose' (the English translator – Hugh Chisholm – has missed the beauty of this

---

[1] '*Toute la terre aux arbres, par là-bas, sur fond de vignes noires, comme une Bible d'ombre et de fraîcheur dans le déroulement des plus beaux textes de ce monde*'; '*Et la terre à longs traits, sur ses plus longues laisses, courant, de mer à mer, à de plus hautes écritures*'; '*Et ces grandes proses hivernales, qui sont aux laines du Vieux Monde la louveterie du Nouveau Monde*'; '*Ces vols d'insectes par nuées qui s'en allaient se perdre au large comme des morceaux de textes saints, comme des lambeaux de prophéties errantes et des récitations de généalogistes, de psalmistes*'. (*Vents*, II, 1–4.)

comparison of the misty moon with the familiar fungoid blight
to which white roses are particularly subject); or, from one of his
earliest poems, '*Images à Crusoe*', 'Hear the hollow creatures
rattling in their shells – Against a bit of green sky a sudden puff
of smoke is the tangled flight of mosquitoes . . . and other gentle
creatures, listening to the evening, sing a song purer than their
announcing of the rains: It is the swallowing of two pearls
swelling their yellow gullets.'[1] You can hear and see the like on
any shore or by any pond where the frogs make their continuous
music. The exotic strangeness of some images (the 'two pearls' in
the frog's gullet, or 'Anhinga, the bird, fabled water-turkey,
whose existence is no fable . . . it is enough for me that he lives')[2]
is diffused upon all, reminding us that common and rare alike
participate in the same marvel of existence, the *magia*. This world
which seems remote and unreal to poets and their readers is one
in which any naturalist would feel at home; the world of the
scientists which often seems infinitely more poetic than the dull
round of poets and their readers, who notice, as a rule, very little,
and have lost the habit of regarding knowledge of many kinds –
or even of any kind – as the material of poetry.

At my first meeting with the poet, I listened with enchantment while he spoke of the wildest shores and deserts of the world
(his conversation is like his poems, rich in marvels) and I asked
if living in Georgetown he did not miss such things. He pointed
to the sky where two vultures were wheeling; spoke of W. H.
Hudson who had studied dispersal of tropical plants and insects
brought ashore at English sea-ports, and those fungi which thrive
on the paste used for bill-sticking; for St. John Perse the great
cities are themselves only another wave-crest raised by the ocean
of inexhaustible life. The 'marvels', purified from all commonplace associations and the unreal values utility assigns are, in his
poetry, revealed in their absolute nature.

If at first sight the vocabulary of St. John Perse seems difficult,
his themes exotic, there is an underlying simplicity about this
poetry of 'the many', 'the ten-thousand creatures'. Its amplitude
is tremendous but it is not as Joyce, semantically, or, as Eliot, in

---

[1] '*Entends claquer les bêtes creuses dans leurs coques – Il y a sur un morceau de ciel vert une
fumee hative qui est le vol emmêlé des moustiques. . . . Et d'autres bêtes qui sont douces,
attentives au soir, chantent un chant plus pur que l'annonce des pluies: c'est la déglutition de
deux perles gonflant leur gosier jaune*'. (*Eloges – La Ville.*)

[2] '*Et l'Oiseau Anhinga, la dinde d'eau des fables, dont l'existence n'est point fable . . .
et c'est assez pour moi qu'il vive –*' (*Vents*, II, 4.)

historical and literary allusiveness, or, as Yeats, in metaphysical and mythological import, complex poetry at all. That may well be part of its difficulty for readers more attuned (since Empson taught a generation to look for such complexities) to a trivial complexity than to a simple grandeur. It is 'nature-poetry'; but upon a scale which is to the the nature-poetry of the post-Wordsworthians as the ocean to a village pond.

In one of his very few prose statements the poet defined certain attributes of poetry which are presumably those he would wish us to find in his own work.[1] Poetry and science, he said, are alike ways of exploring an 'original night' in itself unknowable;

if poetry is not itself, as some have claimed, 'reality absolute', it is poetry which shows the strongest passion for, and the keenest apprehension of it, to that extreme limit of complicity where reality seems to shape itself within the poem.

By means of analogical and symbolic thinking, by means of the far-reaching light of the mediating image and its play of correspondences, by way of a thousand chains of reactions and unusual associations, by virtue also of a language through which is transmitted the very rhythm of Being, the poet clothes himself in a surreality to which the scientist cannot aspire. Is there, for man, any dialectic more compelling, or capable of engaging him more fully? When the philosophers themselves abandon the threshold of the metaphysical, it falls to the poet to take the place of the metaphysician; and at such times it is poetry and not philosophy which is revealed as the true 'daughter of wonder', to use the phrase of the ancient philosopher who most mistrusted her.[2]

Claudel wrote of the eyes of the poet as 'two round holes which I am tempted to refer to as magnets'.[3] My own first impression

---

[1] *Poesie* (Speech of acceptance upon the award of the Nobel Prize for Literature delivered in Stockholm, 10 December 1960).

[2] *Car si la poésie n'est pas, comme on l'a dit, 'le réel absolu', elle en est bien la plus proche convoitise et la plus proche appréhension, à cette limite extrême de complicité où le réel dans le poème semble s'informer lui-même.*

Par la pensée analogique et symbolique, par l'illumination lointaine de l'image médiatrice, et par le jeu de ses correspondances, sur milles chaînes de réactions et d'associations étrangères, par la grâce enfin d'un langage où se transmet le mouvement même de l'Etre, le poète s'investit d'une surréalité qui ne peut être celle de la science. Est-il chez l'homme plus saisissante dialectique et qui de l'homme engage plus? Lorsque les philosophes eux-mêmes desertent le seuil métaphysique, il advient au poète de relever là le métaphysicien; et c'est la poésie alors, non la philosophie, qui se révèle la vraie 'fille de l'étonnement', selon l'expression du philosophe antique à qui elle fut le plus suspecte.

[3] *Un Poème de Saint-John Perse*, in the *Revue de Paris*, November 1949; and *The Hudson Review*, 1951, translated by Hugh Chisholm.

of the poet, whose appearance for the rest is correct and somewhat retiring – was of those eyes, as of a man enchanted by what
he contemplates. St. John Perse's poetry has been described (by
Gaëtan Picon) as 'a magic positivism and pragmatism'. It is true
that a materialist might (disregarding his own confessed concern
with the metaphysical) so read it; but his 'marvels' are more akin
to *maya* than to matter, and suggest his friend Conrad's 'a man
that is born falls into a dream like a man who falls into the sea';
or (from the preface to *The Shadow Line*)

> All my moral and intellectual being is punctuated by an invisible
> conviction that whatever falls under the dominion of our senses must
> be in nature and, however exceptional, cannot differ in its essence
> from all the other effects of the visible and tangible world of which
> we are a self-conscious part. The world of the living contains enough
> marvels and mysteries acting upon our emotions and intelligence in
> ways so inexplicable that it would almost justify the conception of
> life as an enchanted state.

For St. John Perse it is true, as Blake claimed for himself, that
'I see everything I paint In This World'. Blake also said that 'to
the Eyes of the Man of Imagination, Nature is Imagination
itself'; and that the world perceived by the senses is the fourth
region of consciousness, externalized by the illusory philosophy
of materialism, 'although it appears without, it is within, in
your imagination'. In the poetry of Perse, the sensible world is
restored as a region of the imagination; for the content of his
imagination is 'nature' itself.

The unbounded nature of the poet's theme, free in time as it
is uncircumscribed by space, determines the prodigality of his
metre. Accustomed as we are to minimal vision, our attention
solicited by, and for, the pathological, the criminal, the immature
the uneducated, the ignorant, and the unskilled of all sorts
presenting the articulations of ignorance as communications
of knowledge and achievements of art, we have all but lost the
capacity for the total response his poetry demands. The 'self-
expression' of the individual (always more or less handicapped
in one or more of the above ways) has no place in his art. Claudel
called him 'a Mont St. Michel immensely accentuated in an
ebbing tide'; and if this mountain is generally unnoticed in post-
war England this may well be because, by standards designed
for measuring mole-hills, mountains are unperceived. Yet his

unbounded vision of 'the visible and tangible world of which we are a self-conscious part' is a liberation offered to whoever is willing to entrust himself to the great open sea (*'le mouvement même de l'Etre'*) of St. John Perse's poetry.

As against the continuous and relentless attrition, the dwindling of knowledge, the coarsening of sensibility, the abdication in thought, feeling and conduct of even the conception of the best, tacitly demanded and too often accorded in deference to the all-too-common common man, he summons to an expansion of consciousness, to a total realization of being. He speaks as the 'free man of high caste', reminding those who prefer to forget how great are the demands made by the aristocratic view of man, which alone protects and fosters the highest human potentialities: knowledge, and the freedom to translate knowledge and imagination into action (the prince) and into art (the poet, who is 'brother' to the prince). For Perse, as for Plato, and Manu, the superiority of the 'man of high caste' lies not in his status but in his quality of being; his superior knowledge and freedom of action whether as acknowledged leader, or as exile from a fallen civilization, 'the superior man' remains such by virtue of what he is. The prince-poet has given himself totally to the fullest attainable human experience by accepting those hard terms upon which alone freedom of act and thought are given. We are again reminded of Conrad, whose heroes also were free men of high caste, and of his phrase about 'the unknown disciplines of the self-imposed task'. Sex and the dead, Yeats somewhere said, are the only matters serious enough to angage the thoughts of an ageing poet; and erotic love and death are the frontiers which alone bound the world of St. John Perse's prince-poet. Mortal, we are possessed by, but cannot possess, the immortal life which the sexual mystery confers, and death takes away; no other limitations can take away the freedom of act and thought of whoever fears neither the loss of life nor of possessions. Courage, magnanimity, and knowledge – the aristocratic virtues – are the fruits of this proud detachment. The plebeian whine comes from those (of whatever social class, since caste and class are not coterminous) who have not looked at life and death. The experience of immortality is lost precisely when we seek to bind it to our transient selves. *'Il faut que vous mettez la tête dans la gueule du lion'* was the memorable advice the poet once gave me; for such is the condition accorded by reality itself, that lion's-mouth ever open before us.

One same wave throughout the world, one same wave since Troy
Rolls its haunch towards us. On a far-off open sea this gust was long
ago impressed.[1]

The sea, ancient and universal symbol of material flux, impressed by the 'breath of life' in the beginning is an image from
Genesis acceptable alike to Platonist and evolutionist.

With the thought of Teilhard de Chardin M. Léger admitted
a certain affinity, at the same time denying indebtedness and
withholding that kind and degree of admiration for the Jesuit to
be found in 'certain Paris salons'. Such ideas, he said, had long
been in the air. Yet both are discernibly of the same generation,
and the vision common to both lends to the modern experience
of nature an amplitude, spaciousness and purity to be found in
no living or recent English writer known to me. (It is characteristic that after disclaiming any indebtedness to Teilhard he
added: 'But for one thing I admire him: his Order offered him
freedom from his vows of obedience, in all honour; and he
refused.' The admiration of the poet, like the action of the
Jesuit, was that of the 'free man of high caste'.)

'One law of harmony governs the whole world of things.' The
amplitude of that harmony, of the free-flowing 'wave throughout the world' characterizes the cadences of the verse of St. John
Perse; for verse it is (so he insists) though of very long lines, and
in no way to be confused with prose-poetry; or, in England, with
with the cadenced poetic prose of David Jones. (Readers of
Proust will remember that the two maids at Balbec were in-
credulous when Marcel, reading *Éloges*, told them that this was
'poetry'.) It is difficult to attune a foreign ear, not to the sweep of
the larger pattern, but to the very subtle internal cross-patterns,
again like waves, whose regularity of rhythm breaks down into
such variety of rhythm, assonance, even internal rhyme. The
ruling pattern is liturgical, with returning phrases which, as in
an Introit psalm, define and continually re-affirm the theme.

One same wave throughout the world, one same wave reaching to
us, in the very great distance of the world and of its age . . . and such
a surge, from all sides, that rises and finds its way up into us.[2]

---

[1] *Une même vague par le monde, une même vague depuis Troie/Roule sa hanche jusqu'à
nous. Au très grand large loin de nous fut imprimé jadis ce souffle. (Amers, IX, 1.)*

[2] *Une même vague par le monde, une même vague jusqu'à nous, au très lointain du monde
et de son âge. . . . Et tant de houle, et de partout, qui monte et fraye jusqu'en nous. (Amers,
IX, 3.)*

One same wave throughout the world, one same wave and course. . . . Narrow the measure, narrow the caesura, which breaks the woman's body at the middle like an ancient metre. . . .[1]

One same wave throughout the world, one same wave among us, raising, rolling the hydra enamoured of its force. . . . And from the divine heel, that very strong pulsation, which rules everywhere. . . . Love and the sea of the same bed, love and the sea in the same bed. . . .[2]

One same wave throughout the world, one same wave throughout the city. . . . Lovers, the sea follows us! Death is not! The gods hail us in the port. . . .[3]

In *Vents* (the 'very great winds over all the faces of this world' . . . 'over all the trails of this world'), recurring themes are 'Let us be gone! be gone! Cry of the living' and 'of the Prodigal'; 'favoured by the favourable dream'; 'Ea, god of the abyss'; 'oh you whom the storm refreshes'[4] (St. John Perse makes ridiculous the timid fear of the orator's vocative).

No two poems are alike, nor their imagery interchangeable. A superficial reader of Perse will be impressed by the consistency of his inimitable style, his 'breath', but a closer reading reveals the architectural unity of theme, imagery and even metre within each.

Concluding his analysis of *Vents*, Claudel (after quoting long sections of particularly magnificent evocations of that spacious cosmology of Perse's world) exclaims, 'We are a long way from Marcel Proust'. Guadeloupe with its swarms of green insects and boats with white sails on tropical seas may be a long way from Combray with its lilacs and its hawthorn, the nomadic horde and the anonymous exile from the Boulevard St. Germain. St. John Perse is himself by no means a Proustian; yet ceitain themes belong to the period to which both have given expression. Both are impressionists imaginatively re-creating the 'minute

---

[1] *Une même vague par le monde, une même vague notre course.* . . . *Étroite la mesure, étroite la césure, qui rompt en son milieu le corps de femme comme le mètre antique.* . . . (*Amers*, IX, 3.)

[2] '*Une même vague par le monde, une même vague parmi nous, haussant, roulant l'hydre amoureuse de sa force.* . . . *Et du talon divin, cette pulsation très forte, et qui tout gagne.* . . . *Amour et mer de même lit, amour et mer au même lit.* . . .' (*Amers*, IX, 6.)

[3] '. . . *Une même vague par le monde, une même vague par la Ville.* . . . *Amants, la mer nous suit! La mort n'est point! Les dieux nous hèlent à l'escale.* . . . (*Amers*, IX, 7.)

[4] '. . . *très grands vents sur toutes faces de ce monde*' . . . '*sur toutes pistes de ce monde*'. '*S'en aller! S'en aller! Parole de vivant!*' and '*Parole de Prodigue; Eâ, dieu de l'ambîme*'; *Et le poète aussi est avec nous*'; '*O vous, que refraîchit l'orage*'.

particulars' of the sensible world; above all both are concerned with palingenesis, the restoration of all things to their primal perfection, the state of Paradise: Proust by the emancipation of memory from the bondage of time; St. John Perse by the freedom and simultaneity of all existence within the single Now of 'nature'. For Proust, the element in which all is freed from time is mind itself, the only paradise the paradise we have lost, for only when twice-born in memory do things enter upon this timeless and immortal contemporaneity. For St. John Perse all in nature is immortal and contemporaneous in so far as the many participate in the one. Like Proust too the poet places the supreme value not in the qualities of things but in their mere existence. In a passage in *Jean Sauteuil* (a hundred others may be found, but I happened to be reading the lesser book) the narrator, sitting in the kitchen of the family house at Etreuilles (Combray) is speechlessly happy as the cook stirs her pans on the open fire and takes his damp shoes to dry them:

> At such moments the sound of the cook's voice, saying 'I should just think those shoes of yours *are* wet!' is pleasant in your ears, because it is something that *exists*, as, too, the sight of the old chemist standing by his window, absorbed in the concoction of some mixture and brightly illumined by the lamp, is also full of charm because he *is*.[1]

If this be existentialism both Proust and Perse are existentialists in the existential not in the theoretical sense: for both the marvel of '*les merveilles*' is that *they are*.

But if Claudel's phrase is intended to praise the poet at the expense of the novelist, admirers of both may well see in the passage quoted an element entirely absent from the writings of St. John Perse – the human as such. The poet stops short, in his account of man, precisely with what is (in terms of all the higher religions) precisely human in man, his individual being. The gods whom he invokes are the old pantheistic gods: '*Eâ, dieu de l'abîme*'; '*mer de Baal, mer de Mammon*'; Dionysus with the rigging of his ship entwined with vines; the many-armed, skull-adorned fertility goddess of southern India. Nor does he shrink from those more barbaric Mexican deities to whom blood sacrifice was

---

[1] *Dans ces moments le bruit de la voix de la cuisinière disant: 'Ce qu'elles étaint mouillées, tout de même, vos chaussures', vous impressione agréablement parce que le bruit de voix c'est une chose qui est, comme par la fenêtre le vieux pharmacien absorbé dans un mélange et vivement éclairé par la lampe vous charme aussi parce qu'il est. (Jean Sauteuil, 1, p. 186)*

made, from a sense (so I remember the poet saying) of the inexhaustible abundance of life. Some might see in this re-immersion of man in the pre-human a post-Christian vision (if we may
so describe a mode of apprehending life which Teilhard's Alpha
and Omega perhaps insufficiently consecrate) essentially nihilistic. Upon the charge of nihilism this most life-praising of poetry
must be acquitted; even though (as Edwin Muir said also of
D. H. Lawrence) the 'life' he praises is not human life as such.
It is, however, a 'divine' life, not some mechanistic nihil. But
the creator of the Baron de Charlus is within the Christian tradition, the poet of *Amers* outside it; his world is pre-human.

Erotic love (and *Amers* is the most splendid poem known to me
upon that theme) celebrates the re-immersion of man and
woman, in the act of love, in the 'one same wave' of the immortal
and indivisible life of the cosmos: 'In the divine promiscuity and
man's depravation in the gods . . .'[1] who here represents the
immortal cosmic life. For the poet man is but the crest of the
advancing wave of nature; the life and the joy in which he participates is impersonal: 'In the destructive element, immerse' –
such, following Conrad (whose Stein was quoting his Goethe) is
the invitation of his poetry.

Individual woman is but an aspect of that 'universal bride' the
fecund sea of life:

Towards you, the universal bride in the midst of the congregating
waters, towards you, the licentious bride in the abundance of her
springs and at the high flood-tide of her maturity, all earth itself
streaming descends the gorges of love.[2]

A long way – Claudel might have said – from Dante's
vision of Beatrice; yet it is a sacred poem. Having in *Vents*
said all he (and through him the former diplomat) wished to
say of our *'rendez-vous avec la fin d'un age'*, the poet, like some
modern Anthony who has risen out of his own defeat, divests himself of the prince and becomes the lover. There is in Perse's
erotic poem some of that dazzling quality of the barge of Cleo-
patra – his imagery is indeed of truly Shakespearian fertility – as
she, mediating the goddess Isis herself, advances to meet her
lover (worthy, in the eyes of her love, to be set at 'Jove's side' and

---

[1] *Dans la promiscuité divine et la dépravation de l'homme chez les dieux. . . .*

[2] *Vers toi l'Épouse universelle au sein de la congrégation des eaux, vers toi l'Épouse
licencieuse dans l'abondance de ses sources et le haut flux de sa maturité, toute la terre elle-
même ruisselante descend les gorges de l'amour. (Amers, Chœur, 3.)*

attended by the page Eros). In Perse's poem woman is herself the ship in which the lover puts to sea upon the ocean of existence, carried by that 'one same wave' in the act of love, obscene and sacred, in which every mortal creature participates, in the *hieros gamos* with *l'Epouse éternelle*.

We may reflect, in passing, how little, for all the current obsession with sex, has been written on this theme, in English, which, beside *Amers*, does not seem vulgar and trivial. Is it an after-image of Protestant puritanism that in place of the erotic, in Anglo-Saxon countries, has left only the pornographic?

The sea as symbol of material existence and its flux is age-old and universal – Hebraic, neo-Platonic, Hermetic, Vedantic; and woman as the *foederis area* who in her body bears immortal life over those dangerous waves where Odysseus sailed among marvels and perils. But in the poetry of Perse it is the existential reality rather than the symbolic analogies on other planes of the real, which are made apparent. The wave of the sea that with such a surge . . . rises and finds its way up into us' might be (like the hot heart of the bird in *Oiseaux* whose burning is its life) the '*simple fait biologique*'; for the salinity of blood biologists relate to the salinity of the sea where all organic life originated; 'The Sea, woven in us, to the last weaving of its tangled deeps, the Sea, in us weaving its great hours of light and its great trails of darkness.'[1]

Neither of St. John Perse's two subsequent poems is on the same scale, or so magnificent, as *Vents* and *Amers*. *Chronique* (1960) is on the theme of age; and the approach to death is still a setting-forth, an *éloge*. *Oiseaux* (1966), illustrated by four lithographs by Georges Braque (a collaboration in which the poem existed first), is the poet's definition and exploration of the relation of art to nature, nature to consciousness. Classical, economical ('laconic') in contrast with the superb prodigality and amplitude of *Amers*, this poem is not an essay in criticism but itself exemplifies what it explores – an existential identity of thought and expression, comparable with the identity, in nature, of existence and being, form and life.

Man has rejoined the innocence of the wild creature, and the bird painted in the hunter's eye has become the hunter himself in the eye of the creature, as it does in Esquimaux art. Wild things and

[1] *La Mer, en nous tissée, jusqu'à ses ronceraies d'abîme, la Mer, en nous tissant ses grandes heures de lumière et ses grandes pistes de ténèbres. . . . (Amers, I, 4.)*

hunter together cross the ford of a fourth dimension. From the difficulty of being to the ease of loving they move in step at last, two real beings who form a pair.[1]

Of inner and outer worlds the bird (a symbol especially apt perhaps because of all creatures the bird is the most free to move in all elements and to 'lose its shadow') is the unifying image. In the immediacy of primitive art, related rather to the skills of the hunter than to aesthetics, the poet finds the very point at which, in the transition from sky to eye, the image passes from nature into art; and whereas for Proust memories are alone freed from the restrictions of time and place, for St. John Perse whatever enters art enters the paradisal state of co-existence and unity; while at the same time art is itself but another region of nature. In this superb image we see what the *ars poetica* can achieve by means of the 'mediating image and its play of correspondences, by way of a thousand chains of reactions and unusual associations' without being symbolic. Again we may think of Proust, whose rejection of 'realism' was not on metaphysical grounds, but because it is in the nature of sensations to evoke those thousand associations. It is these alone, their resonances and evocations, which enrich and give meaning to the sensations which occasion them. Or again,

At the hypnotic point of an immense eye inhabited by the painter, like the very eye of a cyclone in its course – all things referred to their distant causes and all fires crossing – there is unity at last re-knitted and diversity reconciled. After such and so long a consummation of flight, behold the great round of birds painted on the zodiacal wheel and the gathering of an entire family of wings in the yellow wind, like one vast propeller in quest of its blades.[2]

In entering consciousness, multiplicity enters the state of unity.

None of the poet's translators is in all ways excellent. Eliot's knowledge of French seems the most perfect; his polished ren-

[1] *L'homme a rejoint l'innocence de la bête, et l'oiseau peint dans l'œil du chasseur devient le chasseur même dans l'œil de la bête, comme il advient dans l'art des Eskimos. Bête et chasseur passent ensemble le gué d'une quatrième dimension. De la difficulté d'être à l'aisance d'aimer vont enfin, du même pas, deux êtres vrais, appariés. (Oiseaux, 5.)*

[2] *Au point d'hynose d'un œil immense habité par le peintre, comme l'œil même du cyclone en course – toutes choses rapportées à leurs causes lointaines et tous feux se croisant – c'est l'unité enfin renouée et le divers réconcilié. Après telle et si longue consummation du vol, c'est la grande ronde d'oiseaux peints sur la roue zodiacale, et le rassemblement d'une famille entière d'ailes dans le vent jaune, comme une seule et vaste hélice en quête de ses pales. (Oiseaux, XI.)*

derings are faultless, linguistically, though his own dignified and processional *lento* at times slows down Perse's 'rhythm of Being itself'. Sometimes he misses the naked simplicity of St. John Perse's images, as in the sedate seventeenth-century 'earth is brought to bed of wonders' for *'la terre enfante des merveilles'*. Eliot's own practice as a poet is to evoke literary overtones and and to call up the past echoed in every word and image; whereas St. John Perse's images all alike seem to belong to a 'nature' which has no past, no history, in which fossil, ephemerae, or modern city alike belong to the one here and now. His language is without echoes or penumbra. Hugh Chisholm's *Vents* seems to me best to catch the rhythm of the original, while Wallace Fowlie's *Amers* fails to do so. Denis Devlin's *Exil* is perhaps (after Eliot) the most poetic. Robert Fitzgerald (whose knowledge of French seems less good than any of these) does nevertheless (as in the above quotations from *Oiseaux*) capture the poet's absolutely modern quality, places his work in the present of the 1960's and not of the 1920's. It is not for an English reader to discuss the many untranslatable aspects of his style; every language places on reality itself different contours; even simple nouns are untranslatable; but the 'play of correspondences' of his 'mediating image' is generally not semantic, and is therefore not greatly weakened in translation. As in (to take another example from *Oiseaux*) 'The more they fly, the more wholly they come to the delight of being: birds of the longest day and the longest resolve, with brows like new-born infants or the dolphins of old fables'.[1]

The complexity here is not verbal, yet the internal so-to-say valencies of the figure are as firmly established as the forces which hold together a molecule. The 'long day' of the birds who follow the sun; the strength of the instinct which urges the migrant on is implicit in the 'brows like new-born infants', doubly apt from the projecting rounded form of the bird's head, and the implication of a perpetual setting-forth, the creature at every moment new-born into the future. The beautiful modulation to the brow of the dolphin (bulbous also) and the swiftest-travelling creature of another element is introduced like a change of key in music. The poet (a man of the sea) has doubtless seen many dolphins in the water; but the deliberate evocation here of the dolphin

---

[1] *Plus qu'ils ne volent, ils viennent a part entière au délice de l'être : oiseaux du plus long jour et du plus long propos, avec leurs fronts de nouveau-nés ou de dauphins des fables. . . .* (*Oiseaux*, 10.)

of art ('old fables') brings in the legend of Arion and the dolphin
as the vehicle of the poet, and of poetry itself; so that the bird
with its '*longue propos*' (and we are here reminded that Braque's
birds belong not to nature but to art) becomes also the vehicle
of imagination and its 'long purpose'. None of this is stated yet
all is implicit in the configuration of the image. Such poetry is,
in Shelley's full sense, 'the language of the imagination', expressing essences and relationships entirely qualitative.

St. John Perse's existentialism (if such it is) might seem opposed
to the symbolist tradition which (under whatever name) stems
from some form of Platonism. Neither poetic practice can be
detached from that view of the nature of things in which it is
grounded. The symbol presumes multiple planes of being linked
both by cause and by analogy; without understanding of this
metaphysical ground, symbolist poetry becomes meaningless. In
Perse's existentialist use of the image a metaphysical ground is
no less implicit, by his own confession. No less than the poetry
of Yeats his work must remain opaque to vulgar positivism, for
he too uses the term 'divine', though for him divinity is existen-
tially implicit. Perhaps the two apparently opposite modes may
be compared to different phases of waves; at their point of inter-
section we have the existential image; at the limit of their
amplitude, the analogies and resonances of the symbol. And like
the symbolists, St. John Perse not only assumes but affirms and
uses as the instrument of his art the law of harmony which sub-
sists in and unifies the cosmos; his universe is neither arbitrary
not indeterminate, and governed by that symmetry, unity, and
accord in which Plotinus discovers the essence of 'the beautiful'.

The symbol is, besides, itself rooted in nature, and in that reading of the great Bible of the world which precedes all written
books, those remote copies of the intrinsic meanings of things.
I was myself dramatically reminded of this when in the summer of
1966 I saw flying over the Temple of Aesculapius at Epidaurus
(of all places) an eagle with a writhing serpent in its beak. This
symbol, first used as a metaphor by Homer, has accompanied
European poetry and symbolic thought throughout its history,
gathering on its way the symbolic associations profound and
various. The alchemists made of eagle and serpent figures of their
mythology; Ovid, Spenser, Blake and Shelley have in turn
clothed the image in literary form and symbolic connotations.
But seeing the thing itself (as if a piece of writing in the sky torn

loose from all these books) I thought of St. John Perse; whose poetry re-immerses all our used images in 'that original night' of Orpheus, contemporaneous with every period of history and every moment of life, and gives back to us a world at every moment newly created.

1967

INDEX